THE DUEL AND THE OATH.

HENRY CHARLES LEA

With additional original documents in translation

BY

ARTHUR C. HOWLAND

Edited, with an Introduction

BY

EDWARD PETERS

UNIVERSITY OF PENNSYLVANIA PRESS

PHILADELPHIA

First published in 1866, as Parts I and II of
Superstition and Force, by Henry Charles Lea

Introduction © 1974 by the University of Pennsylvania Press,
Inc.

Library of Congress Catalog Card Number 74–16828

ISBN (cloth) : 0–8122–7681–7

ISBN (paper) : 0–8122–1080–8

Manufactured in the United States of America

CONTENTS.

INTRODUCTION.

Henry Charles Lea published his first major historical work, *Superstition and Force*, in 1866. That book, chiefly a study of various aspects of the relations between legal procedure and cultural and religious history in medieval Europe, has been reprinted as three separate paperback volumes, *The Ordeal* (1973), *Torture* (1973) and the present volume, *The Duel and the Oath*. This volume contains parts I and II of Lea's work, originally entitled "Wager of Law" and "Wager of Battle." As a historian, Lea was self-taught. He lacked the large libraries of ancillary material and the wealth of published and catalogued manuscript sources, the availability of which has helped to transform historical investigation between the end of the nineteenth and the mid–twentieth century. Moved as much by his own curiosity about what he called the progress "from primitive savagism to civilised enlightenment," as by his fascination with the history of the Roman Catholic Church, Lea might have become one of those many liberal nineteenth-century anticlerical historians whose works form as much a part of confessional as of professional historiography. Yet Lea developed several techniques in his research that checked this direction. As Walter Ullmann has summed them up, they are:

> Three factors that were to influence his future historical work: (1) that the study of the sources is indispensable if a period or a movement or an institution is to be

properly understood: the reliance on secondary authorities is to be discouraged, because they in one way or another have succumbed to purely subjective assessments; (2) that in order to see and explain and understand an institution or the actuality of living in an historical period or in a particular country, there is no better guide and no more reliable mirror than the law enacted and practised: in this realization Lea was far ahead of all his contemporaries and of many historians in later decades; (3) that in the medieval period it was the Church which dominated the social and political life both by its practices and its laws; its sources were on the whole well preserved; its canon law was the best possible guide to an understanding of medieval institutions, at least in the predominantly ecclesiastical field.[1]

Research directly among the sources, a focus on the law and an awareness of the varied and complex role of the Church have remained, since Lea's day, the ground rules for some of the most important historical studies of early Europe. The author of the best history of the American interest in the Middle Ages during the nineteenth and twentieth centuries accurately assesses Lea's importance:

Henry Charles Lea, the businessman and self–taught scholar, was the first American historian of the critical generation who as such attained that actual distinction in Europe. That this was the case not only in the circles of specialized professional scholars, but in the fact that his historiographical works on the old continent also won glory as weapons in the struggle for freedom of the spirit, gives him a particular importance, not only in the development of the American awareness of the Middle Ages, but especially also in the overall history of American historiography.[2]

Lea's studies in *Superstition and Force* were focused upon the complex relations between forms of legal procedure and the cultural values they represented. In *The Duel and the Oath* he focused upon the limitations of what modern jurists would term private law (or civil cases), the concept of immanent justice, which maintained that divine intervention in the regulation of human affairs was a regular and predictable occurrence, and the consequent forms of compurgation and judicial combat that these institutions entailed. Compurgation (co-purging, or co-swearing) was the practice by which either the accuser or the accused was compelled to bring to court a specified number of "oath-helpers" who agreed to take a particular oath on his behalf, not, to be sure, as witnesses, which they were not, but, in a sense, as backers, supporters of his person and his cause. The number of oath helpers and the form of the oath varied in ecclesiastical and temporal courts, in cases and in localities. Judicial combat, an alternative to compurgation and, in special cases, mandatory, required accuser and accused, or their designated representatives, to engage in a duel—to the victor going the verdict. Both compurgation and judicial combat depended for their value upon the idea that God might intervene, in the case of the former by preventing the oath–helpers from saying the oath verbatim or by permitting the oath to be repeated perfectly, and in the case of the latter, by aiding the combatant who represented the more just cause. Such practices and the cultural world they reveal are so remote from modern notions of jurisprudence that some indication of their origins and purpose ought to be given.

The modern form of trial procedure—involving the forms of accusation, rules and presentation of evidence, the treatment of witnesses' evidence, the concept of due process and the professionalization of at least part of the judicial personnel—did not emerge as widespread in most of Europe until the late twelfth and thirteenth centuries. As with other changes in the twelfth and thirteenth centuries, changes in the law and in legal procedure reflect a transformation of old, deeply rooted cultural values during a period that may well be the most significant turning–point in modern history. In the course of this revolution, the practice of compurgation became generally restricted to a narrower spectrum of cases, and the judicial duel became a part of the complex formalization of aristocratic status, being retained by the European aristocracy (and the American citizenry) chiefly until the nineteenth century. Even though their contemporary manifestations may be in the figure of the hopeful character witness on the one hand and the gunfighters in modern western films on the other, both compurgation and the judicial combat have a long history whose roots touch the entire history of the settlement of Europe and the formation of a European culture and civilization.

Compurgation, judicial duel and the ordeal fell generically into the category of *judicium Dei*, or judgements of God, an increasingly satisfactory expression of the Romano–Germanic idea of immanent justice, which survived with much criticism until the beginning of the thirteenth century.[3] "I will defend this charge with my body," was the formal response to a denial of accusation. Compurgation itself required a defense by a specific group of supporters—kindred, neighbors, or friends. The law of the Germanic kingdoms of Europe did not touch free men in quite the way the law of a modern industrial state touches its members. Unless the accused had been caught in the act, the court was stopped from proceeding further after accusation and denial, except for one recourse—the submission of the case decision to God. The spectrum of individual freedom upon which the mechanisms of the law impinged was narrow, and the duel, the ordeal, or compurgation were the forms by which rulers commended the case to God when they, with their restricted judicial capacities and rules of evidence, found themselves unable to make a holding.[4] Compurgation, as opposed to the judicial duel, survived in ecclesiastical courts longer than in secular courts. The judicial duel, sublimated in the complex process of formalizing aristocratic status in Euorpe after the twelfth century, took on its romantic dimensions and influenced the character of personal antagonism in university debates, tournaments and literature.[5]

The motif of the single combat over a point of law and honor had a much longer history than the process of compurgation. By the end of the eleventh century, the distinction between legal procedure and vindication of personal honor had begun to blur, as may be seen in the final sections of *The Song of Roland* during the trial of Ganelon. The appeal of the judicial combat/duel to an increasingly selfconscious aristocracy remained powerful, in some cases extending down to the present century. The ritual, combat and resolution became a theme that must be considered from an anthropological and legal–historical viewpoint.[6]

The idea that legal rules and institutions operate uniformly through a society, regardless of status, wealth, power or honor is a peculiarly modern one. The infinite gradation of status in the early European world meant that in law courts as well as in courtyards each individual carried a legal identity with him, and this identity reflected in the law court what the individual and his society knew already—that status determined both the extent of legal control over individuals and the character of that control. Thus, the focus upon legal customs, regardless of how remote from any experience of ours that we can recognize, is an essential part of studying the history of the European past. As Lea discovered, and Ullmann has reminded us, "the history of jurisprudence is the history of civilization." Under its aspect as a manifestation of culture, law is among the most revealing and expansive areas of historical study.

Edward Peters
Philadelphia, 1974

NOTES

1. Walter Ullmann, "Historical Introduction" to H. C. Lea, *The Inquisition of the Middle Ages* (New York, 1963), p. 12.

2. Hans Rudolf Guggisberg, *Das europäische Mittelalter im amerikanischen Geschichtsdenken des 19. und des frühen 20. Jahrhunderts* (Basel, Stuttgart, 1964), pp. 100–101.

10 INTRODUCTION.

3. See John W. Baldwin, "The Intellectual Preparations for the Canon of 1215 Against Ordeals," *Speculum* 36 (1961), pp. 613–636, and the bibliography in Henry C. Lea, *The Ordeal* (Philadelphia, 1973).

4. See *La Preuve,* Vol. XVII of the *Receuils de la société Jean Bodin* (Brussells, 1965).

5. See Robert Baldick, *The Duel* (New York, 1965), an informal history; George Neilson, *Trial by Combat* (London, 1890). Friedrich Prinz, *Klerus und Krieg im früheren Mittelalter* (Stuttgart, 1971) traces one aspect of this complex problem. The following works offer some suggestion of the duel's later stages: Bertrand de Loque, *Discourses of Warre and Single Combat,* ed. Alice Shalvi (London, 1968); F. R. Bryson, *The Sixteenth-Century Italian Duel* (Chicago, 1938); Giovanni da Legnano, *Tractatus de Bello, De Represaliis et De Duello,* ed. T. H. Holland (Oxford, 1917). See also Jean Yver, *L'Interdiction de la guerre privée dans le très ancien droit normand,* separately printed from the *Travaux de la semaine d'histoire du droit normand* (Caen, 1928).

6. In general, see Marc Bloch, *Feudal Society,* trans. L. A. Manyon (Chicago, 1961), pp. 109–122, 359–374. For *The Song of Roland*, see Robert Harrison, trans., *The Song of Roland* (New York, 1970); George Fenwick Jones, *The Ethos of the Song of Roland* (Baltimore, 1963); Pierre LeGentil, *The Chanson de Roland,* trans., F. Beer (Cambridge, Mass., 1969). On the concept of "immanent justice," see Paul Rousset, "La croyance en la justice immanente à l'époque féodale," *Le Moyen Age* 54 (1948), pp. 225–248. A number of chronicles give many accounts of both compurgation, e.g., Gregory of Tours, *History of the Franks,* trans. E. Brehaut (rep. New York, 1969), Paul the Deacon, *History of the Lombards,* trans. W. D. Foulke (rep. ed., Philadelphia, 1974). For an example from the Germanic law codes, see Katherine Fischer Drew, trans., *The Burgundian Code* (Philadelphia, 1972), XLV, pp. 52–53.

THE DUEL AND THE OATH.

I.

THE WAGER OF LAW.

CHAPTER I.

RESPONSIBILITY OF THE KINDRED.

THE conception of crime as a wrong committed against society is too abstract to find expression in the institutions of uncivilized communities. The slayer or the spoiler is an enemy, not of his fellows in general, but only of the sufferer or of his kindred; and if society can provide means for the wronged to exact reparation, it has done its duty to the utmost, and has, indeed, made a notable advance on the path that leads from barbarism to civilization. How recent has been our progress beyond this stage of development is illustrated in the provisions of a code granted so lately as 1231 by the Abbey of St. Bertin to the town of Arques. By these laws, when a man was convicted of intentional homicide, he was handed over to the family of the murdered person, to be slain by them in turn.[1] It still was vengeance, and not justice, that was to be satisfied.

In early times, therefore, the wrong-doer owed no satisfaction to the law or to the state, but only to the injured party. That injured party, moreover, was not a mere individual. All the races of the great Aryan branch of mankind have developed through a common plan of organization, in which each family —sometimes merely the circle of near kindred, at others enlarged into a *gens* or sept—was a unit with respect to the other

---

[1] Legg. Villæ de Arkes § xxviii. (D'Achery Spicileg. III. 608).

2

similar aggregations in the tribe or nation, presenting, with respect to personal rights, features analogous to their communal holding of land.[1] Within these units, as a general rule, each individual was personally answerable for all, and all were answerable for each. A characteristic incident of this system was the *wer-gild* or blood-money, through which offences were condoned and the aggrieved were satisfied by a payment made, when the crime was homicide, to the kindred of the slain, and generally contributed by the kindred of the slayer.

The fragments of the Avesta are the earliest records of Aryan legislation that have reached us, and in them we find distinctly marked evidence of this common responsibility of the kindred.[2] Among the Hindus, the ancient code, known as the Manava Dharma Sastra, represents a highly complex social organization, in which primitive institutions have been completely overlaid by the later and antagonistic elements of caste and Brahmanism, but yet it reveals the existence of village communities which were a direct development of the primal system of the family;[3] and the ancient solidarity of these communities is shown in the provision that if a murder or robbery could not be traced, the village in which it occurred was obliged to make it good, or that to which the track of the offender could be followed.[4] In the adventures of the Kauravas and Pandavas, moreover, the Mahabharata preserves fragments of traditions conveying some indications of a pre-existing solidarity among kindred.[5] Much more clearly defined were the Hellenic

[1] See Pictet, Origines Indo-Européennes (Paris, 1878, T. II. pp. 372–6; T. III. pp. 5–8), for the philological evidence of the development of society from the family in all the Aryan nations.

[2] Vendidad, Farg. IV. 24–35 (Bleeck's Translation, Hertford, 1864, pp. 30–1).

[3] Manava Dharma Sastra, VIII. 295 sqq. Comp. Maine's Ancient Law, pp. 260 sqq.

[4] Yajnavalkya, II. 272 (Stenzler's Translation).

[5] Even among the remnants of the pre-Aryan races of India the same customs are traceable. Early in the present century Lieutenant Shaw described the hill-tribes of Rajmahal, to the north of Bengal, as recognizing

organizations of the *patræ* and *phratriæ ;* while the institution
of the *wer-gild* is seen in the wages earned by Heracles in
serving Omphale, to be paid to the kinsmen of the murdered
Iphitus ; and its existence can be traced to historic times in the
payments provided by the Trallian laws to the families of the
subject Leleges and Minyans who might be slain.   Sir Henry
Maine has acutely suggested, also, that the belief in an hereditary curse, which plays so awful a part in Grecian legend, is
derived from the primal idea of the solidarity of the family
group.[1]   In Rome, notwithstanding the powerful Latin tendency to absorb all minor subdivisions into the state, the institution of the *gens*, and the relationship between the patron and
his clients, bear striking analogies to the organizations which
we find among the Teutonic tribes as they emerge into history ;
while the fine imposed on the elder Horatius, to expiate for
his son the crime of slaying his sister, shows a remnant still
existing of the *wer-gild* levied on the relatives.[2]   The early
legislation of the Celts, both in the Irish and Welsh tribes, as
we shall presently see, carried the solidarity of the family to
its highest point of development.   The same institutions form
a prominent feature of social organization among the Slavs.
The Russian Mir, or communal society, is evidently a development of the original family ; while the Ruskaia Prawda, the
earliest extant code, promulgated by Yaroslav Vladomirovich
in the eleventh century, allows the relatives of a murdered
man either to kill the murderer or to accept a *wer-gild* from
him.   The district, moreover, in which a homicide occurs is

the responsibility of the injurer to the injured ; compensation was assessed
at the pleasure of the complainant, and the kindred of the offender were
compelled to contribute to it, exactly as among the barbarians who occupied
Europe (Asiatic Researches, Vol. IV.).

[1] Dicæarchi Frag. (Didot, Frag. Hist. Græcor.).—Apollodor. Biblioth. II.
vi. 2-3.—Diodor. Siculi IV. 31.—Plut. Quæst. Græc. 46.—Maine's Ancient
Law, p. 127.

[2] Tit. Liv. I. 26; V. 32.—Appiani de Bell. Hannibal. xxviii.—Dion.
Halicar. II. 10; XIII. 5.

liable to a fine, unless the victim is an unknown stranger: as such, there are none to claim compensation for him, he is outside of all family organization, and the law has no protection for him.[1] In Poland, the laws in force until the close of the fifteenth century provided no other penalty for murder than a *wer-gild* to be divided among the kindred and friends of the slain; and during the fifteenth century there was only a short term of imprisonment added.[2] Among the southern Slavs the Zadruga takes the place of the Russian Mir, and is a still more absolute and primitive form of family organization.[3]

In obedience to this all-pervading tendency of organization, the barbarian tribes which overthrew the Roman Empire based their institutions on two general principles—the independence of the individual freeman and the solidarity of the family group—and on these were founded their simple forms of jurisprudence. As the criminal was not responsible to the state, but to the injured party, personal punishments were unknown, and the law made no attempt to decree them. All that it could do was to provide rude courts before which a plaintiff could state his case, and a settled tariff of pecuniary compensation to console him for his sufferings.[4] If he disdained this peaceful process, he was at liberty to assemble his kindred and friends, and exact what satisfaction he could with sword and axe. The offender, moreover, could not legitimately refuse to appear when summoned before the *mallum*, or judicial assembly of the tribe; nor could he, as a rule, claim the right of

[1] Esneaux, Hist. de Russie, I. 172 sqq.

[2] Jo. Herburti de Fulstin Statut. Reg. Polon. tit. *Homicid.* (Samoscii, 1597, pp. 200 sqq.). In cases, however, of homicide committed by a *kmetho*, or serf, upon another, a portion of the *wer-gild* was paid to the magistrate.

[3] See an abstract of Bojisic's work on the customs of the southern Slavs, in the "Penn Monthly" Magazine, Phila, Jan. 1878, pp. 15 sqq.

[4] Gradually, however, a portion of the composition money was attributed, under the name of *fredum*, to the king or the magistrate, as a compensation for readmitting the criminal to the public peace.

armed defence, if the complainant preferred to receive the money payment provided for the offence of which he might prove his antagonist guilty.

This *wer-gild* was in no sense a fine inflicted as a punishment for guilt, but only a compensation to induce the injured party to forego his right of reprisals, and the interest which society felt in it was not in the repression of crime, but in the maintenance of peace by averting the endless warfare of hostile families. An Anglo-Saxon proverb, quoted approvingly in the laws of Edward the Confessor, as collected by William the Conqueror, says: "Bicge spere of side oðer bere"—Buy off the spear from thy side or endure it.[1] The application of the system is to be seen in the minute and complex tariffs of crime which form so large a portion of the barbarian codes. Every attempt against person and property is rated at its appropriate price, from the theft of a sucking pig to the armed occupation of an estate, and from a wound of the little finger to the most atrocious of parricides. To what extent this at last was carried may be seen in the Welsh codes, where every hair of the eyelash is rated at a penny.[2]

This system introduced into legal proceedings a commercial spirit which seems strangely at variance with the savage heroism commonly attributed to our barbarian ancestors. In the translation by Mr. Dasent of the old Icelandic Saga of Burnt Njal is vividly set forth the complex procedure which arose from the development of these principles, whereby suits could be sold and assigned by one party to another, and a plaintiff with a promising claim for damages would part with it to some speculator who undertook the chances of the suit; or, if the prospects were not encouraging, he would pay some shrewd lawyer or mighty warrior to prosecute it in his stead. As either party in the primitive Icelandic code could at any

---

[1] Ll. Edwardi c. xii. (Thorpe's Ancient Laws, I. 467).

[2] Gwentian Code, Bk. II. chap. vii. § 8. (Aneurin Owen's Ancient Laws, etc. of Wales, I. 701.)

moment interrupt the proceedings with a challenge to single
combat, or a powerful pleader might collect his friends for a
raid on the Althing, and thus break up the court, this traffic in
suits was a speculation well fitted to vary the monotony of a
sea-rover's life on shore.

In the application of this principle of compensation the
solidarity of the family bore a part as conspicuous as in the
alternative of private warfare. The kindred of the offender
were obliged to contribute shares proportionate to their degrees
of relationship; while those of the man who was wronged
received respective percentages calculated on the same basis.
Thus the most ancient Barbarian code that has reached us—
that of the Feini, or primitive Irish—in a fanciful quadripar-
tite enumeration of the principles in force in levying fines,
alludes to the responsibility of kindred—"And because there
are four things for which it is levied : 'cin' (one's own crime),
and 'tobhach' (the crime of a near kinsman), 'saighi' (the
crime of a middle kinsman), and the crime of a kinsman in
general."[1] A very complete example of the development of
this system is to be found in the Icelandic legislation of the
twelfth century, where the fines exacted diminish gradually, as
far as the relatives in the fifth degree on both sides, each grade
of the criminal's family paying its rate to the corresponding
grade of the sufferer's kindred.[2] When, however, the next of
kin were females, and were thus incompetent to prosecute for
murder, the person who undertook that office was rewarded
with one-third of the fine.[3] It was not until about 1270 that
King Haco, in his unsuccessful attempt to reform these laws,
ventured to decree that in cases of murder the blood-money
should not be divided among the family of the victim, but
should all be paid to the heir.[4] On the other hand, in Denmark, Eric VII., in 1269, relieved the kindred of the murderer

---

[1] Senchus Mor, I. 259 (Hancock's ed. Dublin, 1865).

[2] Grágás, Sect. IV. cap. cxiv.   [3] Ibid. Sect. VIII. cap. lv.

[4] Jarnsida, Mannhelge, cap. xxix.—Cf. Legg. Gulathingenses, Mann-
helgi, cap. xii.

from contributing to the *wer-gild*, although it continued to be divided among the relatives of the slain.[1]

Among the Welsh the provisions for levying and distributing the fines were almost as complex as those of the early Icelandic law, one body of jurisprudence extending the liability even as far as sixth cousins;[2] and perhaps the quaintest expression of the responsibility of the kindred is to be found in the regulation that if any one should draw blood from the abbot of either of the seven great houses of Dyved, the offender should forfeit seven pounds, while a female of his kindred should become a washerwoman in token of disgrace.[3] The firm hold which this practical solidarity of the family had upon the jurisprudence of the European races is shown by a clause in the statutes of the city of Lille, as late as the fourteenth century, where the malefactor had the right to collect from his relatives a portion of the *wer-gild* which he had incurred; and elaborate tables were drawn up, showing the amount payable by each relative in proportion to his degree of kinship, the liability extending as far as to third cousins.[4] A still more pregnant example of the responsibility of kindred is found in the customs of Aspres, in 1184, where the kindred of a homicide, if they would abjure him by oath on relics, were entitled to the public peace; but, if they refused to do so, it became the duty of the Count of Hainault, the Abbot of St. Vaast, and the relatives of the slain, to hunt them down, and seize all their property.[5]

The introduction of Christianity, with the all-pervading sacerdotalism of the church, rendered necessary an innovation on the primeval form of social organization, for ecclesiastical ties dissolved those of the family. By the Carlovingian

---

[1] Constit. Eric. Ann. 1269 § vii. (Ludewig, Reliq. MSS. T. XII. p. 204).

[2] Dimetian Code, Bk. II. ch. i. §§ 17–31.—Bk. III. ch. iii. § 4.—Anomalous Laws, Bk. IV. ch. iii. § 11.

[3] Dimetian Code, Bk. II. chap. xxiv. § 12.

[4] Roisin, Franchises, etc. de la ville de Lille, pp. 106–7.

[5] Charta Balduini Hannoniens. (Martene, Collect. Ampliss. I. 964.)

legislation, when a priest was slain his *wer-gild* was paid to the church, which was held to be nearer to him than any relative,[1] though this regulation subsequently was modified so as to divide the composition into three parts, of which one was paid to the church of the deceased, one to his bishop, and the third to his kindred.[2]   As a general rule, therefore, the clerk could claim no share of the blood-money collected for the murder of his kinsmen, nor be called upon to contribute to that incurred by his family;[3] though it is true that, by the Welsh laws of Hoel the Good, compiled in the tenth century, children, even prospective, were a link through which the liability might be again incurred.   "Neither clerks nor women are to have a share of the *galanas*, since they are not avengers; however, they are to pay for their children or to make oath that they shall never have any."[4]

With this exception, therefore, in its relations to the community, each family in the barbaric tribes was a unit, both for attack and defence, whether recourse was had to the jealously preserved right of private warfare, or whether the injured parties contented themselves with the more peaceful processes of the *mallum* or *althing*.   This solidarity of the kindred is the key to much that would otherwise appear irrational in their legislation, and left, as we have seen, its traces late in the customary law.

---

[1] Capitul. Lib. IV. cap. 15.   [2] Concil. Tribur. an. 895, can. iv.
[3] Dimetian Code, Bk. II. chap. i. § 32.
[4] Venedotian Code, Bk. III. chap. i. § 21.

CHAPTER II.

THE OATH AND ITS ACCESSORIES.

BETWEEN the commission of an offence and its proof in a court of justice there lies a wide field for the exercise or perversion of human ingenuity. The subject of evidence is one which has taxed man's reasoning powers to the utmost; and the subtle distinctions of the Roman law, with its *probatio, præsumptio juris, præsumptio juris tantum :* the endless refinements of the glossators, rating evidence in its different grades, as *probatio optima, evidentissima, apertissima, legitima, sufficiens, indubitata, dilucida, liquida, evidens, perspicua,* and *semiplena;* and the artificial rules of the common law, so repugnant frequently to human common sense, all alike show the importance of the subject, and its supreme difficulty. The semi-barbarian, impatient of such expenditure of logic, arrived at results by a shorter process.

The time has passed for the romantic school of writers who assume that the unsupported oath of the accused was originally sufficient to clear him of a charge, when the fierce warrior disdained to shrink from the consequences of his act. It was not, indeed, until long after the Teutonic tribes had declined from the assumed virtues of their native forests, that an unsupported oath was receivable as evidence, and the introduction of such a custom may be traced to the influence of the Roman law, in which the importance of the oath was overwhelming.[1]

[1] The oath may be regarded as the foundation of Roman legal procedure —" Dato jurejurando non aliud quæritur, quam an juratum sit; remissa quæstione an debeatur; quasi satis probatum sit jurejurando"—L. 5, § 2, D. XII. ii. The *jusjurandum necessarium* could always be administered by the judge in cases of deficient evidence, and the *jusjurandum in jure* proffered by the plaintiff to the defendant was conclusive: " Manifestæ tur-

The Wisigoths, who moulded their laws on the Roman jurisprudence, were the only race of barbarians who permitted the
accused, in the absence of definite testimony, to escape on his
single oath,[1] and this exception only tends to prove the rule,
for at the council of Valence, in 855, the Wisigothic custom
was denounced in the strongest terms as an incentive to perjury.[2] It is true that the oath of a master could clear a slave
accused of certain crimes,[3] which was no less an incentive to
perjury, for the master was liable in case of conviction, but
presumably in such case he took upon himself the responsibility and laid himself open to an accusation of perjury. As
a rule, however, we may assume that the purgatorial power of
a single oath was an innovation introduced by the church,
which was trained in the Roman institutions and claimed for
its members the privilege, when testimony was deficient, of
clearing themselves by appealing in this manner to God.[4]
Continued contact with the remains of Roman civilization
strengthened the custom, and its development was to a great
extent due to the revival of the study of the imperial jurisprudence in the twelfth century.[5] The primitive principle is well

pitudinis et confessionis est nolle nec jurare nec jusjurandum referre"—Ibid.
l. 38.

[1] Ll. Wisigoth. Lib. II. Tit. ii. c. 5.

[2] Concil. Valentin. ann. 855, c. xi.

[3] Ll. Ripuar. Tit. XII. § 1 ; ix. 17.—Capit. Ludov. Pii. ann. 819 add. ad
L. Salicam, c. 15.—Capitul. L. IV. c. 29.—Ivonis Decr. XVI. 239.

[4] De presbytero vero, si quilibet sacerdos a populo fuerit accusatus, si
certi non fuerint testes qui criminis illati approbent veritatem, jusjurandum
erit in medio, et illum testem proferat de innocentiæ suæ puritate cui nuda
et aperta sunt omnia; sicque maneat in proprio gradu.—Gregor. PP. II.
Epist. XIV. ad Bonifacium. Cf. Hincmari Remens. Epist. XXII.

[5] Thus Alfonso the Wise endeavored to introduce into Spain the mutual
challenging of the parties involved in the Roman *jusjurandum in jure*, by
his *jura de juicio* (Las Siete Partidas, P. III. Tit. xi. l. 2. Cf. Espéculo,
Lib. V. Tit. xi. ley 2). Oddly enough, the same procedure is found incorporated in the municipal law of Rheims in the fourteenth century, probably
introduced by some over-zealous civilian; " Si alicui deferatur jusjurandum,

expressed in the Frisian code, where the pleader says, " I swear alone, if thou darest, deny my oath and fight me,"[1]

necesse habet jurare vel referre jusjurandum, et hoc super quovis debito, vel inter quasvis personas"—Lib. Pract. de Consuetud. Remens. § 15 (Archives Législat. de Reims, P. I. p. 37). By this time, however, the oaths of parties had assumed great importance. In the legislation of St. Louis, they occupy a position which was a direct incentive to perjury. Thus he provides for the hanging of the owner of a beast which had killed a man, if he was foolish enough not to swear that he was ignorant of its being vicious. " Et si il estoit si fox que il deist que il seust la teche de la beste, il en seroit pendus pour la recoignoissance"—Établissements, Liv. I. chap. cxxi.

A charter granted to the commune of Lorris, in 1155, by Louis le Jeune, gives to burghers the privilege of rebutting by oath, without conjurators, an accusation unsupported by testimony—Chart. Ludovic. junior. ann. 1155, cap. xxxii. (Isambert, Anciennes Lois Françaises I. 157.) And, in comparatively modern times, in Germany, the same rule was followed. " Juramento rei, quod purgationis vocatur, sæpe etiam innocentia, utpote quæ in anima constitit, probatur et indicia diluuntur;" and this oath was administered when the evidence was insufficient to justify torture. (Zangeri Tract. de Quæstionibus, cap. iii. No. 46.) In 1592, Zanger wrote an elaborate essay to prove the evils of the custom.

It is a noteworthy fact, however, that of all the medieval codes the one least affected by the influence of the Roman law was the Saxon, and in this the purgatorial power of the oath was admitted to a degree unknown elsewhere. The accused was allowed in certain cases to clear himself, however notorious were the facts, and no evidence was admitted to disprove his position, unless it were a question of theft, and the stolen articles were found in his possession, or he had suffered a previous conviction. (Jur. Provin. Saxon. Lib. I. Art. 15, 18, 39; Lib. II. Art. 4, 72.) Even this was an improvement on the previous custom, if we may believe Cardinal Henry of Susa, who denounces the practice in Saxony and Dacia, where a man can clear himself, even if he holds the stolen article in his hand and the loser has ample witnesses present (Hostiensis Aureæ Summæ Lib. v. De Purg. canon. § 3). This irrational abuse was long in vogue, and was denounced by the council of Bâle in the fifteenth century (Schilter. Thesaur. II. 291). It only prevailed in the north of Germany; the Jus

[1] " Ego solus jurare volo, tu, si audes, nega sacramentum meum et armis mecum contende."—Ll. Ripuar. Tit. IX. § 3.

where the oath is only the preliminary to proof by the judgment of God.

The exceptions to this in the early legislation of the barbarians are merely special immunities bestowed on rank.
Thus in one of the most primitive of the Anglo-Saxon codes,
which dates from the seventh century, the king and the bishop
are permitted to rebut an accusation with their simple asseveration, and the thane and the mass-priest with a simple oath,
while the great body both of clerks and laymen are forced to
clear themselves by undergoing the regular form of canonical
compurgation which will be hereafter described.[1] So, in the
Welsh legislation, exemption from the oath of absolution was
accorded to bishops, lords, the deaf, the dumb, men of a
different language, and pregnant women.[2] Instances of class-
privileges such as these may be traced throughout the whole
period of the dark ages, and prove nothing except the
advantages claimed and enjoyed by caste. Thus, by the law
of Southern Germany, the unsupported oath of a claimant
was sufficient, if he were a person of substance and repute,
while, if otherwise, he was obliged to provide two conjurators,[3]
and in Castile, the *fijodalgo*, or noble, could rebut a claim in
civil cases by taking three solemn oaths, in which he invoked
on himself the vengeance of God in this world and the next.[4]

So far, indeed, were the Barbarians from reposing implicit
confidence in the integrity of their fellows that their earliest
records show how fully they shared in the common desire of

Provin. Alaman. (cap. ccclxxxi. ⸹ 3), which regulated Southern Germany,
alludes to it as one of the distinguishing features of the Saxon code.

So, also, at the same period a special privilege was claimed by the inhabitants of Franconia, in virtue of which a murderer was allowed to rebut with
his single oath all testimony as to his guilt, unless he chanced to be caught
with the red hand—Jur. Provin. Alaman. cap. cvi. ⸹ 7.

[1] Laws of Wihtræd, cap. 16–21. Comp. Ll. Henrici I. Tit. lxiv. ⸹ 8.

[2] Anomalous Laws, Book IV. chap. i. ⸹ 11.

[3] Jur. Provin. Alaman. cclxiv. 7, 8.

[4] Fuero Viejo, III. ii.

mankind to place the oath under the most efficient guarantees that ingenuity could devise. In its most simple form the oath is an invocation of some deity or supernatural power to grant or withhold his favor in accordance with the veracity of the swearer, but at all times men have sought to render this more impressive by interposing material objects dear to the individual, which were understood to be offered as pledges or victims for the divine wrath. Thus, among the Hindus, the ancient Manava Dharma Sastra prescribes the oath as satisfactory evidence in default of evidence, but requires it to be duly reinforced—

" In cases where there is no testimony, and the judge cannot decide upon which side lies the truth, he can determine it fully by administering the oath.

" Oaths were sworn by the seven Maharshis, and by the gods, to make doubtful things manifest, and even Vasishtha sware an oath before the king Sudama, son of Piyavana, when Viswamitra accused him of eating a hundred children.

" Let not the wise man take an oath in vain, even for things of little weight; for he who takes an oath in vain is lost in this world and the next.

" Let the judge swear the Brahman by his truth; the Kshatriya by his horses, his elephants, or his arms; the Vaisya by his cows, his corn, and his gold; the Sudra by all crimes."[1]

And in the more detailed code of Vishnu there is an exceedingly complicated system of objects to be sworn upon, varying with the amount at stake and the caste of the swearer.[2]

---

[1] Book VII. 109–13 (after Delongchamps' translation).

The corresponding passage in the Institutes of Vishnu (VIII. 20–3) renders this somewhat more intelligible. When the judge swears the witness—

" A Brahmana he must address thus, ' Declare.'

" A Kshatriya he must address thus, ' Declare the truth.'

" A Vaisya he must address thus, ' Thy kine, grain, and gold (shall yield thee no fruit if thou wert to give false evidence).'

" A Sudra he must address thus, ' Thou shalt have to atone for all (possible) heavy crimes (if thou wert to give false evidence).' "

[2] Institutes of Vishnu, IX. (Jolly's Translation).

3

We see the same custom in Greece, where Homer represents Hera as exculpating herself by an oath on the sacred head of Zeus, and on their marriage-bed, a practice which mortals imitated by swearing on the heads of their children, or on that of their patron, or of the king.[1] Under the Roman law, oaths were frequently taken on the head of the litigant, or on those of his children.[2] The Norse warrior was sworn, like the Hindu Kshatriya, on his warlike gear:

> " Oaths shalt thou
> First to me swear,
> By board of ship,
> By rim of shield,
> By shoulder of steed,
>
> By edge of sword,
> That thou wilt not slay
> The wife of Volund,
> Nor of my bride
> Cause the death."[3]

When these material pledges were not offered, the sanctions of religion have in all ages been called into play to impress the imagination of the swearer with the awful responsibility incurred, the presence of the deity being obtained by the offer of a sacrifice, or his interposition being assured by the use of some object of peculiar sacredness.   In Deuteronomy, when the corpse of a murdered man was found, the elders of the nearest city disculpated themselves and their fellow-citizens before the Levites over the body of a heifer slain for the purpose.[4] We see the same principle applied to promissory oaths in the horse which Tyndareus sacrificed and buried when he exacted from the suitors of Helen the oath that they would accede to her choice of a bridegroom and defend her and her husband against all comers ;[5] and it is only necessary

---

[1] Iliad. xv. 36–40.—Luciani Philopseud. 5 ; Cataplus 11.

[2] Ll. 3, 4, D. XII. ii.

[3] Volundarkvida 31 (Thorpe's Sæmund's Edda). A curious remnant of this is seen in the burgher law of Northern Germany in the thirteenth century, by which a man reclaiming a stolen horse was bound to kick its left foot with his right foot, while with his left hand he took hold of the animal's ear and swore by its head that it was his.—Sachsisches Weichbild, art. 135.

[4] Deuteron. xxi. 4–8.   [5] Pausan. III. xx. 9.

to allude to the well-known Ara Maxima of Hercules in Rome to show the prevalence of the same customs among the Italiotes. Similar practices were familiar to the Norsemen. Among them the Godi was both priest and judge, the judgment-seat adjoined the temple, and all parties to a suit, including judge and witnesses, were solemnly sworn upon the sacred ring kept for that purpose on the altar. It was sprinkled with the blood of a sacrificial bull, and then the oath was taken by invoking Freyr and Niord, and the almighty As to help the swearer as he should maintain truth and justice.[1] Yet so little did all these precautions serve to curb the untruthfulness of the cunning sea-kings that in Viga-Glums Saga we find Glum denying a charge of murder by an oath taken in three temples, in which he called Odin to witness in words so craftily framed that while he was in reality confessing his guilt he apparently was denying it most circumstantially.[2]

Similarly in Christian times, the most venerated forms of religion were, from a very early period, called in to lend sanctity to the imprecation, by devices which gave additional solemnity to the awful ceremony. In this the natural tendency of the church to follow the traditional customs of the populations from which its members were drawn was reinforced by the example of the practices of Judaism. The " covenant between the pieces," by which Yahveh confirmed his promises to Abram, and by which the Jews renewed their promises to him, was a sacrificial ceremony of the most impressive character, only to be used on occasions of supreme importance. As soon as a permanent place of worship was provided, the altar in the temple was resorted to by litigants in order that the oath might be taken in the presence of Yahveh himself; and so powerful was the impression of this upon the Christian mind that in the early ages of the church there was a popular

---

[1] Islands Landnamabok IV. 7 ; II. 9 (Ed. 1774, pp. 299, 83).
[2] Keyser's Religion of the Northmen, Pennock's Translation, p. 238.

superstition that an oath taken in a Jewish synagogue was more binding and more efficient than one taken elsewhere.[1] These beliefs developed into a great variety of formulas, which would reward an examination more detailed than that which I can give them here.

In the middle of the sixth century, Pope Pelagius I. did not disdain to absolve himself from the charge of having been concerned in the troubles which drove his predecessor Vigilius into exile, by taking a disculpatory oath in the pulpit, holding over his head a crucifix and the gospels;[2] and in the eighth century a priest accused without witnesses to prove his guilt was enabled to absolve himself by placing the cross upon his head and declaring his innocence by the Everlasting God.[3] So, when the holy Gregory of Tours was accused of reproachful words truly spoken of Queen Fredegonda, a council of bishops decided that he should clear himself of the charge by oaths on three altars, after celebrating mass on each, which he duly performed, doubtless more to his corporeal than his spiritual benefit.[4] This plan of reduplicating oaths on different altars was an established practice among the Anglo-Saxons, who, in certain cases, allowed the plaintiff to substantiate his assertion by swearing in four churches, while the defendant could rebut the charge by taking an oath of negation in twelve.[5] Seven altars are similarly specified in the ancient Welsh laws in cases where a surety desired to deny his suretyship;[6] and, according to the *Fleta*, as late as the thirteenth century, a custom was current among merchants of proving the payment

---

[1] Gen. xv. 9–17.—Jer. xxxiv. 18–19.—I. Kings, viii. 31–2.—Chrysost. Orat. adv. Jud. I. 3.

[2] Anastas. Biblioth. No. LXII.

[3] Ecgberti Dialog. IV. (Haddan and Stubbs's Councils of Great Britain, III. 405).

[4] Gregor. Turon. Hist. Lib. v. cap. xlix. Gregory complains that this was contrary to the canons, of which more hereafter.

[5] Dooms of Alfred, cap. 33.

[6] Dimetian Code, Bk. II. chap. vi. § 17 (Owen, I. 431).

of a debt by swearing in nine churches, the abuse of which led to its abrogation.[1]

The intense veneration with which relics were regarded, however, caused them to be generally adopted as the most effective means of adding security to oaths, and so little respect was felt for the simple oath that, ere long, the adjuncts came to be looked upon as the essential feature, and the imprecation itself to be divested of binding force without them. Thus, in 680, when Ebroin, mayor of the palace of Burgundy, had defeated Martin, Duke of Austrasia, and desired to entice him from his refuge in the stronghold of Laon, two bishops were sent to him bearing the royal reliquaries, on which they swore that his life should be safe. Ebroin, however, had astutely removed the holy remains from their cases in advance, and when he thus got his enemy in his power, he held it but a venial indiscretion to expose Martin to a shameful death.[2] How thoroughly this was in accordance with the ideas of the age is shown by the incorporation, in the canons of the church, of the doctrine that an oath was to be estimated by its externals and not by itself. The penitential of David, dating from the latter half of the sixth century, provides that perjury committed in a church shall be punished by a fine of four times the value of that for which the false oath was taken,[3] but no penalty is provided for false swearing elsewhere. As the theory developed itself this tacit condoning of such perjury was boldly declared to be good ecclesiastical law, and the venerable code of morality which passes under the name of

[1] Fleta, Lib. II. cap. lxiii. § 12. The Moslem jurisprudence has a somewhat similar provision for accusatorial oaths in the Iesameh by which a murderer can be convicted, in the absence of testimony or confession, by fifty oaths sworn by relatives of the victim. Of these there must be at least two, and the fifty oaths are divided between them in proportion to their respective legal shares in the Deeyeh, or blood-money for the murder.—Du Boys, Droit Criminel des Peuples Modernes, I. z69.—Seignette, Code Mussulman, Constantine, 1878, p. lvi.

[2] Fredegarii Chron. cap. xcvii.

[3] Excerpt. de Libro Davidis No. xvi. (Haddan and Stubbs, I. 120).

3*

Theodore Archbishop of Canterbury assumes that a false oath taken on a consecrated cross requires, for absolution, three times the penance necessary in cases where the oath had been taken on an unconsecrated one, while, if the ministration of a priest had not been employed, the oath was void, and no penalty was inflicted for its violation.[1] In a similar mood the penitential known as that of Gregory III. provides that three years' penance will absolve for perjury committed on a consecrated cross or on the hand of a bishop or priest, while seven years are requisite if the oath has been taken on the gospels or on an altar with relics.[2] This rule took its final shape in the canon law, which provides one year's penance for perjury committed on an unconsecrated cross, and three years' for that on a consecrated one, or on the hand of a bishop.[3]

These principles were adopted as the fundamental basis of all legal procedures in Wales. Every prosecution and defence required relics to give validity to the oaths of both parties, and even in the fifteenth century a collection of laws declares that a plaintiff coming into court without a relic on which to make his oath, not only lost his cause, but incurred a fine of nine-score pence. The same tendency is shown in the rule by which a man who suspected another of theft could go to him with a relic, and in the presence of witnesses demand an oath of ne-gation, a failure in which was a conviction of the crime im-

---

[1] Si in manu episcopi . . . aut in cruce consecrata perjurat III. annos pœniteat. Si vero in cruce non consecrata perjurat, I. annum pœniteat; si autem in manu hominis laici juraverit nihil est.—Theodori Cantuar. Pœnit. cap. xxiv. § 2. (Thorpe, Ancient Laws, vol. II. p. 29.) Cf. Haddan and Stubbs, III. 423; Wasserschleben, Bussordnungen, pp. 190, 226.

[2] Pœnitent. Pseudo-Gregor. III. vii. (Wasserschleben, p. 539).

[3] Pœnitent. Cummeani cap. v. § 3 (Wasserschleben, p. 477).—Gratiani Decr. c. 2. Caus. XXII. Q. v. In the fourteenth century this was repeated in the penitential canons of Astesanus (§ 23), which continued until the Reformation to be a recognized authority in the confessional. Astesanus, however, explains that the obligation is equal to God, but unequal as regards the church, whence the difference in the penance.—Astesani Summa de Casibus Conscientiæ, P. I. Lib. I. Tit. xviii.

puted, without further trial.[1]   In the same spirit, ecclesiastical
authority was even found to admit that a powerful motive might
extenuate the sin of perjury.   If committed voluntarily, seven
years of penitence were enjoined for its absolution; if invol-
untarily, sixteen months, while if to preserve life or limb, the
offence could be washed out with four months.[2]   When such
doctrines were received and acted upon, we can hardly wonder
at the ingenious device which the sensitive charity of King
Robert the Pious imitated from the duplicity of Ebroin, to save
the souls of his friends.   He provided two reliquaries on which
to receive their oaths—one for his magnates, splendidly fabri-
cated of crystal and gold, but entirely empty, the other for the
common herd, plainer and enshrining a bird's egg.   Knowing
in advance that his lieges would be forsworn, he thus piously
sought to save them from sin in spite of themselves, and his
monkish panegyrist is delighted in recounting this holy deceit.[3]

It was easy, from a belief such as this, to draw the deduc-
tion that when an oath was sworn on relics of peculiar sanctity, immediate punishment would follow perjury; and thus it
followed that some shrines obtained a reputation which caused
them to be resorted to in the settlement of disputed judicial
questions.   Even as early as St. Augustin there are traces of

---

[1] Anomalous Laws, Book IX. chap. v. § 3; chap. xxxviii. § 1 (Owen,
II. 233, 303).   The definition of relics, however, was somewhat vague—
" There are three relics to swear by: the staff of a priest; the name of God;
and hand to hand with the one sworn to." Bk. XIII. ch. ii. § 219 (Ibid. II.
557).

[2] Regino de Eccles. Discip. Lib. I. cap. ccc.   See also Jur. Provin.
Saxon, Lib. III. c. 41.   Notwithstanding the laxity of these doctrines, it
is not to be supposed that the true theory of the oath was altogether lost.
St. Isidor of Seville, who was but little anterior to Theodore of Canterbury,
well expresses it (Sentent. Lib. II. cap. xxxi. § 8): " Quacunque arte ver-
borum quisque juret, Deus tamen, qui conscientiæ testis est, ita hoc accipit,
sicut ille cui juratur intelligit," and this, being adopted in successive collections of canons, coexisted with the above as a maxim of ecclesiastical law
(Ivon. Decret. P. XII. c. 36.—Gratian. c. 13, Caus. XXII. Q. ii.).

[3] Helgaldi Vit. Roberti Regis.

such practices, which that Father of the Church not only records, but imitated,[1] and at a later period the legends are
numerous which record how the perjured sinner was stricken
down senseless or rendered rigid and motionless in the act of
swearing falsely.[2] From this point of view oaths were really
ordeals, and as such we shall consider them hereafter. At present it suffices to observe that the profit which the church derived from thus administering oaths on relics affords an easy
explanation of her teachings, and of the extension of these
practices. Their resultant advantages are well illustrated by
the example of the holy taper of Cardigan, in Wales. A
miraculous image of the Virgin was cast ashore, bearing this
taper burning in its hand. A church was built for it, and
the taper "contynued styll burnynge the space of nyne yeres,
without wastynge, until the tyme that one forsware himselfe
thereon, so then it extincted, and never burned after." At
the suppression of the house under Henry VIII., the prior,
Thomas Hore, testified : "Item, that since the ceasynge of
burnynge of the sayd taper, it was enclosed and taken for a
greate relyque, and so worshipped and kyssed of pylgremes,
and used of men to sweare by in difficill and harde matters,
whereof the advauntage admounted to great sommes of money
in tymes passed, payenge yerely to the same XXti nobles for a
pencion unto thabbott of Chersey."[3]

In all this Spain would seem to be exceptional. In the
thirteenth century the rule is expressed that a pleader must

---

[1] Augustin. Epist. 78, §§ 2, 3 (Ed. Benedict.).

[2] Gregor. Turon. de Gloria Martyr. cap. 58, 103.

[3] Suppression of Monasteries, p. 186 (Camden Soc. Pub.). The Priory
of Cardigan was dependent upon the Abbey of Chertsey, and the sum named
was apparently the abbot's share of the annual "alms."

Perhaps the most suggestive illustration of the reverence for relics is a
passage in the ancient Welsh laws limiting the protection legally afforded
by them—"If a person have relics upon him and does an illegal act under
the relics, he is not to have protection or defence through those relics, for
he has not deserved it."—Venedotian Code, Bk. I. chap. x. § 7.

take the oath required of him by his antagonist; if he is required to swear by God, it will not suffice for him to swear by some saint, or by his own head. Oaths could indeed be taken on crosses or altars, but they could also be reduced to the simplest asseveration. Thus, there is a provision that if one party says "Swear to me on your simple word," then the reply "know that it is so," or "believe me that it is so," suffices, and has all the force of the most solemn adjuration.[1]

CHAPTER III.

CONJURATORS, OR PARTAKERS IN THE OATH.

NOTWITHSTANDING the earnestness with which these teachings were enforced, it may readily be believed that the wild barbarian, who was clamoring for the restoration of stolen cattle, or the angry relatives, eager to share the *wer-gild* of some murdered kinsman, would scarce submit to be balked of their rights at the cost of simple perjury on the part of the criminal. We have seen that both before and after their conversion to Christianity they had little scruple in defiling the most sacred sanctions of the oath with cunning fraud, and they could repose little confidence in the most elaborate devices which superstition could invent to render perjury more to be dreaded than defeat. It was therefore natural that they should perpetuate an ancestral custom, which had arisen from the structure of their society, and which derived its guarantee from the solidarity of families alluded to above. This was the custom which was subsequently known as canonical compurgation, and which long remained a part of English jurisprudence, under the name of the Wager of Law. The defendant, when denying the allegation under oath,

---

[1] Espéculo, Lib. v. Tit. xi. leyes 14, 15. The oaths required of Jews and Moors were much more elaborate (Ibid. 16, 17).

appeared surrounded by a number of companions—*juratores, conjuratores, sacramentales, collaudantes, compurgatores,* as they were variously termed—who swore, not to their knowledge of the facts, but as sharers and partakers in the oath of denial.

This form of procedure derives importance from the fact that it is an expression of the character, not of an isolated sept, but of nearly all the races that have moulded the destinies of modern Europe. Although unknown to the Roman law, there are traces of it in the ancient Hellenic legislation.[1] The Ostrogoths in Italy, and the Wisigoths of the south of France and Spain were the only nations in whose extant codes it occupies no place, and they, as has already been remarked, at an early period yielded themselves completely to the influence of the Roman civilization.[2]   On the other hand, the Salians, the Ripuarians, the Alamanni, the Baioarians, the Lombards, the Frisians, the Norsemen, the Saxons, the Angli and Werini, the Anglo-Saxons, and the Welsh, races whose common origin must be sought in the prehistoric past, all gave to this form of purgation a prominent position in their jurisprudence, and it may be said to have reigned from Southern Italy to Scotland.[3]

The earliest text of the Salic law presents us with the usages of the Franks unaltered by any allusions to Christianity, and it may therefore be presumed to date from a period not later than the conversion of Clovis. In this primitive code there are directions for the employment of conjurators, which show that the procedure was a settled and established form at that period.[4]   So in the Frisian law, which, although compiled in

---

[1] Patetta, Le Ordalie, Torino, 1890, p. 130.

[2] Yet compurgators appear in the Spanish laws of the twelfth century. See Fuero de Balbás, ann. 1135 (Coleccion de Privilegios, etc. Madrid, 1833, T. VI. p. 85).

[3] The primitive Scottish procedure appears to have been based on compurgation.—Neilson's Trial by Combat, London, 1890, p. 78.

[4] First Text of Pardessus, Tit. xxxix. § 2, and Tit. xlii. § 5 (Loi Salique,

the eighth century, still reveals pagan customs and the primitive condition of society, the practice of compurgation evidently forms the basis of judicial proceedings. The Islands Landnamabok also exhibits it as a form of regular procedure among the heathen Norsemen. Although the other codes have only reached us in revisions subsequent to the conversion of the several tribes, still, the universal use of the practice shows that its origin must be traced to a period anterior to the separation of the several races from the original common stock.

The church, with the tact which distinguished her dealings with her new converts, was not long in adopting a system which was admirably suited for her defence in an age of brute force. As holy orders sundered all other ties, and as the church was regarded as one vast family, ecclesiastics speedily arrogated to themselves and obtained the privilege of having men of their own class as compurgators, and, thus fortified for mutual support, they were aided in resisting the oppressors who invaded their rights on every hand. This claim, with all its attendant advantages, was fully conceded when Charlemagne, in the year 800, went to Rome for the purpose of trying Pope Leo III. on a grave charge, and in that august presence the Pontiff, whom no witnesses dared to accuse, cleared himself of the crimes imputed to him by solemnly taking the oath of denial in company with twelve priests as compurgators.[1] Three years afterwards, the Emperor decreed

Paris, 1843, pp. 21, 23). It is somewhat singular that in the subsequent recensions of the code the provision is omitted in these passages.

[1] Eginhard. Annal. ann. 800.—The monkish chroniclers have endeavored to conceal the fact that Leo underwent the form of trial like a common criminal, but the evidence is indubitable. Charlemagne alludes to it in the *Capitularium Aquisgranense* ann. 803, in a manner which admits of no dispute.

The monk of St. Gall (De Gestis B. Carol. Mag. Lib. i. cap. 28), whose work is rather legendary in its character, describes the Pope as swearing to his innocence by his share at the day of judgment in the promises of the gospels, which he had placed upon his head.

that, in all doubtful cases, priests should defend themselves with three, five, or seven ecclesiastical compurgators, and he announced that this decision had been reached by the common consent of pope, patriarchs, bishops, and all the faithful.[1] It is true that a few months later, on being shown a decretal of Gregory II.[2] ordering the clergy to rebut with their single oaths all accusations unsupported by witnesses, he modified his previous command, and left the matter to the discretion of his prelates ; but this had no practical result, for Charlemagne's capitulary was adopted in the canon law and ascribed to Leo himself.[3] The custom soon received the papal sanction again in the most solemn manner. In 823, Pope Pascal I. was more than suspected of complicity in the murder of Theodore and Leo, two high dignitaries of the papal court.

[1] Capit. Aquisgran. ann. 803, cap. vii.

[2] Bonifacii Epist. cxxvi.

The subject of the oaths of priests was one of considerable perplexity during the dark ages. Among the numerous privileges assumed by the sacerdotal body was exemption from the necessity of swearing, an exemption which had the justification of the ancient Roman custom; " Sacerdotem, Vestalem, et Flaminem Dialem in omni mea jurisdictione jurare non cogam" (Edict. Perpet. ap. Aul. Gell. x. 15). The effort to obtain the reversion of this privilege dates from an early period, and was sometimes allowed and sometimes rejected by the secular authorities, both as respects promissory, judicial, and exculpatory oaths. The struggle between church and state on this subject is well exemplified in a case which occurred in 1269. The Archbishop of Reims sued a burgher of Chaudardre. When each party had to take the oath, the prelate demanded that his should be taken by his attorney. The defendant demurred to this, alleging that the archbishop had in person presented the complaint. Appeal was made to the Parlement of Paris, which decided that the defendant's logic was correct, and that the personal oath of the prelate was requisite (Olim, I. 765).

In Spain, a bishop appearing in a secular court, either as plaintiff or defendant, was not exempt from the oath, but had the singular privilege of not being compelled to touch the gospels on which he swore.—Siete Partidas, P. iii. Tit. xl. l. 24.

[3] Gratian. c. 19, Caus. ii. Q. v.

Desirous to avoid an investigation by the commissioners sent by Louis le Débonnaire, he hastily purged himself of the crime in anticipation of their arrival, by an oath taken with a number of bishops as his compurgators;[1] and it is a striking example of the weight accorded to the procedure that, although the assumed fault of the victims had been their devotion to the imperial party, and though the pope had by force of arms prevented any pursuit of the murderers, the emperor was powerless to exact satisfaction, and there was nothing further to be done.   Pope Pascal stood before the world an innocent man.

It is true that, in the tenth century, Atto of Vercelli complains bitterly that a perverse generation refused to be satisfied with the single oath of an accused priest, and required him to be surrounded by compurgators of his class, which that indignant sacerdotalist regarded as a grievous wrong.[2]   As the priesthood, however, failed in obtaining the entire immunity for which they strove during those turbulent times, the unquestioned advantages which compurgation afforded recommended it to them with constantly increasing force.   Forbidden at length to employ the duel in settling their differences, and endeavoring, in the eleventh and twelfth centuries, to obtain exemption from the ordeal, they finally accepted compurgation as the special mode of trial adapted to members of the church, and for a long period we find it recognized as such in all the collections of canons and writings of ecclesiastical jurists.[3] From this fact it obtained its appellation of *purgatio canonica*, or canonical compurgation.

---

[1] Eginhard. Annal. ann. 823.
[2] Atton. de Pressuris Ecclesiast. P. 1.
[3] Buchardus, Ivo, Gratianus, *passim.*—Ivon. Epist. 74.

CHAPTER IV.

SELECTION OF COMPURGATORS.

As already remarked, the origin of the custom is to be traced to the principle of the unity of families. As the offender could summon his kindred around him to resist an armed attack of the injured party, so he took them with him to the court, to defend him with their oaths. Accordingly, we find that the service was usually performed by the kindred, and in some codes this is even prescribed by law, though not universally.[1] This is well illustrated in the Welsh laws, where the *raith*, or compurgation, was the basis of almost all procedure, and where consequently the system was brought to its fullest perfection. Complicated rules existed as to the proportion of paternal and maternal kindred required in various cases, and the connection between the *wer-gild* and the obligation of swearing in defence of a kinsman was fully

---

[1] L. Longobard. Lib. II. Tit. xxi. § 9; Tit. lv. § 12.—L. Burgund. Tit. vii.—Laws of Ethelred, Tit. ix. §§ 23, 24.—L. Henrici I. cap. lxxiv. § 1. Feudor. Lib. v. Tit. ii.

This point illustrates the essential distinction between witnesses and compurgators. The Roman law exercised great discrimination in admitting the evidence of a relative to either party in an action (Pauli Sentent. Lib. v. Tit. xv.—Ll. 4, 5, 6, 9. Dig. XXII. v.). The Wisigoths not only adopted this principle, but carried it so far as to exclude the evidence of a kinsman in a cause between his relative and a stranger (L. Wisigoth. Lib. II. Tit. iv. c. 12), which was adopted into the Carlovingian legislation (Benedict. Levit. Capitul. Lib. VI. c. 348) under the strong Romanizing influence which then prevailed. The rule, once established, retained its place through the vicissitudes of the feudal and customary law (Beaumanoir, Coutumes du Beauvoisis, cap. xxxix. § 38.—Cout. de Bretagne, Tit. vii. art. 161, 162). In the ancient Brahmanic legislation the evidence of both friends and enemies was excluded (Institutes of Vishnu, viii. 3).

recognized—"Because the law adjudges the men nearest in worth in every case, excepting where there shall be men under vows to deny murder," therefore the compurgators were required to be those "nearest to obtain his worth if killed."[1] Under these circumstances, the *raithman* could be objected to on the score of not being of kin, when the caths of himself and his principal were received as sufficient proof of relationship;[2] and the *alltud*, or foreigner, was not entitled to the raith unless he had kindred to serve on it.[3] How the custom sometimes worked in practice among the untameable barbarians is fairly illustrated by a case recounted by Aimoin as occurring under Chilperic I. in the latter half of the sixth century. A wife suspected by her husband offered the oath of purgation on the altar of St. Denis with her relatives, who were persuaded of her innocence; the husband not yet satisfied, accused the compurgators of perjury, and the fierce passions of both parties becoming excited, weapons were speedily drawn, and the sanctity of the venerable church was profaned with blood.[4]

It was manifestly impossible, however, to enforce the rule of kinship in all cases, for the number of compurgators varied in the different codes, and in all of them a great number were required when the matter at stake was large, or the crime or criminal important. Thus when Chilperic I. was assassinated in 584, doubts were entertained as to the legitimacy of his son Clotair, an infant of four months—doubts which neither the character of Queen Fredegonda nor the manner of Chilperic's death had any tendency to lessen—and Gontran, brother of the murdered king, did not hesitate to express his belief that the royal child's paternity was traceable to some one of the minions of the court, a belief doubtless stimulated by the promise it afforded him of another crown. Fredegonda, however, repaired her somewhat questionable reputation and

[1] Anomalous Laws, Bk. IX. chap. ii. § 4; chap. v. § 2 (Owen, II. 225, 233). This collection of laws is posterior to the year 1430.

[2] Anomalous Laws, Bk. v. chap. ii. § 117 (Ibid. II. p. 85).

[3] Ibid. § 144 (p. 95).　　　　[4] Aimoini Lib. III. c. 29.

secured the throne to her offspring, by appearing at the altar
with three bishops and three hundred nobles, who all swore
with her as to the legitimacy of the little prince, and no further
doubts were ventured on the delicate subject.[1] A similar case
occurred in Germany in 899, when Queen Uta cleared herself
of an accusation of infidelity, by taking a purgatorial oath
with eighty-two nobles.[2] So in 824, a dispute between Hubert,
Bishop of Worcester, and the Abbey of Berkeley, concerning
the monastery of Westbury, was settled by the oath of the
bishop, supported by those of fifty mass-priests, ten deacons,
and a hundred and fifty other ecclesiastics.[3] These were,
perhaps, exceptional instances, but in Wales the law required,
as a regular matter, enormous numbers of compurgators in
many cases. Privity to homicide, for instance, was divided
into three triads, or nine classes of various degrees of guilt.
Of these, the first triad called for one hundred raithmen to
establish the denial ; the second triad, 200, and the third,
300 ;[4] while, to rebut an accusation of killing with savage
violence or poisoning, the enormous number of six hundred
compurgators was considered necessary.[5] Even these armies
of oath-takers did not widen the circle from which selection
was allowed, for the law absolutely specifies that "the oaths
of three hundred men of a kindred are required to deny
murder, blood, and wound,"[6] and the possibility of finding
them is only explicable by the system of tribes or clans in
which all were legally related one to another. This is illustrated by a further regulation, according to which, under the

---

[1] Greg. Turon. Lib. VIII. c. 9.   [2] Herman. Contract. ann. 899.

[3] Spelman. Concil. I. 335.

[4] Venedotian Code, Book III. chap. i. §§ 1–10.—Dimetian and Gwentian
Codes, Book II. chap. i. §§ 10–12 (Owen I. 219–21, 407, 689).—There is
very great confusion in these laws as to the numbers requisite for many
crimes, but with respect to the accessories of *galanas*, or homicide, the
rule appears to have been absolute.—Cf. Spelman, Glossary s. v. *Assath.*

[5] Venedotian Code, Book III. chap. i. § 18. Anomalous Laws, Book IV.
chap. iii. §§ 12, 13 (Ibid. I. 231, II. 23).

[6] Ibid. § 17 (p. 231); cf. Book II. chap. viii. § 4 (p. 137).

Gwentian code, in an accusation of theft, with positive evidence, the thief was directed to clear himself with twenty-four raithmen of his own *cantrev* or district, in equal number from each *cymwd* or sub-district.[1]

Under a different social organization, it is evidently impossible that a kindred sufficiently large could have been assembled in the most numerous families, and even when the requirements were more reasonable, the same difficulty must frequently have occurred. This is recognized in the Danish laws of the thirteenth and fourteenth centuries, where the conjuratorial oaths of kindred, known as *neffn i kyn*, were requisite, unless the accused could swear that he had no relations, in which case he was allowed to produce twelve other men of proper character, *lag feste men.*[2] In a constitution of Frederic II. in 1235, the compurgators are required to be of the same class as their principal, and to be *sinodales homines*, men of undoubted character.[3] Thus the aid of those not connected by ties of blood must often have been necessary, and as it was a service not without danger, as we shall see hereafter, it is not easy to understand how the requisite number was reached. In certain cases, no doubt, the possibility of obtaining those not bound by kindred to undertake the office is traceable to the liability which in some instances rested upon a township for crime committed within its borders;[4] while the system of

---

[1] Gwentian Code, Book II. chap. iii. § 11 (Ibid. I. 691).

[2] Leg. Cimbric. Lib. II. c. 9.—Constit. Woldemari Regis §§ 9, 52, 56, 86. Throughout Germany a minor son could be cleared, even in capital accusations, by the single purgatorial oath of his father, if it was the first time that they had been defendants in court.—Jur. Provin. Alaman. cap. clxix. § 1 ; Sachsische Weichbild, art. 76.

[3] Böhlau, Nove constitutiones Dom. Alberti, pp. 2, 6, 12, 38 (Weimar, 1858). "Cum duobus viris bone opinionis et integri status, sinodalibus hominibus." The expression is doubtless derived from the *testes synodales* —men of standing and reputation selected in episcopal synods to act as a kind of grand jury and report the sins of their neighbors.

[4] This has been denied by those who assume that the *frithborgs* of Edward the Confessor are the earliest instance of such institutions, but traces

guilds in which the members shared with each other a responsibility resembling that of kinship rendered participation in the
oath of denial almost a necessity when a comrade was
prosecuted.[1]

It would be endless to specify all the variations in the
numbers required by the different codes in all imaginable cases
of quarrel between every class of society. Numerous elements
entered into these regulations; the nature of the crime or
claim, the station of the parties, the rank of the compurgators,
and the mode by which they were selected. Thus, in the
simplest and most ancient form, the Salic law merely specifies
twenty-five compurgators to be equally chosen by both parties.[2]
Some formulas of Marculfus specify three freeholders and
twelve friends of the accused.[3] A Merovingian edict of 593
directs the employment of three peers of the defendant, with
three others chosen for the purpose, probably by the court.[4]

of communal societies are to be found in the most ancient text of the Salic
law (First text of Pardessus, Tit. XLV.), and both Childebert and Clotair II.,
in edicts promulgated near the close of the sixth century, hold the hundreds
or townships responsible for robberies committed within their limits (Decret.
Childeberti ann. 595, c. 10; Decret. Chlotarii II. c. 1).

It is not improbable that, as among all the barbarian races, the family
was liable for the misdeeds of its members, so the tribe or clan of the
offender was held responsible when the offence was committed upon a
member of another tribe, and such edicts as those of Childebert and Clotair were merely adaptations of the rule to the existing condition of society.
The most perfect early code that has reached us, that of the ancient Irish,
expresses in detail the responsibility of each sept for the actions not only
of its members, but of those also who were in any way connected with it.
" And because the four nearest tribes bear the crime of each kinsman of
their stock. . . . And because there are four who have an interest in every
one who sues and is sued: the tribe of the father, the chief, the church,
the tribe of the mother or foster-father. . . . Every tribe is liable after the
absconding of a member of it, after notice, after warning, and after lawful
waiting."—Senchus Mor, I. 263–5.

[1] See Mr. Pike's very interesting " History of Crime in England," Vol.
I. pp. 61–2. London, 1873.

[2] First text of Pardessus, Tit. XLII. § 5.

[3] Marculf. App. xxxii.; xxix.　　　　[4] Pact. pro Tenore Pacis cap. vi.

Alternative numbers, however, soon make their appearance, depending upon the manner in which the men were chosen. Thus among the Alamanni, on a trial for murder, the accused was obliged to secure the support of twenty designated men, or, if he brought such as he had selected himself, the number was increased to eighty.[1] So, in a capitulary of 803, Charlemagne prescribes seven chosen conjurators, or twelve if taken at random,[2] a rule which is virtually the same as that laid down by the Emperor Henry III. in the middle of the eleventh century.[3] In 922 the council of Coblentz directs that accusations of sacrilege could be rebutted with twenty-four chosen men, or seventy-two freemen not thus selected.[4] In Bigorre the law thus discriminated against the *cagots*—an infamous wandering race of uncertain origin—for cases in which the oaths of seven conjurators ordinarily sufficed required thirty *cagots*, when the latter were called upon to act.[5] In an English record of the fifteenth century we find a defendant called upon to prove his innocence with six of his neighbors or twelve strangers.[6]

Strangely enough, the church at one time adopted the principle that the higher the rank of the accused the more he must present of his peers as compurgators. Thus the bishop required eleven bishops, the priest five priests, and the deacon two deacons; but Cardinal Henry of Susa who enunciates this says it is an error, and that the number is at the discretion of the judge.[7] The rule, moreover, that the compurgators must be of the same rank and class as the accused was waived

---

[1] L. Alaman. Tit. lxxvi.   [2] Capit. Car. Mag. IV. ann. 803, cap. x.

[3] Goldast. Constit. Imp. I. 231.

[4] Hartzheim Concil. German. II. 600.

[5] Lagrèze, Hist. du Droit dans les Pyrénées, p. 47, Paris, 1867.

[6] Pike, op. cit. I. 451.

[7]   Pontificem parium manus expurgat duodena.
        Sexta sacerdotem, levitam tertia purgat.
        Maior maiori, minor est adhibenda minori.
        Quem plebs infamat purgabitur in manifesto.
    Hostiensis Aureæ Summæ Lib. v. Tit. *De Purgat. canon.* § 4.

when they were presumably inimical to him or the proper number could not be had, and thus a cleric might be cleared by the oaths of laymen.[1]

Variations likewise occur arising from the nature of the case and the character of the plaintiff. Thus in the Scottish law of the twelfth century, in a criminal charge, a man could defend himself against his lord with eleven men of good reputation, but if the king were the accuser, twenty-four were requisite, who were all to be his peers, while in a civil case twelve were sufficient.[2] So in the burgher laws of David I., ordinary cases between citizens were settled with ten conjurators, but eleven were necessary if the king were a party, or if the matter involved the life, limb, or lands of one of the contestants; and in cases occurring between a citizen and a countryman, each party had to provide conjurators of his own class.[3] In the complicated rules for compurgation which form the basis of the Welsh jurisprudence, there are innumerable details of this nature. We have seen that for some crimes many hundred *raith-men* were required, while similar numbers were enjoined in some civil suits respecting real property.[4] From this the number diminishes in proportion to the gravity of the case, as is well illustrated by the provisions for denying the infliction of a bruise. If the mark remained until the ninth day, the accused could deny it with "two persons of the same privilege as himself;" if it remained until the eighteenth day, the oaths of three conjurators were necessary; if till the twenty-seventh day, four *raith-men* were required.[5]

---

[1] Ibid. § 5.

[2] Quoniam Attachiamenta cap. xxiv. §§ 1, 4; cap. lxxv. §§ 1, 4. In another subsequent code, in simple cases of theft, when the accuser had no testimony to substantiate his claim, thirty conjurators were necessary, of whom three must be nobles (Regiam Majestatem Lib. IV. c. 21). For the disputed date of the *Regiam* see Neilson, Trial by Combat, ch. 30.

[3] Leg. Burgorum cap. xxiv. §§ 1, 3.

[4] Anomalous Laws, Book XIII. chap. ii. § 94 (Owen II. 521).

[5] Gwentian Code, Bk. II. chap. vii. § 10 (Ibid. I. 701).

The character of the *raith-men* also affected the number demanded. Thus, in a collection of Welsh laws of the fifteenth century there is an explanation of the apparent anomaly that privity to theft or homicide required for its defence a vastly greater number of compurgators than the commission of the crime itself. The large bodies prescribed for the former consisted simply of any men that could be had—of course within the recognized grades of kindred—while, for the latter, rules of varying complexity were laid down. Thus, of the twenty-four required for theft, in some texts it is prescribed that two-thirds are to be of the nearest paternal kin, and one-third of the nearest maternal; or, again, one-half *nod-men*.[1] So, in accusations of homicide, the same proportions of paternal and maternal kindred were required, all were to be proprietors in the country of the *raith*, and three, moreover, were to be men under vows of abstinence from linen, horses, and women, besides a proper proportion of *nod-men*.[2]

Instances also occur in which the character of the defendant regulated the number required. Among the Welsh, the laws of Hoel Dda provide that a wife accused of infidelity could disprove a first charge with seven women; if her conduct provoked a second investigation, she had to procure fourteen; while, on a third trial, fifty female conjurators were requisite for her escape.[3] Another application of the same

---

[1] Anomalous Laws, Bk. IX. chap. ii. § 4; chap. xx. § 12; chap. xxi. § 3.—Book XIV. chap. xxxviii. § 16.—Book v. chap. ii. § 112 (Ibid. II. 225, 261, 709, 83).

Under the primitive Venedotian Code (Book III. chap. i. §§ 13, 19) only twelve men were required, one-half to be *nod-men*, two-thirds of paternal, and one-third of maternal kin; while in the Gwentian Code (Book II. chap. ii. § 10) and in the Dimetian Code (Book II. chap. iii. § 10, Book III. chap. i. § 24), fifty are prescribed.

The *nod men*, as will be seen hereafter, were conjurators who took a special form of oath.

[2] Anomalous Laws, Book XIV. chap. xxxviii. § 16; Book IX. chap. xx. § 12; chap. xxi. § 1.

[3] Leges Wallice, Lib. II. cap. xxiii. § 17 (Owen II. 848). It is worthy of remark that one of the few instructions for legal procedures contained in

principle is found in the provision that when a man confessed a portion of the crime imputed to him and denied the remainder, an augmented *raith* was required to support his denial, because it is more difficult to believe a man who has admitted his participation in a criminal act. Thus when only fifty men were requisite to rebut a charge of homicide, and the accused admitted one of the accessories to homicide, his denial of the main charge had to be substantiated by one hundred, two hundred, or three hundred men, according to the nature of the case. On the other hand, where no criminal act was concerned, confession of a portion diminished the *raith* for the remainder. Thus in a claim for suretyship, six compurgators were necessary to the defendant; but if he admitted part of the suretyship, his unsupported oath was sufficient to rebut the remainder, as the admission of a portion rendered him worthy of belief.[1] In the Anglo-Saxon jurisprudence, the *frangens jusjurandum,* as it was called, also grew to be an exceedingly complex system in the rules by which the number and quality of the conjurators were regulated according to the nature of the crime and the rank of the accused. In cases of peculiar atrocity, such as violation of the sanctity of the grave, only thanes were esteemed competent to appear.[2] In fact, among the Anglo-Saxons, the value of a man's oath was rated according to his rank, that

the Korán relates to cases of this kind. Chapter xxiv. 6–9 directs that a husband accusing his wife of infidelity, and having no witnesses to prove it, shall substantiate his assertion by swearing five times to the truth of the charge, invoking upon himself the malediction of God; while the wife was able to rebut the accusation by the same process. As this chapter, however, was revealed to the Prophet after he had writhed for a month under a charge brought against his favorite wife Ayesha, which he could not disregard and did not wish to entertain, the law is rather to be looked upon as *ex post facto* than as indicating any peculiar tendency of the age or race.

[1] Anomalous Laws, Book XI. chap. v. §§ 40, 41 (Ibid. II. 445).

[2] Wealreaf, *i. e.,* mortuum refere, est opus nithingi; si quis hoc negare velit, faciat hoc cum xlviii. taynis plene nobilibus.—Leg. Æthelstani, de Ordalio.

of a thane, for instance, being equal to those of seven villeins.[1] The same peculiarity is observable among the Frisians,
whose laws required that compurgators should be of the same
class as their principal, and the lower his position in the State,
the larger was the number requisite.[2]

It was, however, not only the number of compurgators required that affected the result, but the method by which they
were chosen, and this gave rise to wide variations in practice.
Originally, it is probable that the selection was left to the
accused, who gathered them from among his kindred. This
would lead almost inevitably to his acquittal, as forcibly
pointed out by Hincmar in the ninth century. In objecting
to admit the purgation of an offending priest with ecclesiastics
of his own choice, he states that evil-minded men combined
together to defeat justice and secure immunity for their crimes
by serving each other in turn, so that when the accused insisted
on offering his companions to the oath, it was necessary to
make them undergo the ordeal to prove their sincerity.[3] His
expressions indicate that the question of selection at that time
was undecided in France, and the alternative numbers alluded
to above show one of the methods adopted to meet the evident
evils of the process. Other nations devised various expedients.
The original Lombard law of King Rotharis gave to the

---

[1] Sacramentum liberalis hominis, quem quidem vocant *twelfhendeman*,
debet stare et valere juramentum septem villanorum (Cnuti Secular. cap.
127). The *twelfhendeman* meant a thane (Twelfhindus est homo plene
nobilis i. Thainus.—Leg. Henrici I. Tit. lxxvi. § 4), whose price was
1200 solidi. So thoroughly did the structure of jurisprudence depend
upon the system of *wer-gild* or composition, that the various classes of
society were named according to the value of their heads. Thus the villein
or *cherleman* was also called *twyhindus* or *twyhindeman*, his *wer-gild*
being 200 solidi; the *radcnicht* (road-knight, or mounted follower) was a
sexhendeman; and the comparative judicial weight of their oaths followed
a similar scale of valuation, which was in force even subsequently to the
Conquest (Leg. Henrici I. Tit. lxiv. § 2).

[2] L. Frision. Tit. I.

[3] Hincmari Epist. xxxiv. So also in his Capit. Synod. ann. 852, II. xxv.

plaintiff the privilege of naming a majority of the compurgators, the remainder being chosen by the defendant,[1] but
even in this the solidarity of the family was recognized, since
it was the duty of the plaintiff to select the nearest relatives
of his adversary, provided they were not personally hostile
to the accused.[2] This same spirit is shown even so late as
1116, in a charter by which Baldwin VII. of Flanders grati-
fied the citizens of Ypres by substituting among them the
process of compurgation for the ordeal and battle trial. According to this, the accuser selected four of the relatives of
the accused to take the purgatorial oath; if they refused
through known enmity, he was bound to select four other of
the kindred, and if none such were to be found then four
legal men sufficed.[3] The English law was the first to educe
a rational mode of trial from the absurdity of the barbaric
traditions, and there the process finally assumed a form
which occasionally bears a striking resemblance to trial by
jury—in fact, it insensibly runs into the latter, to the rise of
which it probably contributed. By the laws of Canute, in
some cases, fourteen men were named to the defendant, among
whom he was obliged to find eleven willing to take the purgatorial oath with him.[4] The selection of these virtual jurors
was probably made by the *gerefa*, or sheriff;[5] they could be

---

[1] L. Longobard. Lib. II. Tit. lv. § 5.   [2] Ibid. Tit. xxi. § 9.

[3] Proost, Récherches sur la Législation des Jugements de Dieu, Brux-
elles, 1868, p. 96.

[4] Nominentur ei XIV., et adquirat XI., et ipse sit duodecimus.—L.
Cnuti c. lxvi. Horne, who probably lived in the reign of Edward II.,
attributes to Glanville the introduction of the jury-trial.—"Car, pur les
grandes malices que lon soloit procurer en testmonage et les grands delaies
qui se fierent en les examinements, exceptions et attestations, ordeina Ran-
dulph de Glanvile celle certeine Assise ou recognitions et jurées se feissent
per XII jurors, les procheins vicines, et issint est cest establissement appelé
assise."—Myrror of Justice, cap. II. sect. xxv. For a minute examination
into the origin of the jury-trial, see a series of articles by Prof. J. B. Thayer
in the Harvard Law Review for 1892.

[5] Laws of Ethelred, Tit. III. c. xiii.

challenged for suspicion of partiality or other competent cause, and were liable to rejection unless unexceptionable in every particular.[1] Very similar to this was the *stockneffn* of the ancient Danish law, by which, in cases where the relatives were not called upon, thirteen men were chosen, a majority of whom could clear the accused by taking the oath with him. They were nominated by a person appointed for the purpose, and if the court neglected this duty, the privilege enured to the plaintiff.[2] More facile for the defence was a process prescribed in a Spanish charter of 1135, where, in cases of homicide, it sufficed for the accused to obtain five conjurators out of twelve selected by the magistrates.[3] A method combining selection and chance is described in the custumal of Ipswich in the twelfth century, to decide questions of debt between the townsfolk. The party on whom proof was incumbent brought in ten men; these were divided into two bands of five each, and a knife was thrown up between them; the band towards which the point of the knife fell was taken, one of the five was set aside, and the remaining four served as conjurators.[4]

The Northern nations were evidently less disposed to favor the accused than the Southern. In Sweden and Denmark, another regulation provides that although the defendant had a right to demand this mode of purgation, yet the plaintiff had the selection of the twelve men who served as conjurators; three of these the accused could challenge for enmity, but their places were supplied by the plaintiff.[5] The evanescent code compiled for Iceland by Haco Haconsen and his son Magnus, towards the close of the thirteenth century, is

[1] L. Henrici I. Tit. xxxi. § 8; Tit. lxvi. § 10.

[2] Constit. Woldemari Regis §§ lii. lxxii.

[3] Fuero de Balbás (Coleccion de Privilegios, etc. Madrid, 1833, T. VI. p. 85).

[4] Prof. J. B. Thayer, in Harvard Law Review, Vol. V. p. 58.

[5] L. Scaniæ Lib. vii. c. 8.—Chart. Woldemari Regis, ann. 1163 (Du Cange s. v. *Juramentum*).

5

more equitable in its provisions.   Though it leaves the nomination of the conjurators to the defendant, the choice is subject to limitations which placed it virtually in the power of
the court.   They were required to be men of the vicinage,
of good repute, peers of the accused, and in no way connected
with him by blood or other ties.[1]   The more lasting code
promulgated at the same time by Magnus for his Norwegian
dominions, a code which became the common law of Norway
for 500 years, provides, for cases in which eleven conjurators
are required, that seven of them shall be selected of intelligent
men of full age, and in no way related to the accused, yet
residents of the vicinage, and acquainted with the facts; the
accused can then add four more of good character, himself
making the twelfth.[2]   We see here, as in the English jurisprudence, how nearly the conjuratorial process approaches to
the jury-trial, and how completely it has departed from its
origin in the solidarity of the family.

Such care in the selection of those on whom duties so responsible devolved did not prevail among the more Southern
races at an earlier age.   Among the Lombards slaves and
women in tutelage were often employed.[3]   The Burgundians
required that the wife and children, or, in their absence, the
father and mother of the accused should assist in making up
the number of twelve,[4] the object being evidently to increase
the responsibility of the family for the action of its head.
The abuses of this custom, however, caused its prohibition
under Charlemagne for the reason that it led to the swearing
of children of tender and irresponsible age.[5]   That legislator,
however, contented himself with forbidding those who had
once been convicted of perjury from again appearing either as
witnesses or conjurators;[6] and the little care that was deemed

---

[1] Jarnsida, Thiofa-Balkr, cap. ix. x.

[2] Leges Gulathingenses, Thiofa-Bolkr, c. xiii.   (Ed. Havniæ 1817, p.
547).

[3] L. Longobard. I. xxxiii. 1, 3.   [4] L. Burgund. Tit. viii.

[5] Capit. Car. Mag. I. ann. 789 c. lxii.   [6] Ibid.

necessary in their selection under the Carlovingian jurisprudence is shown by a law of Louis le Débonnaire ordering
that landless freemen should be allowed to serve as conjurators,
though ineligible as witnesses.[1] A truer conception of the
course of justice is manifested, some centuries later, by the
Béarnese legislation, which required that the *seguidors* or
conjurators, as well as the *testimonis* or witnesses should be
men able to pay the amount at stake, together with the fine
incurred by the losing party,[2] or that they should be fair and
loyal men, not swayed by enmity.[3]

In ecclesiastical trials it would seem that the selection of
compurgators rested with the bishop. In a case occurring in
the thirteenth century, of a priest accused of homicide who
failed in his compurgation, he appealed to the Holy See on the
ground that his accusers were perjurers and that the bishop
had chosen the compurgators to suit himself.[4] As a matter of
course, the result of the trial depended, as it does with the
modern jury, on the fairness with which the choice was made,
and in the universal corruption of the middle ages there is no
reason to suppose that favoritism or bribery was not a controlling influence in a majority of cases.

CHAPTER V.

CONDITIONS OF COMPURGATION.

The conditions under which resort was had to this mode of
deciding litigation have been the subject of some discussion.
It has been assumed that, in the early period, before the
ferocious purity of the Barbarians had become adulterated

---

[1] Capit. Ludov. Pii ann. 829 Tit. III. § vi.

[2] For. de Morlaas, Rubr. xli. art. 146–7.

[3] Que sien boos et loyaus, et que no sien enemicxs.—Fors de Béarn,
Rubr. xxx.

[4] Formulary of the Papal Penitentiary, Philadelphia, 1892, p. 100.

under the influence of Roman civilization, it was used in all
description of cases, at the option of the defendant, and was
in itself a full and satisfactory proof, received on all hands as
equal to any other.[1] The only indication that I have met
with, among the races of Teutonic stock, tending to the support of such a conjecture, occurs in the Lombard code, where
Rotharis, the earliest compiler of written laws, abolishes a
previously existing privilege of denying under oath a crime
after it had been confessed.[2] A much more powerful argument on the other side, however, is derivable from the earliest
text of the Salic law, to which reference has already been
made. In this, the formula shows clearly that conjurators
were only employed in default of other testimony;[3] and what
lends additional force to the conclusion is that this direction
disappears in subsequent revisions of the law, wherein the influences of Christianity and of Roman civilization are fully
apparent. No safe deductions, indeed, can be drawn from
mere omissions to specify that the absence of witnesses was
necessary, for these ancient codes are drawn up in the rudest
manner, and regulations which might safely be presumed to
be familiar to every one would not, in their curt and barbarous
sentences, be repeated with the careful redundancy which
marks our modern statutes. Thus there is a passage in the
code of the Alamanni which declares in the most absolute
form that if a man commits a murder and desires to deny it,

---

[1] Königswarter, Études Historiques. p. 167.

Nam nulli liceat, postquam manifestaverit, postea per sacramentum
negare, quod non sit culpabilis, postquam ille se culpabilem assignavit.
Quia multos cognovimus in regno nostro tales pravas opponentes inten-
tiones, et hæc moverunt nos præsentem corrigere legem, et ad meliorem
statum revocare.—L. Longobard. Lib. II. Tit. lv. § 8.

[3] Si quis hominem ingenuo plagiaverit et probatio certa non fuit, sicut
pro occiso juratore donet. Si juratores non potuerit invenire, VIII M
dinarios, qui faciunt solidos CC, culpabilis judicetur (Tit. xxxix. § 2). A
similar provision—" si tamen probatio certa non fuerit"—occurs in Tit. xlii.
§ 5.

he can clear himself with twelve conjurators.[1] This, by itself, would authorize the assumption that compurgation was allowed to override the clearest and most convincing testimony, yet it is merely a careless form of expression, for another section of the same code expressly provides that where a fact is proved by competent witnesses the defendant shall not have the privilege of producing compurgators.[2]

It therefore seems evident that, even in the earliest times, this mode of proof was only an expedient resorted to in doubtful matters, and on the necessity of its use the *rachinborgs* or judges probably decided. A case recorded in the Landnamabok certainly shows that among the heathen Norsemen the Godi or priest-judge had this power, for when Thorbiorn Digre prosecuted Thorarin of Mafahlid for horse-stealing, and demanded that he should produce twelve conjurators, Arnkell, the Godi, decided that the accused might clear himself with his simple oath on the holy ring of the altar, and thus the prosecution came to naught except as leading to a bloody feud.[3] That this discretion was lodged in the court in subsequent times is generally admitted. It is scarcely worth while to multiply proof; but a few references will show the light in which the custom was regarded.[4]

[1] Si quis hominem occiderit et negare voluerit, cum duodecim nominatis juret.—L. Alaman. Tit. LXXXIX.

[2] L. Alaman. Tit. XLII.   [3] Islands Landnamabok II. ix. (p. 83).

[4] For instance, in the Baioarian law—"Nec facile ad sacramenta veniatur. . . . In his vero causis sacramenta præstentur in quibus nullam probationem discussio judicantis invenerit" (L. Baioar. Tit. VIII. c. 16). In a Capitulary of Louis le Débonnaire—"Si hujus facti testes non habuerit cum duodecim conjuratoribus legitimis per sacramentum adfirmet" (Capit. Ludov. Pii ann. 819, § 1). In one of the Emperor Lothair—"Si testes habere non poterit, concedimus ut cum XII. juratoribus juret" (L. Longobard. Lib. I. Tit. IX. § 37). So Louis II., in 854, ordered that a man accused of harboring robbers, if taken in the act, was to be immediately punished; but if merely cited on popular rumor, he was at liberty to clear himself with twelve compurgators (Recess. Ticinen. Tit. II. cap. 3).

It was the same in subsequent periods. The Scottish law of the thirteenth

As employed by the Church, the rule was distinctly enunciated in the thirteenth century that the accused was not to be
allowed to clear himself by canonical purgation when the
crime was notorious or when the accuser offered to prove the
charge.[1]

The Welsh, however, were exceptional in this respect. The

century alludes to the absence of testimony as a necessary preliminary, but
when an acquittal was once obtained in this manner the accused seems to
have been free from all subsequent proceedings, when inconvenient witnesses might perhaps turn up—" Et si hoc modo purgatus fuerit, absolvetur
a petitione Regis in posterum" (Regiam Majestatem, Lib. IV. c. 21).
So, in the laws of Nieuport, granted by Philip of Alsace, Count of Flanders, in 1163 " Et si hoc scabini vel opidani non cognoverint, conquerens
cum juramento querelam suam sequetur, et alter se excusabit juramento
quinque hominum" (Leg. secundæ Noviportus). See also the Consuetud. Tornacens. ann. 1187, §§ ii. iii. xvi., where two conjurators release a
defendant from a claim of debt unsupported by evidence. In case of assault,
" si constans non fuerit," two conjurators clear the accused; in case of
wounding, six are required if the affair occurred by daylight; if at night,
the cold water ordeal is prescribed (D'Achery, Spicileg. III. 551-2). The
legislation of Norway and Iceland in the next century is even more positive " Iis tantum concessis quæ legum codices sanciunt, juramenta nempe
purgatoria et accusatoria, ubi legitimi defuerint testes" (Jarnsida, Mannhelge, cap. xxxvii.).

On the other hand, an exception to this general principle is apparently
found in a constitution of the Emperor Henry III., issued about the middle
of the eleventh century " Si quem ex his dominus suus accusaverit de
quacunque re, licet illi juramento se cum suis coæqualibus absolvere,
exceptis tribus: hoc est si in vitam domini sui, aut in cameram ejus consilium habuisse arguitur, aut in munitiones ejus. Cæteris vero hominibus
de quacunque objectione, absque advocato, cum suis coæqualibus juramento
se poterit absolvere" (Goldast. Constit. Imp. I. 231).

In a constitution of Frederic II. in 1235, the oaths of six compurgators
clear a man accused of having commenced hostilities without awaiting the
three days term prescribed after defiance, no evidence being alluded to on
either side—" et nisi violator productus super hoc vel septena manu sino-
dalium hominum purgaverit innocentiam suam quod non commiserat contra
hoc statutum perpetuo pene subiaceat quod dicitur erenlos und rehtlos"—
Nove Constitutiones Dom. Alberti, p. 12 (Weimar, 1858).

[1] S. Raymondi Summæ Lib. III. Tit. xxxi. § v. *ad calcem.*

raith was the corner-stone of their system of jurisprudence. It was applied to almost all actions, whether of civil or criminal law, and even cases of doubtful paternity were settled by it, no woman, except one "of bush and brake" who had no legal kindred, being allowed to give testimony or take an oath with respect to the paternity of her illegitimate child.[1] It excluded and superseded all other procedures. If the accused declined to take the oath of denial, then testimony on both sides could be introduced, and the case be settled on the evidence adduced;[2] but where he chose to abide by the *raith*, the Book of Cynog formally declares that "Evidences are not to be brought as to *galanas* [homicide], nor *saraad* [insults], nor blood, nor wound, nor ferocious acts, nor waylaying, nor burning buildings, nor theft, nor surety, nor open assault, nor adultery, nor violence, nor in a case where guardians should be, nor in a case where an established raith is appointed by law; because evidences are not to extinguish a raith."[3] Indeed, the only case which I have found wherein it was refused is where a priest of the same parish as one accused of theft testifies to have seen him in open daylight with the article stolen in his possession, when apparently the sacred character of the witness precludes a denial on the part of the defendant.[4]

Among other races confidence in its ability to supplement absent or deficient testimony was manifested in another form— the *juramentum supermortuum*—which was employed by various nations, at wide intervals of time. Thus, in the earliest legislation of the Anglo-Saxons, we find that when the defendant or an important witness was dead, the oath which he would have taken or the deposition which he would have made

---

[1] Gwentian Code, Book II. chap. xxxix. § 40 (Owen I. 787). So, in disowning a child, if the reputed father were dead, the oaths of the chief of the kindred, with seven of the kinsmen, were decisive, or, in default of the chief, the oaths of fifty kinsmen (Ibid. § 41).

[2] Anomalous Laws, Book IX. chap. ii. § 9 (Ibid. II. 227).

[3] Ibid. Book VIII. chap. xi. § 31 (Ibid. II. 209).

[4] Ibid. Book IX. chap. ii. § 6 (Ibid. II. 227).

was obtained by proceeding to his tomb, where a certain number of conjurators swore as to what he could or would have
done if alive.[1] Two centuries later, the same custom is alluded
to in the Welsh laws of Hoel Dda,[2] and even as late as the
thirteenth century it was still in force throughout Germany.[3]
There were other cases in which evidence of any kind was
almost impossible, and in these the wager of law offered a
convenient resource. Thus, Frederic II., in 1235, decreed
that a man harboring an outlaw should himself be outlawed,
but he was allowed to prove with six conjurators that he was
ignorant of the outlawry.[4]

A remarkable use of conjurators to confirm the evidence of
witnesses occurs in 850 in a dispute between Cantius, Bishop
of Siena, and Peter, Bishop of Arezzo, concerning certain
parishes claimed by both. The occasion was a solemn one,
for it was before a council held in Rome presided over jointly
by Pope Leo IV. and the Emperor Louis II. Peter relied
upon written charters, while Cantius produced witnesses. The
Emperor pronounced the claim of the latter to be just, when
he and twelve priests swore that the oaths of the witnesses were
true and without deceit, whereupon the disputed parishes were
adjudged to him.[5]

The employment of compurgators, however, depended frequently upon the degree of crime alleged, or the amount at
stake. Thus, in many codes, trivial offences or small claims
were disposed of by the single oath of the defendant, while
more important cases required compurgators, whose numbers
increased with the magnitude of the matter in question. This

[1] Dooms of Ine, cap. liii.

[2] Leg. Wallice, Lib. II. cap. xix. § 2 (Owen II. 842).

[3] Ea autem debita de quibus non constat, super mortuum probari debent,
septima manu.—Jur. Provin. Alaman. cap. vii. § 2. (Ed. Schilter.)—
Sachsische Weichbild art. 67.

[4] Nove Constitutiones Dom. Alberti, p. 38.

[5] " Quod in sacramentis supradictorum testium veritas absque ullo dolo
versata est."—Leon. PP. IV. Epist. 5 (Migne, CXV. 664).

principle is fairly illustrated in a charter granted to the Venetians in the year 1111 by Henry V. In suits which involved only the value of a silver pound, the oath of the party was sufficient; but if the claim amounted to twelve pounds or more, then twelve chosen men were requisite to substantiate the oath of negation.[1]

In England in the thirteenth century we find compurgation very generally employed in the manorial courts for the settlement of petty criminal actions. So general was its use, indeed, that it obtained the name of "law," as the legal method *par excellence*, and the process is curtly described in the reports as "facere legem," "esse ad legem," "vadiare legem," whence is derived the term "wager of law." The number of compurgators was generally two or five, and they seem to have been left, as a rule, to the choice of the defendant, so that failure to procure the requisite number was very unusual.[2]

In later times, compurgation was also sometimes used as an alternative when circumstances prevented the employment of other popular modes of deciding doubtful cases. Those, for instance, who would ordinarily be required to defend themselves by the wager of battle, were permitted by some codes to substitute the oaths of a certain number of conjurators, when precluded by advanced age from appearing in the arena. The burgher law of Scotland affords an example of this,[3] though elsewhere such cases were usually settled by the substitution of champions. Class privileges also manifested themselves in this as in so many other features of mediæval law, and we sometimes find compurgation allowed as a favor to those of gentle birth. Thus, in the Council of Reims in 1119, among

[1] Lünig Cod. Ital. Diplom. II. 1955.

[2] Maitland, Select Pleas in Manorial and other Seignorial Courts, pp. 7, 10, 18, 32, 36, 37, 47, 83, 137, 140, 141, 142, 144, 151, 157, 173.

[3] Si burgensis calumniatus præteriit ætatem pugnandi, et hoc essoniaverit in sua responsione, non pugnabit. Sed juramento duodecim talium qualis ipse fuerit, se purgabit.—L. Burgorum cap. 24, §§ 1, 2.

the provisions for the enforcement of the Truce of God, accusations of its violation are rebutted by knights with six compurgators, while common people are required to undergo the ordeal.[1]

CHAPTER VI.

FORMULAS AND PROCEDURE.

THE primitive law-givers were too chary of words in their skeleton codes to embody in them the formula usually employed for the compurgatorial oath. We have therefore no positive evidence of its nature in the earliest times ; but as the forms made use of by several races at a somewhat later period have been preserved, and as they resemble each other in all essential respects, we may reasonably assume that little variation had previously occurred. The most ancient that I have met with occurs in an Anglo-Saxon formulary which is supposed to date from about A. D. 900 : "By the Lord, the oath is clean and unperjured which N. has sworn."[2] A century later, in a compilation of the Lombard law, it appears : "That which the accused has sworn is true, so help me God."[3] The form specified in Béarn, at a period somewhat subsequent, is curt and decisive : "By these saints, he tells the truth ;"[4] while the code in force in Normandy until the sixteenth century directs an oath identical in spirit : "The oath which William has sworn is true, so help me God and his saints."[5]

---

[1] Concil. Remens. ann. 1119 (Harduin. VI. 1986).

[2] On þone Drihten se að is clæne and unmæne þe N. swor.—Thorpe's Ancient Laws, I. 180-1.

[3] Hoc quod appellatus juravit, verum juravit. Sic Deus, etc.—Formul. Vet. in L. Longobard (Georgisch, 1275).

[4] Per aquetz santz ver dits.—Fors de Béarn, Rubr. LI. art. 165.

[5] Du serment que Guillaume a juré, sauf serment a juré, ainsi m'aist Dieu et ses Sainctz.—Ancienne Cout. de Normandie, chap. lxxxv. (Bourdot de Richebourg, IV. 54).

It will be observed that all these, while essentially distinct from the oath of a witness, are still unqualified assertions of the truth of the principal, and not mere asseverations of belief or protestations of confidence. The earliest departure from this positive affirmation, in secular jurisprudence, occurs in the unsuccessful attempt at legislation for Norway and Iceland by Haco Haconsen in the thirteenth century. In this, the impropriety of such oaths is pointed out, and it is directed that in future the compurgator shall swear only, in confirmation of his principal, that he knows nothing to the contrary.[1] In the similar code promulgated in 1274 by his son Magnus in Norway, it is directed that the accused shall take a full oath of denial, and the conjurators shall swear in the same words that his oath is true, and that they know nothing truer.[2]

We shall see that, before the custom fell into total disuse, the change which Haco vainly attempted, came to be generally adopted, in consequence, principally, of the example set by the church. Even before this was formally promulgated by the Popes, however, ecclesiastics occasionally showed that they were more careful as to what they swore, and at a comparatively early period they introduced the form of merely asserting their belief in the oath taken by their principal. Thus, in 1101, we find two bishops endeavoring to relieve a brother prelate from a charge of simony, and their compurgatorial oath ventures no further than "So help me God, I believe that Norgaud, Bishop of Autun, has sworn the truth."[3]

---

[1] Nobis adhæc Deo coram periculosum esse videtur, ejus, cujus interest, jusjurandum purgatorium edendo præeunte, omnes (ab eo productos testes) iisdem ac ille conceptis verbis jurare, incerti quamvis fuerint, vera ne an falsa jurent. Nos legibus illatum volumus ut ille, cujus interest, jusjurandum conceptis verbis solum præstet, cæteri vero ejus firment juramentum adjicientes se nequid verius, Deo coram, scire, quam jurassent.—Jarnsida, Mannhelge, cap. xxxvii.—The passage is curious, as showing how little confidence was really felt in the purgation, notwithstanding the weight attached to it by law.

[2] Leges Gulathingenses, Thiofa-Bolkr, c. xiii.

[3] Credo Norigaudum istum Eduensem episcopum vera jurasse, sicut me Deus adjuvet.—Hugo. Flaviniac. Lib. ii.

In the form of oath, however, as well as in so many other particulars, the Welsh had a more complicated system, peculiar to themselves. The ordinary *raith-man* only was required to take an oath "that it appears most likely to him that what he swears to is true." In many aggravated crimes, however, a certain proportion, generally one-half, had to be *nod-men* who were bound to a more stringent form, as the law specifies that "the oath of a nod-man is, to be in accordance with what is sworn by the criminal."[1] The difference, as we have seen, in the numbers required when a portion were *nod-men* shows how much more difficult it was to find men willing to swear to an absolute denial, and how much more weight was attached to such a declaration than to the lax expression of opinion contained in the ordinary oath of the *raith-man*.

Variations are likewise observable in the form of administering the oath. Among the Alamanni, for instance, the compurgators laid their hands upon the altar, and the principal placed his hand over the others, repeating the oath alone;[2] while among the Lombards, a law of the Emperor Lothair directs that each shall take the oath separately.[3] It was always, however, administered in a consecrated place, before delegates appointed by the judges trying the cause, sometimes on the altar and sometimes on relics. In the Welsh laws of the fifteenth century it is specified that all *raiths* shall be administered in the parish church of the defendant, before the priest shall have disrobed or distributed the sacramental bread.[4] At an earlier period a formula of Marculfus specifies the Capella S. Martini, or cope of St. Martin,[5] one of the most venerated relics of the royal chapel, whence we may perhaps conclude that it was habitually used for that purpose in the business of the royal Court of Appeals.

[1] Anomalous Laws, Book VII. chap. i. § 18 (Owen, II. 135).

[2] L. Alaman. Tit. vi.   [3] L. Longobard. Lib. II. Tit. lv. § 28.

[4] Anomalous Laws, Book IX. chap. vi. § 4; chap. xvii. § 5.—cf. Book VI. chap. i. § 50 (Owen. II. 235, 255, 113).

[5] Marculf. Lib. I. Formul. xxxviii.

Notwithstanding the universality of the custom, and the absolute character of the decisions reached by the process, it is easy to discern that the confidence reposed in it was of a very qualified character, even at an early period. The primitive law of the Frisians describes some whimsical proceedings, prescribed for the purpose of determining the responsibility for a homicide committed in a crowd. The accuser was at liberty to select seven from among the participants of the brawl, and each of these was obliged to deny the crime with twelve conjurators. This did not absolve them, however, for each of them was also individually subjected to the ordeal, which finally decided as to his guilt or innocence. In this, the value of the compurgation was reduced to that of the merest technical ceremony, and yet a failure to procure the requisite number of supporters was tantamount to a conviction, while, to crown the absurdity of the whole, if any one succumbed in the ordeal, his conjurators were punished as perjurers.[1] A similar want of confidence in the principle involved is shown by a reference in the Anglo-Saxon laws to the conjurators of an accused party being outsworn (*overcythed*), when recourse was likewise had to the ordeal.[2] Among the heathen Norsemen, indeed, an offer by either party to produce conjurators could always be met by the antagonist with a challenge to the duel, which at once superseded all other proceedings.[3] As regards the church, although the authoritative use of compurgation among ecclesiastics would seem to demand for it among them implicit faith in its results, yet we have already seen that, in the ninth century, Hincmar did not hesitate to require that in certain cases it should be confirmed by the ordeal; and two centuries later, a remark of Ivo of Chartres implies a strong degree of doubt as to its efficacy. In relating that Sanctio, Bishop-elect of Orleans, when accused of simony by a disappointed rival, took the oath of

[1] L. Frisionum Tit. xiv.

[2] Dooms of King Edward, cap. iii.

[3] Keyser's Religion of the Northmen, Pennock's Transl. p. 246.

6

negation with seven compurgators, he adds that the accused
thus cleared himself as far as he could in the eyes of man.[1]
That the advantages it offered to the accused were duly appreciated, both by criminals and judges, is evident from the case
of Manasses, Archbishop of Reims.   Charged with simony
and other offences, after numerous tergiversations he was
finally summoned for trial before the Council of Lyons, in
1080.   As a last effort to escape the impending doom, he
secretly offered to Bishop Hugh, the Papal legate, the enormous sum of two hundred ounces of gold and other presents
in hand, besides equally liberal prospective payments, if he
could obtain the privilege of compurgation with six suffragan
bishops.   Gregory VII. was then waging too uncompromising
a war with the corroding abuse of simony for his lieutenant to
yield to any bribe, however dazzling; the proffer was spurned,
Manasses confessed his guilt by absence, and was accordingly
deposed.[2]   Incidents like this, however, did not destroy confidence in the system, for, some sixty years later, we find Innocent II. ordering the Bishop of Trent, when similarly accused
of simony, to clear himself with the oaths of two bishops and
three abbots or monks.[3]

The comparative value attached to the oaths of conjurators
is illustrated by the provisions which are occasionally met
with, regulating the cases in which they were employed in
default of witnesses, or in opposition to them.   Thus, in the
Baioarian law, the oath of one competent witness is considered
to outweigh those of six conjurators;[4] and among the Lombards, an accusation of murder which could be met with three
witnesses required twelve conjurators as a substitute.[5]

It is therefore evident that conjurators were in no sense witnesses, that they were not expected to give testimony, and
that they merely expressed their confidence in the veracity of

---

[1] Quantum in conspectu hominum purgari poterat.—Ivon. Epist. liv.
[2] Hugo Flaviniac. Lib. II.   [3] Gratian. c. 17, Caus. II. Q. v.
[4] L. Baioar. Tit. XIV. cap. i. § 2.
[5] L. Longobard. Lib. I. Tit. ix. § 37.

their principal. It may consequently at first sight appear somewhat unreasonable that they should be held guilty of perjury
and subject to its penalties in case of unluckily sustaining the
wrong side of a cause.   It is probably owing to this apparent
injustice that some writers have denied that they were involved
in the guilt of their principal, and among others the learned
Meyer has fallen into this error.[1] The proof, however, is too
clear for dispute. We have already seen that the oath was an
unqualified assertion of the justice of the side espoused, without reservation justifying the escape of the compurgators from
the charge of false swearing, and one or two incidental references have been made to the punishments inflicted on them
when subsequently convicted of perjury. The code of the
Alamanni recognized the guilt involved in such cases when it
denied the privilege of compurgation to any one who had previously been more than once convicted of crime, giving as a
reason the desire to save innocent persons from incurring the
sin of perjury.[2] Similar evidence is derived from a regulation
promulgated by King Liutprand in the Lombard Law, by
which a man nominated as a conjurator, and declining to
serve, was obliged to swear that he dared not take the oath
for fear of his soul.[3] A case in point occurs in the life of St.
Boniface, whose fellow-laborer Adalger in dying left his property to the church. The graceless brothers of the deceased
disputed the bequest, and offered to make good their claim to
the estate by the requisite number of oaths. The holy man
ordered them to swear alone, in order not to be concerned in
the destruction of their conjurators, and on their unsupported
oaths gave up the property.[4]

[1] Institutions Judiciaires, I. 308.

[2] Ut propter suam nequitiam alii qui volunt Dei esse non se perjurent,
nec propter culpam alienam semetipsos perdant.— L. Alaman. Tit. xlii.
§ 1.

[3] Quod pro anima sua timendo, non præsumat sacramentalis esse.—L.
Longobard. Lib. II. Tit. lv. § 14.

[4] Othlon. Vit. S. Bonif. Lib. II. c. xxi.—" Vos soli juratis, si vultis; nolo
ut omnes hos congregatos perdatis."—Boniface, however, did not weakly

The law had no hesitation in visiting such cases with the penalties reserved for perjury. By the Salic code unlucky compurgators were heavily fined.[1] Among the Frisians, they had to buy themselves off from punishment by the amount of their *wer-gild*—the value set upon their heads.[2] A slight relaxation of this severity is manifested in the Carlovingian legislation, by which they were punished with the loss of a hand—the customary penalty of perjury—unless they could establish, by undergoing the ordeal, that they had taken the oath in ignorance of the facts; but even in trifling causes a defeated litigant could accuse his own conjurator of perjury, when both parties were sent to the ordeal of the cross, and if the conjurator broke down he lost a hand.[3] So late as the close of the twelfth century, we find Celestin III. ordering the employment of conjurators in a class of cases about the facts of which they could not possibly know anything, and decreeing that if the event proved them to be in error they were to be punished for perjury.[4] That such liability was fully recognized at this period is shown by the argument of Aliprandus of Milan, a celebrated contemporary legist, who, in maintaining the position that an ordinary witness committing perjury must always lose his hand, without the privilege of redeeming it, adds that no witness can perjure himself unintentionally; but that conjurators may do so either knowingly or unknowingly, that they are therefore entitled to the benefit of the doubt, and if not wittingly guilty, that they should have the privilege of redeeming their hands.[5]

abandon the cause of the church. He freely invoked curses on the greedy brethren, which being fulfilled on the elder, the terror-stricken survivor gladly relinquished the dangerous inheritance.

[1] L. Salic. Tit. I, §§ 3, 4.   [2] L. Frisionum Tit. x.

[3] Capit. Pippini ann. 793 § 15.—Capit. Car. Mag. incert. anni c. x. (Martene Ampl. Collect. VII. 7).

[4] Celest. PP. III. ad Brugnam Episc. (Baluz. et Mansi, III. 382).

[5] Cod. Vatican. No. 3845, Gloss. ad L. 2 Lombard. II. 51, apud Savigny, Geschichte d. Rom. Recht. B. iv.—I owe this reference to the kindness of my friend J. G. Rosengarten, Esq.

All this seems in the highest degree irrational, yet in criticising the hardships to which innocent conjurators were thus exposed, it should be borne in mind that the whole system had become a solecism. In its origin, it was simply summoning the kinsmen together to bear the brunt of the court, as they were bound to bear that of battle ; and as they were liable for a portion of the fine which was the penalty of all crimes —personal punishments for freemen being unknown—they could well afford to incur the risk of paying for perjury in order to avoid the assessment to be levied upon them in case of the conviction of their relative. In subsequent periods, when the family responsibility became weakened or disused, and the progress of civilization rendered the interests of society more complex, the custom could only be retained by making the office one not to be lightly undertaken. A man who was endeavoring to defend himself from a probable charge of murder, or who desired to confirm his possession of an estate against a competitor with a fair show of title, was expected to produce guarantees that would carry conviction to the minds of impartial men. As long as the practice existed, it was therefore necessary to invest it with every solemnity, and to guard it with penalties that would obviate some of its disadvantages.

Accordingly, we find that it was not always a matter of course for a man to clear himself in this manner. The ancient codes have frequent provisions for the fine incurred by those unable to procure the requisite number of compurgators, showing that it was an occurrence constantly kept in mind by legislators. Nor was it only landless and friendless men who were exposed to such failures. In 794, a certain Bishop Peter was condemned by the Synod of Frankfort to clear himself, with two or three conjurators, of the suspicion of being involved in a conspiracy against Charlemagne, and, small as was the number, he was unable to procure them.[1]

[1] Capit. Car. Mag. ann. 794 § 7.

So, in the year 1100, when the canons of Autun, at the Council of Poitiers, accused their bishop, Norgaud, of simony and other irregular practices, and he proposed to absolve himself with the compurgatorial oaths of the Archbishop of Tours and the Bishop of Rédon, the canons went privately to those prelates and threatened that in such event they would bring an accusation of perjury and prove it by the ordeal of fire, whereupon the would-be conjurators wisely abandoned their intention, and Norgaud was suspended.[1] I have already referred (p. 51) to a case before the Papal Penitentiary about 1240, in which a priest accused of homicide was put upon his purgation and failed, whereupon his bishop deprived him of function and benefice, and he hastened to Rome with a complaint that the bishop had not been impartial in the selection of compurgators. The most rigid compliance with the requisitions of the law was exacted. Thus the statutes of Nieuport, in 1163, provide a heavy penalty, and in addition pronounce condemnation, when a single one of the conjurators declines the oath.[2] It goes without saying that failure in compurgation was equivalent to conviction or confession.[3]

---

[1] Hugo. Flaviniac. Lib. ii. ann. 1100. Norgaud, however, was reinstated next year by quietly procuring, as we have already seen, two brother prelates to take the oath with him, in the absence of his antagonists.

[2] Et si quis de quinque juvantibus defecerit, accusatus debit tres libras, et percusso decem solidos.—Leg. Secund. Noviportus (Oudegherst).

[3] Hostiensis Aureæ Summæ Lib. v. *De Purg. Canon.* § 7.—" Sicut puniretur de crimine de quo impetebatur si convinceretur considerato modo agendi, sic punietur si in purgatione deficiat."

CHAPTER VII.

DECLINE OF COMPURGATION.

In a system of which the fundamental principle was so vicious, the best efforts of legislation could prove but a slight palliation, and from an early period we find efforts made for its abrogation or limitation. In 983, a constitution of Otho II. abolished it in cases of contested estates, and substituted the wager of battle, on account of the enormous perjury which it occasioned.[1] In England, a more sweeping denunciation, declaring its abolition and replacing it with the vulgar ordeal, is found in the confused and contradictory compilation known as the laws of Henry I.[2]

We have already seen, from instances of later date, how little influence these efforts had in eradicating a custom so deeply rooted in the ancestral prejudices of all the European races. The hold which it continued to enjoy on the popular confidence is well illustrated by the oath which, according to the Romancero, was exacted of Alfonso VI. of Castile, by the Cid to clear him of suspicion of privity to the death of

---

[1] L. Longobard. Lib. II. Tit. lv. § 34.—Qua ex re mos detestabilis in Italia, improbusque non imitandus inolevit, ut sub legum specie jurejurando acquireret, qui Deum non timendo minime formidaret perjurare.

[2] L. Henrici I. cap. lxiv. § 1. "Malorum autem infestacionibus et perjurancium conspiracione, depositum est frangens juramentum, ut magis Dei judicium ab accusatis eligatur; et unde accusatus cum una decima se purgaret per eleccionem et sortem, si ad judicium ferri calidi vadat." This cannot be considered, however, as having abrogated it even temporarily in England, since it is contradicted by many other laws in the same code, which prescribe the use of compurgators, and we shall see hereafter how persistently its use was maintained.

his brother and predecessor Sancho II. at the siege of Zamora, where he was slain by Bellido Delfos—

> " Que nos fagays juramento
> Qual vos lo querrán tomar,
> Vos y doce de los vuesos,
> Quales vos querays juntar,
> Que de la muerte del Rey
> Non tenedes que culpar . . . .
> Ni tampoco della os plugo,
> Ni a ella distes lugar."[1]

The same reliance on its efficacy is shown in a little ballad by Audefroi-le-Bâtard, a renowned *trouvère* of the twelfth century:—

LA BELLE EREMBORS.[2]

" Quand vient en mai, que l'on dit as lons jors," etc.

> In the long bright days of spring-time,
>   In the month of blooming May,
> The Franks from royal council-field
>   All homeward wend their way.
> Rinaldo leads them onward,
>   Past Erembors' gray tower,
> But turns away, nor deigns to look
>   Up to the maiden's bower.
>   Ah, dear Rinaldo!
>
> Full in her turret window
>   Fair Erembors is sitting,
> The love-lorn tales of knights and dames
>   In many a color knitting.
> She sees the Franks pass onward,
>   Rinaldo at their head,
> And fain would clear the slanderous tale
>   That evil tongues have spread.
>   Ah, dear Rinaldo!

---

[1] Romances Antiguos Españoles.   Londres, 1825, T. I. pp. 246–7.   Cf. Dozy, Recherches sur l'Histoire, etc. de l'Espagne, Leipzig, 1881, II. 108.
[2] Le Roux de Lincy, Chants Historiques Français, I. 15.

" Sir knight, I well remember
  When you had grieved to see
The castle of old Erembors
  Without a smile from me."
" Your vows are broken, princess,
  Your faith is light as air,
Your love another's, and of mine
  You have nor reck nor care."
            Ah, dear Rinaldo!

" Sir knight, my faith unbroken,
  On relics I will swear;
A hundred maids and thirty dames
  With me the oath shall share.
I've never loved another,
  From stain my vows are free.
If this content your doubts and fears,
  You shall have kisses three."
            Ah, dear Rinaldo!

Rinaldo mounts the staircase,
  A goodly knight, I ween,
With shoulders broad and slender waist,
  Fair hair and blue eyes keen.
Earth holds no youth more gifted
  In every knightly measure;
When Erembors beholds him,
  She weeps with very pleasure.
            Ah, dear Rinaldo!

Rinaldo in the turret
  Upon a couch reposes,
Where deftly limned are mimic wreaths
  Of violets and of roses.
Fair Erembors beside him
  Sits clasped in loving hold,
And in their eyes and lips they find
  The love they vowed of old!
            Ah, dear Rinaldo!

In England, although as we have seen (p. 57), the wager of law was the customary resource of the manorial courts in disputed questions, the shrewd and intelligent lawyers who were building up and systematizing the practice of the royal courts were disposed to limit it as much as possible in criminal cases. Towards the close of the twelfth century, Glanville compiled his excellent little treatise "De legibus Angliæ," the first satisfactory body of legal procedure which the history of mediæval jurisprudence affords. Complete as this is in all the forms of prosecution and defence, the allusions to conjurators are so slight as to show that already they were employed rather on collateral points than on main questions. Thus a defendant who desired to deny the serving of a writ could swear to its non-reception with twelve conjurators;[1] and a party to a suit, who had made an unfortunate statement or admission in court, could deny it by bringing forward two to swear with him against the united recollections and records of the whole court.[2] The custom, however, still maintained its hold on popular confidence. In 1194, when Richard I. undertook, after his liberation, to bring about a reconciliation between his chancellor William, Bishop of Ely, and the Archbishop of York, one of the conditions was that the chancellor

---

[1] Glanville, Lib. i. cap. ix. Also, Lib. i. c. xvi., Lib. ix. c. i., Lib. x. c. v.

[2] "In aliis enim curiis si quis aliquid dixerit unde eum pœnituerit, poterit id negare contra totam curiam tertia manu cum sacramento, id se non dixisse affirmando" (Ibid. Lib. viii. c. ix.).—In some other systems of jurisprudence. this unsophisticated mode of beclouding justice was obtained by insisting on the employment of lawyers, whose assertions would not be binding on their clients. Thus, in the Assises de Jerusalem (Baisse Court, cap. 133): "Et por ce il deit estre lavantparlier, car se lavantparlier dit parole quil ne doie dire por celuy cui il parole, celui por qui il parle et son conceau y pueent bien amender ains que le iugement soit dit. Mais se celuy de cui est li plais diseit parole qui li deust torner a damage, il ne la peut torner arieres puis quil la dite." The same caution is recommended in the German procedure of the fourteenth century—" verbis procuratoris non eris adstrictus, et sic vitabis damnum" (Richstich Landrecht, cap. ii. Cf. Jur. Provin. Saxon. Lib. I. art. 60; Lib. II. art. 14). The same abuse existed in France, but was restricted by St. Louis, who made the assertion of the advocate binding on the principal, unless contradicted on the spot (Établissements, Liv. ii. chap. xiv.).

should swear with a hundred priestly compurgators that he had neither caused nor desired the arrest of the archbishop.[1] In the next century Bracton alludes to the employment of conjurators in cases of disputed feudal service between a lord and his vassal, wherein the utmost exactness was rigidly required both as to the number and fitness of the conjurators,[2] and we shall see that no formal abrogation of it took place until the nineteenth century. An outgrowth of the custom, moreover, was the Inquest of Fame, by which "the general character of the accused, as found by a jury, was accepted as an indication of the guilt or innocence of the prisoner."[3]

Soon after the time of Glanville, the system of compurgation received a severe shock from its most important patron, the church. As stated above, in proceedings between ecclesiastics, it was everywhere received as the appropriate mode of deciding doubtful cases. At the same time the absolute character of the compurgatorial oath was too strong an incentive to perjury, ignorant or wilful, for conscientious minds to reconcile themselves to the practice, and efforts commenced to modify it. About 1130 Innocent II., in prescribing compurgation for the Bishop of Trent, accused of simony, orders that the oath of the conjurators shall be simply as to their belief in the bishop's oath.[4] Gratian inserted this in his *Decretum*, and a commentator soon afterwards speaks of it as an opinion held by some authorities.[5] It was reserved for Innocent III. to give this the full sanction of law as a general

[1] Roger. de Hoveden ann. 1194.

[4] Tunc vadiabit defendens legem se duodecima manu.—Bracton. Lib. III. Tract. iii. cap. 37, § 1.—Et si ad diem legis faciendæ defuerit aliquis de XII. vel si contra prædictos excipi possit quod non sunt idonei ad legem faciendam, eo quod villani sunt vel alias idonei minus, tunc dominus incidet in misericordiam.—Ibid. § 3. So also in Lib. v. Tract. v. cap. xiii. § 3.

[3] Pike, History of Crime in England, I. 285.

[4] Gratian, c. 17, C. II. Q. v.—"Deinde vero purgatores super sancta Dei evangelia jurabunt quod sicut ipsi credunt verum juravit." Cf. c. 5 Extra, v. xxxiv.

[5] Summæ Stephani Tornacensis caus. II. Q. 5 (Schulte, 1891, p. 171).

regulation. Compurgation was too valuable a resource for churchmen to be discarded, and he endeavored to check the abuses to which it led, by demanding conjurators of good character, whose intimacy with the accused would give weight to their oaths.[1] At the same time, in endeavoring to remove one of the objections to its use, he in reality destroyed one of its principal titles to respect, for in decreeing that compurgators should only be obliged to swear to their belief in the truth of the principal's oath,[2] he attacked the very foundation of the practice, and gave a powerful impulse to the tendency of the times no longer to consider the compurgator as sharing the guilt or innocence of the accused. Such an innovation could only be regarded as withdrawing the guarantee which had immemorially existed. To recognize it as a legal precept was to deprive the proceeding of its solemnity and to render it no longer a security worthy the confidence of the people or sufficient to occupy the attention of a court of justice.

In the confusion arising from the long and varying contest as to the boundaries of civil and ecclesiastical jurisdiction, it is not easy to determine the exact influence which this decretal may have exercised directly in secular jurisprudence. We have seen above that the ancient form of absolute oath was still employed without change until long after this period, but the moral effect of so decided a declaration from the head of the Christian church could not but be great. Another influence, not less potent, was also at work. The revival of the study of the Roman jurisprudence, dating from

[1] C. 7, Extra, v. xxxiv.

[2] Illi qui ad purgandam alicujus infamiam inducuntur, ad solum tenentur juramento firmare quod veritatem credunt eum dicere qui purgatur.—C. 13, Extra, v. xxxiv. Innocent also endeavored to put an end to the abuse by which ecclesiastics, notoriously guilty, were able to escape the penalty due their crimes, by this easy mode of purgation.—C. 15, eod. loc.

The formula as given about 1240 by St. Ramon de Peñafort is " Nos credimus quod ipse juravit verum, vel, verum esse quod juravit."—Raymondi Summæ Lib. III. Tit. xxxi. § 5.

about the middle of the twelfth century, soon began to exhibit the results which were to work so profound a change in the legal maxims and principles of half of Europe.[1] The criminal procedure of the Barbarians had rested to a great degree on the system of negative proofs. In the absence of positive evidence of guilt, and sometimes in despite of it, the accused was bound to clear himself by compurgation or by the ordeal.

[1] The rapidity with which the study of the civil law diffused itself throughout the schools and the eagerness with which it was welcomed were the subject of indignant comment by the ecclesiastics of the day. As early as 1149 we find St. Bernard regretting that the laws of Justinian were already overshadowing those of God—" Et quidem quotidie perstrepent in palatio leges, sed Justiniani, non Domini" (De Consideratione, Lib. I. cap. iv.). Even more bitter were the complaints of Giraldus Cambrensis towards the end of the century. The highest of high churchmen, in deploring the decline of learning among the prelates and clergy of his age, he attributes it to the exclusive attention bestowed on the jurisprudence of Justinian, which already offered the surest prizes to cupidity and ambition, and he quotes in support of his opinion the dictum of his teacher Mainier, a professor in the University of Paris: " Episcopus autem ille, de quo nunc ultimo locuti sumus, inter superficiales numerari potuit, cujusmodi hodie multos novimus propter leges Justinianas, quæ literaturam, urgente cupiditatis et ambitionis incommodo, adeo in multis jam suffocarunt, quod magistrum Mainerium in auditorio scholæ suæ Parisius dicentem et damna sui temporis plangentem, audivi, vaticinium illud Sibillæ vere nostris diebus esse completum, hoc scilicet ' Venient dies, et væ illis, quibus leges obliterabunt scientiam literarum' " (Gemm. Ecclesiast. Dist. II. cap. xxxvii.). This, like all other branches of learning, was as yet to a great extent in the hands of the clergy, though already were arising the precursors of those subtle and daring civil lawyers who were destined to do such yeoman's service in abating the pretensions of the church.

It is somewhat singular to observe that at a period when the highest offices of the law were frequently appropriated by ecclesiastics, they were not allowed to perform the functions of advocates or counsel. See Horne's Myrror of Justice, cap. II. sect. 5. There was good reason for prohibiting them from serving as judges, as Frederic II. did in 1235—" Idem erit laicus propter sententias sanguinum quas clerico scribere non liceat, et præterea ut si dilinquid in officio suo pena debita puniatur" (Nove Constitutiones Dom. Alberti, p. 46).

7

The cooler and less impassioned justice of the Roman law saw clearly the futility of such attempts, and its system was based on the indisputable maxim that it is morally impossible to prove a negative—unless, indeed, that negative should chance to be incompatible with some affirmative susceptible of evidence—and thus the onus of proof was thrown upon the accuser.[1] The civil lawyers were not long in recognizing the truth of this principle, and in proclaiming it far and wide. The Spanish code of Alfonso the Wise, in the middle of the thirteenth century, asserts it in almost the same words as the Roman jurisconsult.[2] Not long before, the Assises de Jerusalem had unequivocally declared that "nul ne peut faire preuve de non;" and Beaumanoir, in the *Coutumes du Beauvoisis*, approvingly quotes the assertion of the civil doctors to the same effect, "Li clerc si dient et il dient voir, que negative ne doit pas quevir en proeve."

Abstract principles, however, though freely admitted, were not yet powerful enough to eradicate traditional customs rooted deeply in the feelings and prejudices of the age. The three bodies of law just cited contradict their own admissions, in retaining with more or less completeness the most monstrous of negative proofs—the ordeal of battle—and the introduction of torture soon after exposed the accused to the chances of the negative system in its most atrocious form. Still these codes show a marked progress as relates to the kindred procedure of compurgation. The Partidas, promulgated about 1262, record

---

[1] Actor quod adseverat, probare se non posse profitendo, reum necessitate monstrandi contrarium non adstringit: cum per rerum naturam factum negantis probatio nulla sit (Const. xxiii. C. de Probat. IV. 19).—Cum inter eum, qui factum adseverans, onis subiit probationis, et negantem numerationem, cujus naturali ratione probatio nulla est . . . magna sit differentia (Const. x. C. de non numerat. IV. 30). It is a little curious to see how completely this was opposed to the principle of the early Common Law of England, by which in actions for debt "semper incumbit probatio neganti" (Fleta, Lib. II. cap. lxiii. § 11).

[2] La cosa que non es non se puede probar nin mostrar segunt natura.— Las Siete Partidas, P. III. Tit. xiv. l. 1.

the convictions of an enlightened ruler as to what should be law rather than the existing institutions of a people, and were not accepted as authoritative until the middle of the fourteenth century. The absence of compurgation in Spain, moreover, was a direct legacy from the Wisigothic code, transmitted in regular descent through the Fuero Juzgo.[1] The Assises de Jerusalem is a more precious relic of mediæval jurisprudence. Constructed as a code for the government of the Latin kingdoms of the East, in 1099, by order of Godfrey of Bouillon, it has reached us only in the form assumed about the period under consideration, and as it presents the combined experience of the warriors of many Western races, its silence on the subject of conjurators is not a little significant. The work of Beaumanoir, written in 1283, is not only the most perfect embodiment of the French jurisprudence of his time, but is peculiarly interesting as a landmark in the struggle between the waning power of feudalism and the Roman theories which gave intensity of purpose to the enlightened centralization aimed at by St. Louis: and Beaumanoir likewise passes in silence over the practice of compurgation, as though it were no longer an existing institution. All these legislators and lawyers had been preceded by the Emperor Frederic II., who, in 1231, promulgated his "Constitutiones Sicularum" for the government of his Neapolitan provinces. Frederic was Latin, and not Teutonic, both by education and predilection, and his system of jurisprudence is greatly in advance of all that had preceded it. That conjurators should

---

[1] Though absent from the general laws of Spain, yet compurgation had been introduced as an occasional custom. We have seen it above (p. 49) in the Fuero de Balbás in 1135. The Fuero of Madrid in 1202 provides that a man suspected of homicide and other crimes, in the absence of testimony, can clear himself with six or twelve conjurators, according to the grade of the offence (Mem. de la Real. Acad. de la Historia, 1852). We shall see hereafter that it appears in the Fuero Viejo of Castile in 1356. The passage from the Romancero del Cid, quoted above, shows the hold it had on the popular imagination.

find no place in his scheme of legal procedure is, therefore, only what might be expected. The collection of laws known as the *Établissements* of St. Louis is by no means a complete code, but it is sufficiently copious to render the absence of all allusion to compurgation significant. In fact, the numerous references to the Digest show how strong was the desire to substitute the Roman for the customary law, and the efforts of the king to do away with all negative proofs of course included the one under consideration. The same may be said of the *Livres de Justice et de Plet* and the *Conseil* of Pierre de Fontaines, two unofficial books of practice, which represent with tolerable fulness the procedures in vogue during the latter half of the thirteenth century ; while the *Olim*, or records of the Parlement of Paris, the king's high court of justice, show that the same principles were kept in view in the long struggle by which that body succeeded in extending the royal jurisdiction at the expense of the independence of the vainly resisting feudatories. In the *Olim* from 1254 to 1318, I can find but two instances in which compurgation was required—one in 1279 at Noyon, and one in 1284 at Compiègne. As innumerable decisions are given of cases in which its employment would have been equally appropriate, these two can only be regarded as exceptional, and the inference is fair that some local custom rendered it impossible to refuse the privilege on these special occasions.[1]

All these were the works of men deeply imbued with the spirit of the resuscitated jurisconsults of Rome. Their labors bear testimony rather to the influences tending to overthrow the institutions bequeathed by the Barbarians to the Middle Ages, than to a general acceptance of the innovations attempted. Their authority was still circumscribed by the innumerable jurisdictions which yet defied their gradual encroachments and resolutely maintained ancestral customs. Thus, in 1250, we find in the settlement of a quarrel between

---

[1] Olim, II. 153, 237.

Hugues Tirel Seigneur of Poix in Picardy and the commune of that place, that one of the articles was to the effect that the mayor with thirty-nine of the bourgeois should kneel before the dame de Poix and offer to swear that an insult inflicted on her had not been done, or that if it had, it had been in honor of the Seigneur de Poix.[1] Even an occasional instance may be found where the central power itself permitted the use of compurgation, showing how difficult it was to eradicate the prejudices transmitted through ages from father to son, and that the policy adopted by St. Louis and Philippe le Bel, aided by the shrewd and energetic civil lawyers who assisted them so ably, was not in all cases adhered to. Thus, in 1283, when the bailli of Amiens was accused before the Parlement of Paris of having invaded the privileges of the church by trying three clerks accused of crime, it was decided that he should swear with six compurgators as to his ignorance that the criminals were ecclesiastics.[2] So, in 1303, a powerful noble of the court of Philippe le Bel was accused of a foul and treacherous murder, which a brother of the victim offered to prove by the wager of battle. Philippe was endeavoring to abolish the judicial duel, and the accused desired strongly to escape that ordeal. He was accordingly condemned to clear himself of the imputed crime by a purgatorial oath with ninety-nine nobles, and at the same time to satisfy the fraternal claim of vengeance with an enormous fine[3]—a decision which offers the best practical commentary on the degree of faith reposed in this system of purgation. Even the Parlement of Paris in 1353 and a rescript of Charles le Sage in 1357 allude to compurgation as still in use and of binding force.[4]

---

[1] Actes du Parlement de Paris, T. I. p. cccvii. (Paris, 1863).

[2] Actes du Parlement de Paris, T. I. p. 382.

[3] Statuunt . . . se manu centesima nobilium se purgare, et ad huic benedicto juveni bis septem librarum milia pro sui rancoris satisfactione praesentare.—Wilelmi Egmond. Chron.

[4] Is qui reus putatur tertia manu se purgabit, inter quos sint duo qui dicentur denominati.—Du Cange s. v. *Juramentum.*

It was in the provinces, however, that the system manifested its greatest vitality, protected both by the stubborn dislike to innovation and by the spirit of independence which so long and so bitterly resisted the centralizing efforts of the crown. The Roman law concentrated all power in the person of the sovereign, and reduced his subjects to one common level of implicit obedience. The genius of the barbaric institutions and of feudalism localized power. The principles were essentially oppugnant, and the contest between them was prolonged and confused, for neither party could in all cases recognize the ultimate result of the minuter points involved, though each was fully alive to the broad issues of the struggle.

How obstinate was the attachment to bygone forms may be understood when we see even the comparatively precocious civilization of a city like Lille preserve the compurgatorial oath as a regular procedure until the middle of the fourteenth century, even though the progress of enlightenment had long rendered it a mere formality, without serious meaning. Until the year 1351, the defendant in a civil suit was obliged to substantiate the oath of denial with two conjurators of the same sex, who swore to its truth, to the best of their belief.[1] The minutest regulations were enforced as to this ceremony, the position of every finger being determined by law, and though it was the veriest formality, serving merely as an introduction to the taking of testimony and the legal examination of the case, yet the slightest error committed by either party lost him the suit irrecoverably.[2]

[1] Et li deffendans, sour qui on a clamet se doit deffendre par lui tierche main, se chou est hom II. hommes et lui, se chou est fame II. femmes et li à tierche. . . . "Tel sierment que Jehans chi jura boin sierment y jura au mien ensiant. Si m'ait Dius et chist Saint."—Roisin, Franchises, etc. de la Ville de Lille, pp. 30, 35.

[2] Ibid. p. 51. The system was abrogated by a municipal ordinance of September, 1351, in accordance with a special ordonnance to that effect issued by King John of France in March, 1350.

The royal ordonnance declares that the oath was "en langage estra:gne

Normandy was even more faithful to the letter of the ancient traditions. The Coutumier in use until the revision of 1583 under Henry III. retains a remnant of the practice under the name of *desrene*, by which, in questions of little moment, a man could rebut an accusation with two or four compurgators, even when it was sustained by witnesses. The form of procedure was identical with that of old, and the oath, as we have already seen (page 58), was an unqualified assertion of the truth of that of the accused.[1] Practically, however, we may assume that the custom had become obsolete, for the letters patent of Henry III., ordering the revision in 1577, expressly state that the provisions of the existing laws "estoient la pluspart hors d'usage et peu ou point entendu des habitants du pays;" and that compurgation was one of the forgotten formulas may fairly be inferred from the fact that Pasquier, writing previous to 1584, speaks of it as altogether a matter of the past.[2]

The fierce mountaineers of Béarn were comparatively inaccessible to the innovating spirit of the age, and preserved their feudal independence amid the progress and reform of the sixteenth century long after it had become obsolete elsewhere throughout Southern Europe. Accordingly, we find the practice of compurgation maintained as a regular form of procedure in the latest revision of their code, made by Henry II.

---

et de mos divers et non de legier a retenir ou prononchier," and yet that if either party "par quelconques maniere faloit en fourme ou en langage ou que par fragilite de langhe, huirans eu, se parolle faulsist ou oubvliast, ou eslevast se main plus que li dite maniere acoustumee en requeroit ou quelle ne tenist fermement sen poch en se paulme ou ne wardast et maintenist pluiseurs autres frivoles et vaines chozes et manieres appartenans au dit sierment, selonc le loy de la dite ville, tant em parole comme en fait, il avoit du tout sa cause perdue, ne depuis nestoit rechus sur che li demanderes a claim ou complainte, ne li deffenderes a deffensce."—Ibid. p. 390.

[1] Anc. Coutume de Normandie, chap. lxxxv. (Bourdot de Richebourg, IV. 53-4).

[2] Recherches de la France, Liv. IV. chap. iii. Concerning the date of this, see La Croix du Maine, s. v. *Estienne Pasquier*.

of Navarre in 1551, which continued in force until the eighteenth century.[1] The influence of the age is shown, however,
even there, in a modification of the oath, which is no longer
an unreserved confirmation of the principal, but a mere affirmation of belief.[2]

In Castile, a revival of the custom is to be found in the
code compiled by Pedro the Cruel, in 1356, by which, in
certain cases, the defendant was allowed to prove his innocence with the oath of eleven hidalgos.[3] This, however, is so
much in opposition to the principles of the Partidas, which
had but a few years previous been accepted as the law of the
land, and is so contrary to the spirit of the Ordenamiento de
Alcalà, which continued in force until the fifteenth century,
that it can only be regarded as a tentative resuscitation of
mere temporary validity.

The Northern races resisted more obdurately the advances
of the reviving influence of the Roman law. Though we have
seen Frederic II. omitting all notice of compurgation in the
code prepared for his Neapolitan dominions in 1231, he did
not attempt to abrogate it among his German subjects, for it is
alluded to in a charter granted to the city of Regensburg in
1230.[4] The Schwabenspiegel, which during the thirteenth
and fourteenth centuries was the municipal law of Southern
Germany, directs the employment of conjurators in various
classes of actions which do not admit of direct testimony.[5]

[1] Fors et Cost. de Béarn, Rubr. de Juramentz (Bourdot de Richebourg,
IV. 1082).

[2] Lo jurament deu seguidor se fé JURAN PER aquetz sanctz bertat ditz exi
que io crey.

[3] E si gelo negare e non gelo quisier probar, devel' facer salvo con once
Fijosdalgo e èl doceno, que non lo fiço (Fuero Viejo de Castiella, Lib. I.
Tit. v. l. 12). It will be observed that this is an unqualified recognition of
the system of negative proofs.

[4] Du Cange, s. v. *Juramentum.*

[5] Jur. Provin. Alaman. cap. xxiv.; cccix. § 4; cccxxix. §§ 2, 3;
cccxxxix. § 3 (Edit. Schilteri).

The code in force in Northern Germany, as we have already seen, gave great facilities for rebutting accusations by the single oath of the defendant, and therefore the use of conjurators is but rarely referred to in the Sachsenspiegel, though it was not unknown, for either of the parties to a judicial duel could refuse the combat by procuring six conjurators to swear with him that he was related to his antagonist.[1] In the Saxon burgher law, however, the practice is frequently alluded to, and it would seem from various passages that a man of good character who could get six others to take with him the oath of denial was not easily convicted. But where there was satisfactory proof, compurgation was not allowed, and in homicide cases, if a relative of the slain decided to proceed by the duel, his claim of vengeance was supreme, and no other process was admissible.[2] It is evident, however, that compurgation retained its hold on popular respect when we see, about 1300, the Emperor Albert I. substituting it for the duel in a considerable class of criminal cases.[3] In the early part of the sixteenth century, Maximilian I. did much to diminish the use of the compurgatorial procedure,[4] but that he failed to eradicate it entirely is evident from a constitution issued by Charles V. in 1548, wherein its employment is enjoined in doubtful cases in a manner to show that it was an existing resource of the law, and that it retained its hold upon public confidence, although the conjurators were only required to swear as to their belief in the oath of their principal.[5]

In the Netherlands it likewise maintained its position.

---

[1] Jur. Provin. Saxon. Lib. I. c. 63.

[2] Sachsische Weichbild, art. 71, 72, 86, 40, 88.

[3] Goldast. Constitt. Imp. III. 446.

[4] Meyer, Institutions Judiciaires, V. 221.

[5] Sique accusatus tanta ac tam gravi suspitione laboraret ut aliorum quoque purgatione necesse esset, in arbitratu stet judicis, si illi eam velit injungere, nec ne, qui nimirum compurgatores jurabunt, se credere quod ille illive qui se per juramentum excusarunt, recte vereque juraverint.— Constit. de Pace Publica cap. xv. § 1 (Goldast. Constitt. Imp. I. 541).

Damhouder, writing in 1554, after describing its employment in the Courts Christian, adds that by their example it
was occasionally used also in secular tribunals.[1]

In Scotland, as late as the middle of the fourteenth century,
its existence is proved by a statute which provides that if a
thief escaped from confinement, the lord of the prison should
clear himself of complicity with the evasion by the oaths of
thirty conjurators, of whom three were required to be nobles.[2]

The Scandinavian nations adhered to the custom with even
greater tenacity. In the code of Haco Haconsen, issued
towards the close of the thirteenth century, it appears as the
basis of defensive procedure in almost all criminal cases, and
even in civil suits its employment is not infrequently directed,
the number of conjurators being proportioned to the nature
of the crime or to the amount at stake, and regulations for
administering the oath being given with much minuteness.[3]
In Denmark it was not abolished until near the middle of the
seventeenth century, under Christiern IV., after it had become
a crying abuse through the habit of members of families, and
even of whole guilds, entering into formal engagements to
support each other in this manner.[4] The exact date of its
abrogation is a matter of uncertainty, and the stubbornness
with which the people clung to it is shown by the fact that
even in 1683 Christiern V., in promulgating a new code,
found it necessary formally to prohibit accused persons from
being forced to provide conjurators.[5] In Sweden, its existence was similarly prolonged. Directions for its use are contained in the code which was in force until the seventeenth

---

[1] Damhouder. Rerum Criminalium Praxis cap. xliv. No. 6 (Antwerp.
1601).

[2] Statut. Davidis II. cap. i. § 6.

[3] Jarnsida, Mannhelge & Thiofa-Balkr *passim ;* Erfthatal cap. xxiv. ;
Landabrigtha-Balkr cap. xxviii.; Kaupa-Balkr cap. v., ix., etc.

[4] See Sporon & Finsen, Dissert. de Usu Juramenti juxta Leges Daniæ
Antiquas, Havniae 1815-17, P. I. pp. 160-1, P. II. pp. 206-8.

[5] Christiani V. Jur. Danic. Lib. i. c. xiv. § 8.

century;[1] it is constantly alluded to in the laws of Gustavus Adolphus;[2] and an edict of Charles XI. in 1662 reproves the readiness with which men were everywhere prompt to serve as compurgators, and requires the judges, before admitting them, to investigate whether they are proper persons and what are their reasons to believe in the innocence of their principal.[3] By this time, therefore, though not yet witnesses, they were becoming assimilated to them.

The vitality of communal societies among the Slavs naturally led to the maintenance of a custom which drew its origin from the solidarity of families, and it is therefore not surprising to find it in Poland described as in full force as late as the eighteenth century, the defendant being obliged to support his purgatorial oath with conjurators, who swore as to its truth.[4] Yet among the Poles confidence in it as a legal proof had long been undermined. In 1368 Casimir III. decreed that a man of good repute, when accused of theft, could clear himself by his own oath ; but if his character was doubtful, and compurgation was prescribed, then if he fell short by one conjurator of the number required, he should satisfy the accuser, though he should not be rendered infamous for the future. This led to an increase of crime, and a hundred years later Casimir IV. proclaimed a law by which compurgation was only allowed three times, after which a persistent offender was abandoned to the full severity of the law, as being presumably guilty and not deserving of escape. At the same time any one summoned to compurgation, and appearing before the judge without compurgators, was *ipso facto* pronounced infamous. From a case recorded it would appear that twelve conjurators were required to outweigh the

---

[1] Poteritque se tunc purgare cui crimen imponitur juramento xvIII. virorum.—Raguald. Ingermund. Leg. Suecorum Lib. i. c. xvi.

[2] Legg. Civil. Gustavi Adolphi Tit. x.

[3] Caroli XI. Judicum Regulæ, cap. xxxii.

[4] Ludewig. Reliq. MSS. T. VII. p. 401.

single oath of the accuser.[1] Among the southern Slavs the custom was likewise preserved to a comparatively late date. An edict of Hermann, Ban of Slavonia, in 1416, orders that any noble accused of neglect to enforce a decree of proscription against a malefactor, should purge himself with five of his peers as conjurators, in default of which he was subject to a fine of twenty marcs.[2]

The constitutional reverence of the Englishman for established forms and customs, however, nominally preserved this relic of barbarism in the common law to a period later by far than its disappearance from the codes of other nations. The system of inquests and ordeals established by the Assize of Clarendon in 1166 and the rise of the jury system led to its being superseded in criminal matters, but in civil suits it held its own. According to Bracton, in the thirteenth century, in all actions arising from contracts, sales, donations, etc., when there was no absolute proof, the plaintiff came into court with his *secta*, and the defendant was bound to produce two conjurators for each one advanced by the plaintiff, the evidence apparently preponderating according to quantity rather than quality.[3] From the context, it would appear that the

---

[1] Herb. de Fulstin Statut. Reg. Poloniæ. Samoscii, 1597, pp. 186-88, 465.

By the customs of Iglau, about the middle of the thirteenth century, a man could rebut with two conjurators a charge of assault with serious mutilation, and was subject to a fine of fourteen marks if he failed; accusations of complicity required only the oath of the accused.—Statuta Primæva Moraviæ, Brunæ, 1781, pp. 103-4.

[2] Bassani de Sacchi Jura Regni Croatiæ, Dalmatiæ et Sclavoniæ. Zagrabiæ, 1862, Pt. I. p. 182.

[3] Et sic major præsumptio vincit minorem. Si autem querens probationem habuerit, sicut instrumenta et chartas sigillatas, contra hujusmodi probationes non erit defensio per legem. Sed si instrumento contradicatur, fides instrumenti probabitur per patriam et per testes. Bracton. Lib. IV. Tract. vi. cap. 18, § 6.

The word "secta" is a troublesome one to legal antiquarians from its diverse significations. As used in the above text it means the supporters

secta of the plaintiff consisted of his friends and followers willing to take the oath with him, but not absolutely witnesses. The Fleta, however, some twenty-five years later, uses the term in the sense of witnesses, and in actions of debt directs the defence to be made with conjurators double in number the plaintiff's witnesses,[1] thus offering an immense premium on dishonesty and perjury. Notwithstanding this, the nobles and gentry who came to London to attend the court and Parliament apparently were subjected to many annoyances by the citizens who strove to collect their debts, and in 1363 Edward III. relieved them by abrogating the wholesome rule laid down by Bracton, and enacting that a debtor could wage his law with a sufficient number of conjurators in spite of any papers put forward in evidence by the creditor, who is curtly told to find his remedy in some other way.[2] The unquestionable advantages which this offered to not the least influential part of a feudal community probably had something to do with its preservation. The "Termes de la Ley," compiled in the early part of the sixteenth century, states as the existing practice that "when one shall wage his law, he shall bring with him 6, 8, or 12 of his neighbors, as the court shall assign him, to swear with him;" and when in a statute of 1585 imposing severe fines for using wood or charcoal in iron manufacture it is provided that offenders shall not be entitled to defence by

of the plaintiff's case. Elsewhere we find it denoting the hue and cry, which all men were bound to follow; see Stubb's Select Charters, pp. 256, 366, etc. "Facere sectam" also seems to have the sense of holding court (Ib. p. 303), whence it also derives a secondary meaning of jurisdiction (Baildon, Select Civil Pleas, I. 42).

[1] Fleta, Lib. II. c. lxiii. § 10. Sed si sectam [actor] produxerit, hoc est testimonium hominum legalium qui contractui inter eos habito interfuerint praesentes, qui a judice examinati si concordes inveniantur, tunc poterit [reus] vadiare legem suam contra petentem et contra sectam suam prolatam; ut si duos vel tres testes produxerit [actor] ad probandum, oportet quod defensio fiat per quatuor vel per sex; ita quod pro quolibet teste duos producat jurat [ores] usque ad xii.

[2] 38 Edw. III. St. 1. cap. v. (Statutes at Large I. 319. Ed. 1769).

8

the wager of law, it shows that proceeding to be still in common use, though it was recognized as a means of eluding justice.[1] Style's "Practical Register," published in 1657, also describes the process, but an absurd mistake as to the meaning of the traditional expression "jurare manu" shows that the matter was rather a legal curiosity than a procedure in ordinary use; and, indeed, the author expressly states that the practice having been "abused by the iniquity of the people, the law was forced to find out another way to do justice to the nation." Still the law remained unaltered, and a case is recorded occurring in 1708, known as Gunner's case, where "the plaintiff became nonsuit, when the defendant was ready to perfect his law,"[2] and Jacob, in his "Review of the Statutes," published not long after, treats of it as still part of the existing judicial processes. As the wager of law came to be limited to simple actions of debt, shrewd lawyers found means of avoiding it by actions of "trespass upon the case," and other indirect forms which required the intervention of a jury, but Burn in his Law Dictionary (Dublin, 1792) describes the whole process with all its forms as still existing, and in 1799 a case occurred in which a defendant successfully eluded the payment of a claim by producing compurgators who "each held up his right hand, and then laid their hands upon the book and swore that they believed what the defendant swore was true." The court endeavored to prevent this injustice, but was forced to accept the law of the land. Even this did not provoke a change. In 1824, in the case of King v. Williams (2 Barnewell & Cresswell, 528), some black-letter lawyer revived the forgotten iniquity for the benefit of a client in want of testimony, and demanded that the court should prescribe the number of conjurators necessary for the defence, but the court refused assistance, desiring to give the plaintiff the benefit of any mistake that might be made. Williams then got together eleven conjurators, and appeared in court

[1] 27 Eliz. cap. xix. § 1.
[2] Jacob's Review of the Statutes, 2d Ed. London, 1715, p. 532.

with them at his back, when the plaintiff, recognizing the futility of any further proceedings, abandoned his case in disgust.[1] Still, the fine reverential spirit postponed the inevitable innovation, and it was not until 1833 that the wager of law was formally abrogated by 3 and 4 William IV., c. 42, s. 13.[2]

English colonists carried the ancestral custom across the sea and seem to have resorted to it as an infallible mode of settling certain cases for which no positive evidence could be had. Small as was the infant colony of Bermuda, its court records for a little more than six months show four instances of its use, all of which occur in deciding cases of "suspition of incontinency" regularly presented by the grand jury or the ecclesiastical authorities.[3]

---

[1] I owe a portion of these references to a paper in the London "Jurist" for March, 1827, the writer of which instances the wager of law as an evidence of "that jealous affection and filial reverence which have converted our code into a species of museum of antiques and legal curiosities."

[2] Wharton's Law Lexicon, 2d ed., p. 758.

[3] I owe a transcript of these records to the kindness of the late General J. H. Lefroy, then Governor of Bermuda. The quaintness of the proceedings may justify the printing of the sentences.

Nov. Assizes, 1638.—"Arthur Thorne being presented by the minister and church wardens of Pembroke tribe [parish] upon suspition of incontinency with Elizabeth Jenour the wyfe of Mr. Anthony Jenour, was censured [sentenced] in case he could not purge himself to doe open penaunce in two churches." He probably failed in his purgation, for Mrs. Jenour confessed her sin in open court and was referred to her minister for penance.

June Assizes, 1639. "The minister, church wardens, and sydesmen of Sandy's Tribe doe present Mary Eldrington, the wyfe of Roger Eldrington, upon suspition of incontinency grounded on comon fame: upon which presentment she was censured to doe open penaunce in the church in case she could not purge herselfe by the oath of 3 women of credit in the Tribe."

"Edward Bowly, presented upon suspicion of incontinency with Anne, a negro woman, supposed to be the father of her bastard child, was put to his compurgators, and did thereupon purge himself, and the negro woman censured to receave 21 lashes at the whipping-post, which was executed upon her."

"Edward Wolsey and Dorathie Penniston were presented upon common fame for suspition of incontinencie by the grand inquest, and also presented

Doubtless if the early records of Virginia and Massachusetts could be searched similar evidence of its use would be found in them. Indeed it is quite possible that, strictly speaking, the wager of law may still preserve a legal existence in this country. In 1712 an act of the Colony of South Carolina, enumerating the English laws to be held as in force there, specifically includes those relating to this mode of defence, and I am not aware that they have ever been formally abrogated.[1] In 1811 Chancellor Kilty, of Maryland, speaks of the wager of law as being totally disused in consequence of the avoidance of the forms of suit which might admit of its employment, but he evidently regards it as not then specifically abolished.[2]

While the common sense of mankind was gradually eliminating the practice from among the recognized procedures of secular tribunals, the immutable nature of ecclesiastical observances prolonged its vitality in the bosom of the church. We have seen above that Innocent III., about the commencement of the thirteenth century, altered the form of oath from an unqualified confirmation to a mere assertion of belief in the innocence of the accused. That this at once became the standard formula in ecclesiastical cases is probable when we find it adopted for the oaths of the compurgators who, during the Albigensian persecution, were required by the nascent Inquisition in all cases to assist in the purgation of such suspected heretics as were allowed to escape so easily.[3] And

by the minister and churchwardens of Pembroke Tribe upon the like suspition, whereupon they were sentenced to doe penaunce in the church, standing in a whyte sheete during divine service, making confession of that their suspitious walking in case they could not purge themselves by their owne oathes and two sufficient compurgators."

[1] Cooper's Statutes at Large of South Carolina, Columbia, 1837, II. 403.

[2] Kilty's Report on English Statutes, Annapolis, 1811, p. 140.

[3] Ego talis juro . . . me firmiter credere quod talis non fuit Insabbatus, Valdensis, vel pauperum de Lugduno . . . et credo firmiter eum in hoc jurasse verum.—Doctrina de modo procedendi contra Hæreticos (Mar-

this is no doubt the "congruous purgation" to which Innocent III. and Gregory IX. alluded as that by which suspected heretics should clear themselves.[1] Zealous inquisitors, however, paid little attention to such forms which allowed their victims a chance of escape, for it is related of Conrad of Marburg, who for a short time spread terror and desolation throughout Germany, that when the accused confessed he subjected them to torture and the frightful penance provided by the church, but that when they denied their guilt he sent them at once to the stake. The compurgatorial process, however, vindicated itself in a notable manner when Conrad's cruelties at length aroused effective opposition. Count Sayn, whom he had accused, was virtually acquitted at the Council of Mainz, July, 1233, soon after which Conrad was assassinated: the count, however, required formal vindication, and at the Diet of Frankfort, in February, 1234, he cleared himself of the charge of heresy in the most imposing manner with a train of compurgators comprising eight bishops, twelve Cistercian abbots, twelve Franciscan and three Dominican monks, and a number of Benedictine abbots, clergy, and noble laymen. After this, in April, the Council of Mainz declared him and others of Conrad's victims to be innocent and to be restored to reputation and to their possessions.[2]

The practice of compurgation thus introduced at the foundation of the Inquisition was maintained to the last by that terrible tribunal. "Our holy mother church," says Simancas, Bishop of Badajos, a writer of the sixteenth century, " can in no way endure the suspicion of heresy, but seeks by various

tene, Thesaur. T. V. p. 1801).—This is the same as the form prescribed by the Council of Tarragona in 1242, where we learn, moreover, that the number of compurgators was prescribed by the inquisitor in each case (Aguirre, Concil. Hispan. IV. 193).

[1] Conc. Lateran. IV. can. iii.—Decret. Gregor. P. P. IX. (Harduin. VII. 163).

[2] Hartzheim Conc. Germ. III. 542–50.—Alberic. Trium Font. ann. 1233–4.—Gest. Treviror. c. 175.

remedies to cure the suspect.   Sometimes she forces them to
abjure or to purge themselves ; sometimes she elicits the truth
by torture, and very often she coerces them with extraordinary
punishments.'' Therefore, any one whose orthodoxy was
doubtful, if he was unwilling to clear himself, at the command
of the judge, was held to be convicted of heresy.   By the
secular law he had a year's grace before condemnation, but
under the ecclesiastical law he was instantly punishable.[1]

Canonical purgation, according to the rules of the Inquisition, was indicated when public report rendered a man suspected and there was no tangible evidence against him.   The
number of compurgators was left to the discretion of the judge,
who at the same time decided whether the deficiency of one,
two, or more would amount to a condemnation.   They were to
be peers of the accused ; and though he was allowed to select
them, yet the qualification that they were to be good men and
orthodox practically left their nomination to the officials—
even as the customary accusation by the promotor-fiscal was
held to be in itself the requisite amount of suspicion required
as a condition precedent for the trial.   The greater the suspicion, however, the larger was the number of compurgators to
be adduced.

When the accused had chosen his men, and they were
accepted by the judge, they were summoned, and each one
examined separately by the Inquisitors as to his acquaintance
with the defendant—a process by which, it may readily be
conceived, the terrors of the Holy Office might easily be so
used as to render them extremely unwilling to become his
sponsors.   They were then assembled together ; the accused
was brought in, the charge against him was read, and he took
an oath denying it.   Each conjurator was then taken separately and sworn as to his belief in the truth or falsity of the
oath of denegation, and according as they expressed their
conviction of the veracity of the accused the sentence was
usually rendered, absolving or condemning him.

[1] Jacob. Simancæ de Cathol. Instit. Tit. lvi. No. 3, 4 (Romæ, 1575).

No process of administering compurgation can well be conceived more shrewdly adapted to reduce to a minimum the chances of acquittal, or to leave the result subject to the wishes of the officials. The testimony of the doctors of law, both civil and canon, accordingly was that it was blind, deceitful, and perilous.[1] In fact, it is easy to conceive of the difficulty of finding five, or nine, or eleven men willing to risk their lives and families by standing up in support of any one who had fallen into the grasp of the Holy Office. The terrible apprehension which the Inquisition spread abroad among all classes, and the dread which every man felt of being suspected and seized as an accomplice of heresy, are unconsciously intimated by Simancas when, arguing against this mode of trial, he observes that "the morals of mankind are so corrupt at the present day, and Christian charity has grown so cold, that it is almost impossible to find any one willing to join in clearing his neighbor, or who does not easily believe the worst of him and construe all doubtful things against him. When it is enough for the condemnation of the accused that the compurgators shall declare that they are ignorant or doubtful as to his innocence, who is there that will not express doubt when they know that he would not have been condemned to purge himself if he had not been violently suspected?" For these reasons he says that those of Moorish or Jewish stock should never be subjected to it, for it is almost impossible not to think ill of them, and, therefore, to send them to purgation is simply to send them to the stake.[2]

For all this, there was a lively discussion in the time of Simancas, whether if the accused succeeded in thus clearing himself, it was sufficient for acquittal. Many Inquisitors, indeed, held to the older practice that the accused should first be tortured, when if no confession could be forced from him

---

[1] Simancæ, loc. cit. No. 31.—Villadiego, Fuero Juzgo, p. 318 *b* (Madrid, 1600).—Both of these authorities stigmatize it as "fragilis et periculosa, cæca et fallax."

[2] Simancæ, loc. cit. No. 12.

he was put on his purgation; if he passed safely through this, he was then made to abjure the errors of which he had not been convicted, and after all this he was punished at the discretion of the judge.[1] Such an accumulation of injustice seems incredible, and yet Simancas feels himself obliged to enter into an elaborate discussion to prove its impropriety.

In countries where the Inquisition had not infected society and destroyed all feeling of sympathy between man and man this process of purgation was not impossible. Thus, in 1527, during one of the early persecutions of the reformers under Henry VIII., while numbers were convicted, two women, Margaret Cowbridge and Margery Bowgas, were allowed to clear themselves by compurgators, though there were several positive witnesses against them. It is also noteworthy that in these cases a portion of the compurgators were women.[2]

In the regular ecclesiastical courts the practice was maintained. When the Council of Constance, in its futile efforts at reformation, prepared an elaborate code of discipline, it proposed strenuous regulations to correct the all-pervading vice of simony. To prevent the sale of benefices this project of law decreed deprivation of all preferment as the punishment for such offences, and as transactions of the kind were commonly accomplished in secret, it ordained that common report should be sufficient for conviction; yet it nullified the regulation by permitting the accused to clear himself by canonical purgation.[3] Towards the close of the fifteenth century, Angelo da Chiavasco describes it as customary where there is no formal accuser and yet public rumor requires action, although the judge can also order it in cases of accusation: if the defendant fails of his purgation in the latter case he is to be punished as provided for his crime; if there is only rumor, then the

---

[1] Simancæ, loc. cit. No 17.

[2] Strype's Ecclesiastical Memorials, I. 87.

[3] Reformator. Constant. Decretal. Lib. v. Tit. ii. cap. 1, 3 (Von der Hardt, Tom. I. P. XII. pp. 739, 742).

penalty is discretional.[1] The judge determined the number of conjurators, who were all to be of good reputation and familiar with the life of the accused; if he were a monk, they ought if possible to be of the same order; they simply swore to their belief in his oath of denial.[2] A century later Lancelotti speaks of compurgation as the only mode of defence then in use in doubtful cases, where the evidence was insufficient.[3] This applied not only to cases between churchmen, but also to secular matters subject to ecclesiastical jurisdiction. Grillandus, writing about 1530, speaks of six conjurators of the kindred as the customary formula in proceedings for nullity of marriage, and mentions an instance personally known to him, wherein this procedure was successfully adopted by a wife desirous of a divorce from her husband who for three years had been rendered impotent by witchcraft, in accordance with the rules laid down in the canon law for such cases.[4] And among certain orders of monks within the last century, questions arising between themselves were settled by this mode of trial.[5]

In England, after the Anglican Church had received its final shape under Cranmer, during the reign of Edward VI., the custom appears in a carefully compiled body of ecclesiastical law, of which the formal adoption was only prevented accidentally by the untimely death of the young king. By this, a man accused of a charge resting on presumptions and incompletely proved, was required to clear himself with four compurgators of his own rank, who swore, as provided in the decretals of Innocent III., to their belief in his innocence.[6]

---

[1] Angeli de Clavasio Summa angelica, s. v. *Purgatio.*

[2] Baptistæ de Saulis Summa rosella, s. v. *Purgatio.*

[3] Institut. Jur. Canon. Lib. IV. Tit. ii. § 2.—Cf. Concil. Tarraconens. ann. 1591, Lib. IV. Tit. xiv. (Aguirre, VI. 322).

[4] P. Grillandi Tract. de Sortileg. Qu. 6, No. 14; Qu. 3, No. 36.—Decret. II. caus. xxx. q. 1, can. 2.—C. 7 Extra, Lib. IV. Tit. xv.

[5] Du Cange, loc. cit.

[6] Burnet, Reformation, Vol. II. p. 199 (Ed. 1681).

CHAPTER VIII.

ACCUSATORIAL CONJURATORS.

THOUGH not strictly a portion of our subject, the question is not without interest as to the power or obligation of the plaintiff or accuser to fortify his case with conjurators. There is little evidence of such a custom in primitive times, but one or two allusions to it in the *Leges Barbarorum* show that it was occasionally practised. Some of the earlier texts of the Salic law contain a section providing that in certain cases the complainant shall sustain his action with a number of conjurators varying with the amount at stake; a larger number is required of the defendant in reply; and it is presumable that the judges weighed the probabilities on either side and rendered a decision accordingly.[1] As this is omitted in the later revisions of the law, it probably was not widely practised, or regarded as of much importance. Among the Baioarians, a claimant of an estate produced six conjurators who took the oath with him, and whose united efforts could be rebutted by the defendant with a single competent witness.[2] These directions are so precise that there can be no doubt that the custom prevailed to a limited extent among certain tribes, and a clause in the Decree of Childebert in 597, providing that the oaths of five or seven impartial men of good character shall convict a thief or malefactor, would seem evidently to refer to conjurators and not to witnesses.[3] In the treaty between Childebert and Clotair in 593, an accuser in case of theft is obliged to give twelve conjurators, half of them selected by himself, to

---

[1] Tit. LXXIV. of Herold's text; Cap. Extravagant. No. XVIII. of Pardessus.

[2] L. Baioar. Tit. XVI. cap. i. § 2.

[3] Pactus pro Tenore Pacis, § 2, cf. § 5 (Baluze).

swear that a theft has really taken place.[1] That it was, indeed, more generally employed than the scanty references to it in the codes would indicate, may be inferred from one of the ecclesiastical forgeries which Charlemagne was induced to adopt and promulgate. According to this, no accusation against a bishop could be successful unless supported by seventy-two witnesses, all of whom were to be men of good repute; forty-four were required to substantiate a charge against a priest, thirty-seven in the case of a deacon, and seven when a member of the inferior grades was implicated.[2] Though styled witnesses in the text, the number required is so large that they evidently could have been only conjurators, with whom the complainant supported his oath of accusation, and the fabrication of such a law would seem to show that the practice of employing such means of substantiating a charge was familiar to the minds of men.

Among the heathen Northmen, as we have seen, every pleader, whether plaintiff or defendant, was obliged to take a preliminary oath on the sacred *stalla hringr*, or altar ring, duly bathed in the blood of an ox sacrificed for the purpose. This custom was preserved in England, where the Anglo-Saxon laws required, except in trivial cases, a "fore-oath" from the accuser (*forath, antejuramentum, præjuramentum*), and William the Conqueror, in his compilation of the laws of Edward the Confessor, shows that this was sometimes strengthened by requiring the addition of conjurators, who were in no sense witnesses, since their oath had reference, not to the facts of the case, but solely to the purity of intention on the part of the accuser.[3] Indications of the same procedure are to be

---

[1] Decreti Childeberti c. vii. (Baluze). This provision was not merely temporary. It is preserved in the Capitularies (Lib. VII. c. 257), whence it was carried into the Decretum of Ivo of Chartres in the twelfth century (Decr. P. xiii. c. 6; P. xvi. c. 358).

[2] Capit. Car. Mag. VI. ann. 806, c. xxiii. (Concil. Roman. Silvestri PP. I.).

[3] E li apelur jurra sur lui par VII. humes numez, sei siste main, que pur haur nel fait ne pur auter chose, si pur sun dreit nun purchacer.—Ll. Guillel. I. cap. xiv.

found in the collection known as the laws of Henry I.[1] Probably to the development of this may be attributed the peculiar device of the *secta* already referred to (p. 84), consisting of those who supported the plaintiff by their oaths while in no sense absolute witnesses.   They were not even examined unless the defendant demanded it.   The bringing of the *secta* or suit remained a matter of form long after the actual production of the witnesses had become obsolete in the fourteenth century, and it was not finally abolished until 1852.[2]

In an age of comparative simplicity, it is natural that men should turn rather to the guarantees of individual character, or to the forms of venerable superstition, than to the subtleties of legal procedure.   Even as the defendant was expected to produce vouchers of his truthfulness, so might the plaintiff be equally required to give evidence that his repute among his neighbors was such as to justify the belief that he would not bring a false charge or advance an unfounded claim.   The two customs appear to arise from the same process of reasoning and to be identical in spirit, leading to a contest between the two parties as to which could bring forward the largest and most credible number of conjurators, and the position of the accused being outsworn was a recognized circumstance in jurisprudence.   Thus, the Council of Tribur in 895 provides that in such case he must either confess or undergo the ordeal.[3] In process of time accusatorial conjurators became commonly used in many places.   In Béarn the laws of the thirteenth century provide that in cases of debt under forty sous, where there was no testimony on either side, the claimant could substantiate his case by bringing forward one conjurator, while the defendant could rebut it with two.[4]   A similar rule obtained in

[1] Omnis tihla tractetur antejuramento plano vel observato.—Ll. Henrici I. Tit. lxiv. § 1.   Antejuramentum a compellante habeatur, et alter se sexto decime sue purgetur; sicut accusator precesserit.—Ibid. Tit. lxvi. § 8.

[2] Prof. J. B. Thayer in Harvard Law Review, Vol. V. pp. 47–51.

[3] C. Tribur. ann. 895 c. xxii.

[4] For de Morlaas, Rubr. xxxviii. art. 63.

England in all actions arising from contracts and sales;[1] and in the laws of Soest in Westphalia, compiled at the end of the eleventh or the commencement of the twelfth century, an accusation of homicide could be proved by six conjurators swearing with the prosecutor, while if this failed the accused could then. clear himself with eleven compurgators.[2] Throughout Germany, in the thirteenth century, we find the principle of accusing conjurators generally received, as is evident from the *juramentum supermortuum* already referred to, and other provisions of the municipal law.[3] So thoroughly, indeed, was this established that, in some places, in prosecutions for highway robbery, arson, and other crimes, the accuser had a right to require every individual in court, from the judge to the spectator, to help him with an oath or to swear that he knew nothing of the matter, and even the attorney for the defendant was obliged to undergo the ceremony.[4] In Sweden it was likewise in use under the name of *jeffniteed;*[5] and in the compilation of the laws by Andreas, Archbishop of Lunden, in the thirteenth century, there is a curious provision for cases of secret murder by which the accuser could force nine men successively to undergo the hot-iron ordeal, after which, if thus far unsuccessful, he could still force a tenth man to trial on producing twelve conjurators to swear to the guilt of the accused—these conjurators, in case of acquittal, being each liable to a fine of three marks to the accused and as much to the church.[6] In Norway and Iceland, in certain cases of imputed crime, the accuser was bound to produce ten companions, of whom eight

[1] Bracton. Lib. IV. Tract. vi. cap. 18, § 6.

[2] Statuta Susatensia, No. 10 (Hæber in, Analecta Medii Ævi, p. 509). —The same provision is preserved in a later recension of the laws of Soest, dating apparently from the middle of the thirteenth century (Op. cit. p. 520).

[3] Jur. Provin. Alaman. cap. cccix. § 4 (Ed. Schilter).—Jur. Provin. Saxon. Lib. III. art. 88.—Sachsische Weichb. art. 115.

[4] Jur. Provin. Alaman. cap. cccxcviii. §§ 19, 20.

[5] Du Cange *sub voce.*

[6] Legg. Scan. Provin. Lib. v. c. 57 (Ed. Thorsen, p. 140).

appeared simply as supporters, while two swore that they had heard the offence spoken of, but that they knew nothing about it of their own knowledge—the amount of weight attached to which asseveration is shown by the fact that the accused required only two conjurators to clear himself.[1]

Perhaps the most careful valuation of the oath of a plaintiff is to be found in the Coutumier of Bordeaux, which provides that, in civil cases not exceeding four sols in amount, the claimant should substantiate his case by an oath on the Gospels in the Mayor's Court; when from four to twenty sols were at stake, he was sworn on the altar of St. Projet or St. Antoine; from twenty sols to fifteen livres, the oath was taken in the cemetery of St. Seurin, while for amounts above that sum it was administered on the "Fort" or altar of St. Seurin himself. Persons whose want of veracity was notorious were obliged in all cases, however unimportant, to swear on the Fort, and had moreover to provide a conjurator who with an oath of equal solemnity asserted his belief in the truth of his companion.[2]

The custom of supporting an accusatorial oath by conjurators was maintained in some portions of Europe to a comparatively recent period. Wachter[3] prints a curious account of a trial, occurring in a Suabian court in 1505, which illustrates this, as well as the weight which was still attached to the oath of a defendant. A woman accused three men on suspicion of being concerned in the murder of her husband. They denied the charge, but when the oath of negation was tendered to them, with the assurance that, if they were Suabians, it would acquit them, they demanded time for consideration. Then the advocate of the widow stepped forward to offer the oath of accusation, and two conjurators being found willing to support him the accused were condemned without further

---

[1] Ideo manus libro imponimus sacro, quod audivimus (crimen rumore sparsum), at nobis ignotum est verum sit nec ne.—Jarnsida, Mannhelge, cap. xxiv.

[2] Rabanis, Revue Hist. de Droit, 1861, p. 511.

[3] Du Boys, Droit Criminel des Peuples Modernes, II. 595.

examination on either side. A similar process was observed in the Vehmgericht, or Court of the Free Judges of West-phalia, whose jurisdiction in the fourteenth and fifteenth centuries became extended over the whole of Germany. Accusations were supported by conjurators, and when the defendant was a Frei-graff, or presiding officer of a tribunal, the complainant was obliged to procure seven Frei-schöppen, or free judges, to take the accusatorial oath with him.[1]

The latest indication that I have met with of established legal provisions of this nature occurs in the custom of Britanny, as revised in 1539. By this, a man claiming compensation for property taken away is to be believed on oath as to his statement of its value, provided he can procure companions worthy of credence to depose " qu'ils croyent que le jureur ait fait bon et loyal serment."[2] Even this last vestige disappears in the revision of the Coutumier made by order of Henry III. in 1580.

---

[1] Freher. de Secret. Judic. cap. xvii. § 26.
[2] Anc. Cout. de Bretagne, Tit. viii. art. 168.

II.

THE WAGER OF BATTLE.

CHAPTER I.

WHEN man is emerging from barbarism, the struggle between the rising power of reason and the waning supremacy of brute force is full of instruction. Wise in our generation, we laugh at the inconsistencies of our forefathers, which, rightly considered as portions of the great cycle of human progress, are rather to be respected as trophies of the silent victory, won by almost imperceptible gradations. When, therefore, in the dark ages, we find the administration of justice so strangely interrupted by appeals to the sword or to chance, dignified under the forms of Christianized superstition, we should remember that even this is an improvement on the all-pervading first law of violence. We should not wonder that barbarous tribes require to be enticed to the acknowledgment of abstract right through pathways which, though devious, may reach the goal at last. When the strong man is brought, by whatever means, to yield to the weak, a great conquest is gained over human nature; and if the aid of superstition is invoked to decide the struggle, it is idle for us, while enjoying the result, to contemn the means which the weakness of human nature has rendered necessary to the end. With uneducated nations, as with uneducated men, sentiment is stronger than reason, and sacrifices will be made for the one which are refused to the other. If, therefore, the fierce warrior, resolute to maintain an injustice or a usurpation, can be brought to submit his claim to the chances of an equal com-

9*

bat or of an ordeal, he has already taken a vast step towards acknowledging the supremacy of right and abandoning the personal independence which is incompatible with the relations of human society. It is by such indirect means that individuals, each relying on his own right hand, have been gradually led to endure regular forms of government, and to cherish the abstract idea of justice as indispensable between man and man. Viewed in this light, the ancient forms of procedure lose their ludicrous aspect, and we contemplate their whimsical admixture of force, faith, and reason, as we might the first rude engine of Watt, or the "Clermont," which painfully labored in the waters of the Hudson—clumsy and rough it is true, yet venerable as the origin and prognostic of future triumphs.

There is a natural tendency in the human mind to cast the burden of its doubts upon a higher power, and to relieve itself from the effort of decision by seeking in the unknown the solution of its difficulties. Between the fetish worshippers of Congo and the polished sceptics who frequented the *salon* of Mlle. le Normant, the distance, though great, is bridged over by this common weakness; and whether the information sought be of the past or of the future, the impulse is the same. When, therefore, in the primitive *mallum*, the wisdom of the *rachinborgs* was at fault, and the absence or equal balance of testimony rendered a verdict difficult, what was more natural than to appeal for a decision to the powers above, and to leave the matter to the judgment of God?[1] Nor, with the warlike instincts of the race, is it

---

[1] Thus, as late as the thirteenth century, the municipal law of Southern Germany, in prescribing the duel for cases destitute of testimony, says with a naïve impiety: "Hoc ideo statutum est, quod causa hæc nemini cognita est quam Deo, cujus est eandem juste decidere." Early in the sixteenth century the pious Aventinus regretfully looks back upon the time when princes and priests, assembled to witness the combat, "divinam opem implorabant, beneficia memoriter commemorabant quæ in simili negotio

surprising that this appeal should be made to the God of battles, to whom, whether they addressed him as Odin or Sabaoth, they looked in every case for a special interposition in favor of innocence. The curious mingling of procedure, in these untutored seekings after justice, is well illustrated in a form of process prescribed by the primitive Bavarian law. A man comes into court with six conjurators to claim an estate; the possessor defends his right with a single witness, who must be a landholder of the vicinage. The claimant then attacks the veracity of the witness—"Thou hast lied against me. Grant me the single combat, and let God make manifest whether thou hast sworn truth or falsehood;"[1] and, according to the event of the duel is the decision as to the truthfulness of the witness and the ownership of the property.

In discussing the judicial combat, it is important to keep in view the wide distinction between the wager of battle as a judicial institution, and the custom of duelling which has obtained with more or less regularity among all races and at all ages.

Deus immortalis Christus servator noster ipsis pro sua benignitate atque clementia contulisset . . . . comprecabantur ut summa potestas in re præsenti, pollicita re, hactenus semper factitasset, comprobaret" (Aventini Annal. Baior. Lib. IV. cap. xiv. n. 28). Even as late as 1617, August Viescher, in an elaborate treatise on the judicial duel, expressed the same reliance on the divine interposition: "Dei enim hoc judicium dicitur, soli Deo causa terminanda committitur, Deo igitur authore singulare hoc certamen suscipiendum, ut justo judicio adjutor sit, omnisque spes ad solam summæ providentiam Trinitatis referenda est" (Vischer Tract. Juris Duellici Universi, p. 109). This work is a most curious anachronism. Viescher was a learned jurisconsult who endeavored to revive the judicial duel in the seventeenth century by writing a treatise of 700 pages on its principles and practice. He exhibits the wide range of his studies by citations from no less than six hundred and seventy-one authors, and manages to convey an incredibly small amount of information on the subject. Ephraim Gerhardt, moreover, taxes him with wholesale plagiarism from Michael Beuther's *Disputatio de duello* (Strassburg, 1609) and with false citations of authorities.—Eph. Gerhardi Tract. de Judicio Duellico, præfat.

[1] L. Baioar. Tit. XLV. c. i. § 2.

When the Horatii met the Curiatii, or when Antony challenged Octavius to decide the empire of the world with their two swords, or when Edward III. in 1340 proposed to Philippe de Valois to settle their rival claims to the heritage of France army to army, a hundred to a hundred, or body to body,[1] or when the ancient Hindus were in the habit of averting the carnage of battles in the same manner[2]—these were simply expedients to save the unnecessary effusion of blood, or to gratify individual hate. When the *raffiné* of the times of Henri Quatre, or the modern fire-eater, has wiped out some imaginary stain in the blood of his antagonist, the duel thus fought, though bearing a somewhat closer analogy to the judicial combat, is not derived from it, but from the right of private vengeance which was common to all the barbarian tribes, and from the cognate right of private warfare which was the exclusive privilege of the gentry during the feudal period.[3] The established euphuistic formula of demanding "the satisfaction of a gentleman," thus designates both the object of the custom and its origin. The abolition of private wars gave a stimulus to the duel at nearly the period when the judicial combat fell gradually into desuetude. The one thus succeeded to the other, and, being kindred in form, it is not surprising that for a time there was some confusion in the minds of men respecting their distinctive characteristics. Yet it is not difficult to draw the line between them. The object of the one was vengeance and reparation ; the theory of the other was the discovery of truth and the impartial ministration of justice.

It is easy to multiply examples illustrating this. John van Arckel, a knight of Holland, followed Godfrey of Bouillon to the first crusade. When some German forces joined the army,

---

[1] Rymer, Fœdera, V. 198–200.   [2] Ayeen Akbery, II. 324.

[3] The early edicts directed against the duel proper (Ordonn. Charles IX., an. 1566; Henri IV., an. 1602—in Fontanon I. 665) refer exclusively to the noblesse, and to those entitled to bear arms, as addicted to the practice, while the judicial combat, as we shall see, was open to all ranks, and was enforced indiscriminately upon all.

a Tyrolese noble, seeing van Arckel's arms displayed before
his tent, and recognizing them as identical with his own, ordered them torn down.   The insult was flagrant, but the injured knight sought no immediate satisfaction for his honor.
He laid the case before the chiefs of the crusade as a judicial
matter ; an examination was made, and both parties proved
their ancestral right to the same bearings.   To decide the
conflicting and incompatible pretensions, the judges ordered
the judicial combat, in which van Arckel deprived his antagonist of life and quarterings together, and vindicated his claim
to the argent 2 bars gules, which in gratitude to Heaven he
bore for eight long years in Palestine.   This was not a quarrel
on a punctilio, nor a mode of obtaining redress for an insult,
but an examination into a legal question which admitted of no
other solution according to the manners of the age.[1]   When,
after the Sicilian Vespers, the wily Charles of Anjou was sorely
pressed by his victorious rival Pedro III. of Aragon, and desired to gain time in order to repress a threatened insurrection
among his peninsular subjects, he sent a herald to Don Pedro
to accuse him of bad faith in having commenced the war without defiance.   The fiery Catalan fell into the snare, and in
order to clear himself of the charge, which was not ill-founded,
he offered to meet his accuser in combat and determine their
rights to the Sicilian throne.   The terms were laboriously settled by six representatives of each king and were signed by the
principals December 26, 1282; they were to meet, with a hundred knights on each side, June 1, 1283, in the neutral territory of Bordeaux and fight it out in the presence of Edward I.
of England or of his deputy, and each swore that if he failed
to be present he would forever hold himself as false and perjured and deprived of the royal station and dignity.   When
Charles applied to his cousin Edward to grant the *champ-clos*

---

[1] Chron. Domin. de Arkel (Matthæi Analect. VIII. 296).   In 1336 a
judicial duel was fought in Bavaria to decide a similar question—the right
of two nobles to a coat of arms.—Würdinger, Beiträge zur Geschichte des
Kampfrechtes in Bayern, München, 1877, p. 14.

the latter emphatically replied that for the crowns of the Two
Sicilies he would not be judge in such a combat; Martin II.
chimed in with a bull forbidding him to serve, and the combat
never took place, Charles of Anjou having obtained his purpose in the intervening suspension of arms.[1] Nothing more
picturesquely romantic is to be found in the annals of chivalry
than Muntaner's relation of Don Pedro's secret ride to Bordeaux and his appearance on the day appointed in the lists
where Edward's seneschal was unable to guarantee him a fair
field.[2] So the challenge which Richard II., in 1383, sent to
Charles VI. wore the aspect of the judicial duel to decide their
claims to the realms of France under the judgment of God.[3]
Though practically these challenges may differ little from that
of Antony, still their form and purport were those of the judicial duel in civil or criminal cases.   So, when Charles V. offered to maintain in single combat the charge that Francis I.
had villainously forfeited his faith in disregarding the treaty
of Madrid, and Francis hotly replied with a demand for a secure field in which to defend his honor, the challenge and its
acceptance wore the form of the judicial duel to decide the
question of guilt; although Charles in appointing the Bidasoa
as the place of meeting gave as his reasons the avoidance of
bloodshed and the ending of the war as well as the maintenance of his just cause.[4] The celebrated duel, fought in 1547,
between Jarnac and La Chastaigneraye, so piteously deplored
by honest old Brantôme, shows the distinction maintained to
the last.   It was conducted with all judicial ceremonies, in

[1] Rymer, Fœdera, II. 226-9, 230-4, 239-40, 242-3.—Lünig. Cod. Ital.
Diplom. II. 986.

[2] Ramon Muntaner, cap. lxxi.   See also Pedro's own brief account of the
matter in a letter of June 20, 1283, to his nephew, the Infante Juan of Castile.—Memorial Histórico Español, 1851, T. II. p. 99.

[3] " Sub speculatoris supremi judicio terminatum."—Rymer, Fœd. VII.
407.

[4] Du Bellay, Mémoires, Liv. III.—The letters are given by Juan de
Valdés in the *Diálogo de Mercurio i Caron* (Dos Diálogos, pp. 243, 247,
287.—Reformistas antiguos Españoles).

presence of Henry II., not to settle a point of honor, but to justify Jarnac from a disgusting accusation brought by his adversary. Resulting most unexpectedly in the death of La Chastaigneraye, who was a favorite of the king, the monarch was induced to put an end to all legalized combats, though the illegal practice of the private duel not only continued to flourish, but increased beyond all precedent during the succeeding half century—Henry IV. having granted in twenty-two years no less than seven thousand letters of pardon for duels fought in contravention of the royal edicts. Such a mode of obtaining "satisfaction" is so repugnant to the spirit of our age that it is perhaps not to be wondered at if its advocates should endeavor to affiliate it upon the ancient wager of battle. Both relics of barbarism, it is true, are developments from the same primitive habits and customs, yet they are essentially distinct and have coexisted as separate institutions; and, however much occasionally intermingled by the passions of periods of violence, they were practised for different ends, and were conducted with different forms of procedure. We have only to deal with the combat as a strictly judicial process, and shall, therefore, leave untouched the vast harvest of curious anecdote afforded by the monomachial propensities of modern times.

CHAPTER II.

ORIGIN OF THE JUDICIAL DUEL.

THE mediæval panegyrists of the wager of battle sought to strengthen its title to respect by affirming that it was as old as the human race, and that Cain and Abel, unable to settle their conflicting claims in any other mode, agreed to leave the decision to the chances of the duel; while the combat between David and Goliath was considered by the early schoolmen as an unanswerable proof of the favor with which God regarded such encounters. Leaving such speculations aside, it is enough for us to know that all the tribes which settled in Europe practised the combat with so general a unanimity that its origin must be sought at a period anterior to their separation from the common stock, although it has left no definite traces in the written records which have reached us of the Asiatic Aryans.[1]

That some vague notions of Divine justice making itself manifest through the sword must have existed in prehistoric Hellenic times is apparent from Homer's elaborate description of the duel between Menelaus and Paris. This has all the characteristics of a judicial combat to decide the guilt or innocence of the claimants for the possession of the fair Helen. A preliminary sacrifice is offered to Zeus; Hector and Ulysses measure out the ground; lots are cast to decide which of the antagonists shall have the first throw of the spear; and the assembled armies put up a prayer to Zeus, entreating him to send to Hades the guilty one of the two combatants.[2] This is not merely a device to put an end to the slaughter of brave warriors—it is an appeal to Heaven to elicit justice by means of arms.

The Italiote branch of the Aryans affords us a more definite illustration of the same belief in the custom of the Umbrians, who settled quarrels by single combat, and deemed that he who slew his adversary thus proved that his cause was just.[3]

Although Cæsar makes no mention of such a custom in Gaul, it evidently prevailed among the Celtic tribes. Livy describes how some Spaniards seized the opportunity of a show of gladiators, given by Scipio, to settle various civil suits by combat, and he proceeds to particularize a case in which two

---

[1] An outlying fragment of the same belief is to be seen in the ancient Japanese practice of deciding knotty questions by the judicial duel (Griffis's Mikado's Empire, New York, 1876, p. 92). Even the most savage of existing races, the aborigines of Australia, have a kind of duel under certain rules by which private controversies are settled, and among the Melanesians the custom prevails, champions even being sometimes employed (Patetta, Le Ordalie, Torino, 1890, pp. 55, 60).

[2] Iliad. III. 277-323.

[3] Nicholaus Damascenus (Didot Frag. Hist. Græcor. III. 457).

rival cousins decided in this manner a disputed question in
the law of descent, despite the earnest remonstrances of the
Roman commander.[1]   Among the Irish Celts, at their appearance in history, we find the judicial duel established with
fixed regulations.   In the Senchus Mor, a code claiming to be
compiled under the supervision of St. Patrick, the delay of
five days in a distress is explained by the history of a combat
between two long previous in Magh-inis.   "When they had
all things ready for plying their arms, except a witness alone,
they met a woman at the place of combat, and she requested
of them a delay, saying, 'If it were my husband that were
there I would compel you to delay.'   'I would delay,' said
one of them, 'but it would be prejudicial to the man who sues
me; it is his cause that would be delayed.'   'I will delay,'
said the other.   The combat was then put off, but they did
not know till when it was put off, until Conchubhur and
Sencha passed judgment respecting it; and Sencha asked,
'What is the name of this woman?'   'Cuicthi,' (five) said
she, 'is my name.'   'Let the combat be delayed,' said Sencha,
'in the name of this woman for five days.'"[2]   The combative
ardor of the Feini, indeed, was so strong, and the appeal to
the wager of battle so general, that on their conversion to
Christianity they found it difficult to understand that the holy
ministers of Christ should be restricted from vindicating their
rights by arms, and St. Patrick, in a synod held in 456, was
obliged to threaten his clergy with expulsion from the church
if they endeavored to escape by appeal to the sword from
settling obligations which they had incurred by giving security
for heathens.[3]

This prevalence of the wager of battle among the Irish Celts
renders probable its existence likewise among the early inhabitants of Britain.   If so, the long domination of the Romans
was doubtless sufficient to extinguish all traces of it.   The

[1] Liv. XXVII. 21.   [2] Senchus Mor, I. 251.
[3] Synod. S. Patricii ann. 456, c. 8.

10

Welsh laws attributed to Hoel Dda in the early part of the tenth century, which are exceedingly minute and precise in their directions as to all forms of legal procedure, make no allusion to it whatever. It is true that an ancient collection of laws asserts that the code of Dyvnwal-moel-mud, a British king, prescribed the ordeals of battle, of hot iron, and of boiling water, and that Hoel in his legislation considered them unjust, abrogated them, and substituted the proof by men, or *raith*.[1] This legend, however, is very apocryphal. There is no allusion to such customs in the Welsh codes up to the close of the twelfth century, and the few indications which occur in subsequent collections would seem to indicate that these were rather innovations due to the influence of the English conquest than revivals of ancient institutions.

Among the Slavs, as they emerge into history, the duel occupies a controlling position in the administration of justice. Ibn Dost, an Arab traveller in Russia in the tenth century, relates that a pleader dissatisfied with the judgment of the king could always appeal to the sword, and this decision was regarded as so absolute that the defeated party, his family and possessions were all at the disposition of the victor. In Bohemia at a later period the successful combatant was required to decapitate his antagonist.[2] The earliest records of the various other Slavic lands give evidence of the prevalence of the judicial combat, showing that it formed part of their ancestral customs prior to their occupation of their present territories.[3]

Among the Norræna branch of the Teutons the wager of battle can be traced back to the realm of legend and tradition. Saxo Grammaticus informs us that about the Christian era Frotho III., or the Great, of Denmark, ordered the employment of the duel to settle all controversies, preferring that

---

[1] Anomalous Laws, Book XIV. chap. xiii. § 4 (Owen II. 623).

[2] Patetta, Le Ordalie, p. 156.

[3] Königswarter, op. cit. p. 224; Patetta, pp. 158 sqq.; Eph. Gerhardi Tract. Jurid. de Judic. Duellico, c. ii. § 12.

his warriors should accustom themselves to rely, not on elo-
quence, but on courage and skill;[1] and however doubtful the
chronology may be, the tradition shows that the origin of the
custom was lost in the depths of antiquity. Among the heathen
Norsemen, indeed, the *holm-gang*, or single combat, was so
universal an arbiter that it was recognized as conferring a
right where none pre-existed. Any athlete, who confided in
his strength and dexterity with his weapons, could acquire
property by simply challenging its owner to surrender his land
or fight for it. When Iceland, for instance, was in process of
settlement, Kraku Hreidar sailed thither, and on sighting land
invoked Thor to assign to him a tract of ground which he
would forthwith acquire by duel. He was shipwrecked on
reaching the shore, and was hospitably received by a compa-
triot named Havard, with whom he passed the winter. In the
spring he declared his purpose of challenging Sæmund Sudu-
reyska for a sufficient holding, but Havard dissuaded him,
arguing that this mode of acquiring property rarely prospered
in the end, and Eirek of Goddolom succeeded in quieting him
by giving him land enough. Others of these hardy sea-rovers
were not so amenable to reason as Kraku. When Hallkell
came to Iceland and passed the winter with his brother Ketel-
biorn, the latter offered him land on which to settle, but Hallkell
disdained so peaceful a proposition, and preferred to summon
a neighbor named Grim to surrender his property or meet him
in the *holm-gang*. Grim accepted the defiance, was slain, and
Hallkell was duly installed as his heir. A variation of the
custom is illustrated by the case of Hrolleif, who after some
years' settlement grew dissatisfied with his holding, and challenged his neighbor Eyvind to an exchange of properties or a
combat, alternatives of which the peace-loving Eyvind accepted
the former.[2] The Saga of Egil Skallagrimsson speaks of a
noted duellist known as Ljot the Pale, who had come to the

---

[1] Saxon. Grammat. Hist. Dan. Lib. v.

Islands Landnamabok, III. vii.; v. xii. xiii. See also II. vi. and xiii.

district a landless stranger, and had grown wealthy by thus challenging proprietors and taking their lands, but who met his fate at the hands of Egil, who, while travelling, came to the place where Ljot was about to engage in a holm-gang with a weaker antagonist. Egil volunteered to take his place, and promptly slew Ljot. The holm-gang was so named because the battle was usually fought on a small island or holm ; and that it was regarded as an appeal to the gods is manifested by the custom of the victor sacrificing an ox as soon as he left the spot.[1]

It is true that Tacitus makes no allusion to such a custom among the Germans of his time, a passage which is frequently quoted to that effect being in reality only a description of a mode of divination in which, at the beginning of a war, one of the enemy was captured and made to fight with a chosen champion, the result of the combat being taken to fore-shadow the event of the contest.[2] The object of Tacitus, however, was not to excite the curiosity of his countrymen, but rather to contrast their vices with the uncivilized virtues of the Germans, and his silence on this point is not a nega-tive evidence of weight in comparison with the positive proofs which exist with regard to kindred tribes. Be this as it may, as soon as we obtain an insight into their customs from written laws, we find the wager of battle everywhere recognized. The earliest of these is the code of the Burgundians, collected by King Gundobald towards the close of the fifth century, and in this the duel occupies a place so conspicuous that it obtained in time the name of Lex Gundebalda or Loy Gom-bette, giving rise to a belief that it was of Burgundian origin.

In the ordinary texts of the Salic law no mention is made of it, but in one manuscript it is alluded to as a regular form

---

[1] Keyser's Religion of the Northmen, Pennock's Translation, p. 245–7.

[2] Tacit. de Mor. Germ. x. Du Cange refers to a passage of Paterculus as proving the existence of the judicial duel among the Germans (Lib. ii. cap. 118), but it seems to me only to refer to the law of the strongest.

of procedure.[1] This silence, however, does not justify the conclusion that the battle ordeal was not practised among the Franks. Enough instances of it are to be found in their early history to show that it was by no means uncommon;[2] and, at a later period, the same absence of reference to it is observable in the Lex Emendata of Charlemagne, though the capitularies of that monarch frequently allude to it as a legal process in general use. The off-shoots of the Salic law, the Ripuarian, Allemannic, and Bavarian codes—which were compiled by Thierry, the son of Clovis, revised successively by Childebert and Clotair II., and put into final shape by Dagobert I. about the year 630—in their frequent reference to the "campus," show how thoroughly it pervaded the entire system of Germanic jurisprudence. The Lombards were, if possible, even more addicted to its use. Their earliest laws, compiled by King Rotharis in 643, seventy-six years after their occupation of Italy, make constant allusion to it, and their readiness to refer to its decision the most conspicuous cases is shown in the story of Queen Gundeberga, the wife of Ariovaldus, who was the immediate predecessor of Rotharis. Adalulf, a disappointed lover, brought against her a charge of conspiracy which induced Ariovaldus to cast her in prison, where she lay for three years, until Clotair the Great, to whom she was of kindred, sent an embassy to obtain her release. Diplomacy was of no avail, and all that the Frankish envoys could accomplish was to secure for her a trial by single combat, in which a champion named Pitto overcame Adalulf the accuser, and Gundeberga was restored to the throne with her innocence recognized.[3] Indeed, the tenacious hold which it maintained on the veneration of the Lombards is seen in the fruitless efforts to restrict its employment and to abrogate it

---

[1] Si tamen non potuerit adprobare . . . . et postea, si ausus fuerit, pugnet.—Leyden MS.—Capit. Extravagant. No. xxviii. of Pardessus.

[2] Gregor. Turon. Hist. Franc. Lib. VII. c. xiv.; Lib. X. c. x.—Aimoini Lib. IV. c. ii.

[3] Aimoini Lib. IV. cap. X.

by Rotharis and his successors under the civilizing influence of contact with Roman institutions. Thus Rotharis forbids its use in some cases of importance, substituting conjurators, with a marked expression of disbelief, which shows how little confidence was felt in its results by enlightened men.[1] The next lawgiver, King Grimoald, decreed that thirty years' possession of either land or liberty relieved a defendant from maintaining his title by battle, the privilege of employing conjurators being then conceded to him.[2] In the succeeding century, King Liutprand sought to abolish it entirely, but finding the prejudices of his people too strong to be overcome, he placed on record in the statute-book a declaration of his contempt for it and a statement of his efforts to do away with it, while he was obliged to content himself with limiting the extent of its application, and diminishing the penalties incurred by the defeated party.[3]

While the laws of the Angles, the Saxons, and the Frisians bear ample testimony to the general use of the wager of battle,[4] it is not a little singular that the duel appears to have been unknown among the Anglo-Saxons. Employed so extensively as legal evidence throughout their ancestral regions, by the kindred tribes from which they sprang, and by the Danes and Norwegians who became incorporated with them; harmonizing, moreover, with their general habits and principles

---

[1] Quia absurdum et impossible videtur esse ut tam grandis causa sub uno scuto per pugnam dirimatur.—L. Longobard. Lib. II. Tit. lv. §§ 1, 2, 3.

[2] L. Longobard. Lib. II. Tit. xxxv. §§ 4, 5.

[3] Gravis causa nobis esse comparuit, ut sub uno scuto, per unam pugnam, omnem suam substantiam homo amittat. . . . . Quia incerti sumus de judicio Dei, et multos audivimus per pugnam sine justitia causam suam perdere. Sed propter consuetudinem gentis nostræ Longobardorum legem impiam vetare non possumus (L. Longobard. Lib. I. Tit. ix. § 23). Muratori states that the older MSS. read "legem istam," in place of "impiam," as given in the printed texts, which would somewhat weaken the force of Liutprand's condemnation.

[4] L. Anglior. et Werinor. Tit. I. cap. 3; Tit. xv.—L. Saxon. Tit. xv.—L. Frision. Tit. v. c. i.; Tit. xI. c. 3.

of action, it would seem impossible that they should not likewise have practised it. I can offer no explanation of the
anomaly, and can only state the bare fact that the judicial
combat is not referred to in any of the Anglo-Saxon or Anglo-
Danish codes.[1] There seems, indeed, to be no reason to
doubt that its introduction into English jurisprudence dates
only from the time of William the Conqueror.[2]

The Goths, while yet untainted by the influence of Rome,
were no less given to the employment of the judicial duel
than their Teutonic kindred, and Theodoric vainly endeavored to suppress the custom among those of his subjects

[1] In Horne's Myrror of Justice (cap. II. sect. 13), a work which is supposed to date from the reign of Edward II., there is a form of appeal of
treachery "qui fuit trové en vielx rosles del temps du Roy Alfred," in
which the appellant offers to prove the truth of his charge with his body;
but no confidence can be placed in the accuracy of the old lawyer. Some
antiquarians have been inclined to assume that the duel was practised
among the Anglo-Saxons, but the statement in the text is confirmed by the
authority of Mr. Pike (Hist. of Crime in England, I. 448), whose exhaus-
tive researches into the original sources of English jurisprudence render
his decision virtually final.

In the Saga of Olaf Tryggvesson it is related that he was chosen by an
English queen named Gyda for her husband, to the great displeasure of
Alfin a previous pretender to her hand, who challenged him thereupon,
because "It was then the custom in England, if two strove for anything,
to settle the matter by single combat" (Laing's Heimskringla, I. 400).
Snorro Sturleson, however, can hardly be regarded as of much authority
on a point like this; and as Gyda is represented as daughter of a king of
Dublin, the incident, if it occurred at all, may have taken place in Ireland.

[2] A charter issued by William, which appears to date early in his reign,
gives the widest latitude to the duel both for his French and Saxon subjects
(L. Guillelmi Conquest. II. §§ 1, 2, 3. Thorpe, I. 488). Another law,
however, enabled a Norman defendant to decline the combat when a Saxon
was appellant. "Si Francigena appellaverit Anglum. . . . . Anglus se
defendat per quod melius voluerit, aut judicio ferri, aut duello. . . . . Si
autem Anglus Francigenam appellaverit et probare voluerit, judicio aut
duello, volo tunc Francigenam purgare se sacramento non fracto" (Ibid.
III. § 12. Thorpe, I. 493). Such immunity seems a singular privilege for
the generous Norman blood.

who had remained in Pannonia.[1] That no trace of it is to be found among the extant laws of both Ostrogoths and Wisigoths, framed subsequently to their settlement in Italy, France, and Spain, is easily explained. The effect upon the invaders of the decaying but still majestic civilization of Rome, the Byzantine education of Theodoric, the leader of the Ostrogoths, and his settled policy of conciliating the Italians by maintaining as far as possible the existing state of society, preclude any surprise that no allusion to the practice should occur in the short but sensible code known as the "Edict of Theodoric," which shows how earnestly that enlightened conqueror endeavored to fuse the invaders and the vanquished into one body politic.[2] With regard to the Wisigoths, we must remember that early conversion to Christianity and long intercourse with civilization had already worn off much of the primitive ferocity of a race which could produce in the fourth century such a man as Ulphilas. They were the earliest of the invaders who succeeded in forming a permanent occupation of the conquered territories; and settling, as they did, in Narbonensian Gaul and Spain while the moral influence of Rome was yet all powerful, the imperial institutions exercised a much greater effect upon them than on the subsequent bands of Northern barbarians. Accordingly, we find their codes based almost entirely upon the Roman jurisprudence, with such modifications as were essential to adapt it to a ruder state of society. Their nicely balanced provisions and careful distinctions offer a striking contrast to the shapeless legislation of the races that followed, and neither the judicial combat nor canonical compurgation found a place in them. Even the vulgar ordeal would appear to have been

---

[1] Cassiodor. Variar. Lib. iii. Epist. xxiii., xxiv.

[2] An Epistle from Theodoric to the Gaulish provinces, which he had just added to his empire, congratulates them on their return to Roman laws and usages, which he orders them to adopt without delay. Its whole tenor shows his thorough appreciation of the superiority of the Imperial codes to the customs of the barbarians, and his anxiety for settled principles of jurisprudence (Cassiodor. Variar. Lib. iii. Epist. xvii.).

unknown until a period long subsequent to the conquest of Aquitaine by Clovis, and but little anterior to the overthrow of the Gothic kingdom of Spain by the Saracens. But even as in Italy the Lombard domination destroyed the results of Theodoric's labors, so in France the introduction of the Frankish element revived the barbarian instincts, and in the celebrated combat before Louis le Débonnaire, between Counts Bera and Sanila, who were both Goths, we find the "pugna duorum" claimed as an ancient privilege of the race, with the distinction of its being equestrian, in accordance with Gothic usages, and so thoroughly was the guilt of Bera considered to be proved by his defeat, that his name became adopted in the Catalan dialect as a synonym of traitor.[1]

CHAPTER III.

UNIVERSAL USE OF THE JUDICIAL COMBAT.

THE wager of battle thus formed part of the ancestral institutions of all the races who founded the nations of Europe. With their conversion to Christianity the appeal was transferred from the heathen deities to God, who was expected to intervene and decide the battle in favor of the right.[2] It was an appeal to the highest court and popular confidence in the arbitrament of the sword was rather strengthened than diminished. Enlightened law-givers not only shared, to a greater or less extent, in this confidence, but were also disposed to regard the

---

[1] Ermold. Nigell. de Reb. Gest. Ludov. Pii Lib. III.—Astron. Vit. Ludov. Pii cap. xxxiii.—Marca Hispanica, Lib. III. c. 21.

[2] Even as late as the middle of the thirteenth century St. Ramon de Peñafort thus defines it—"Duellum est singularis pugna inter aliquos ad probationem veritatis, ita videlicet ut qui vicerit probasse intelligitur; et dicitur duellum quasi duorum bellum. Dicitur etiam vulgo in pluribus partibus judicium, eo quod ibi Dei judicium expectatur."—S. Raymondi Summæ Lib. II. Tit. iii.

duel with favor as the most practical remedy for the crime of false swearing which was everywhere prevalent. Thus Gundobald assumes that its introduction into the Burgundian code arose from this cause;[1] Charlemagne urged its use as greatly preferable to the shameless oaths which were taken with so much facility;[2] while Otho II., in 983, ordered its employment in various forms of procedure for the same reason.[3] It can hardly be a source of surprise, in view of the warlike manners of the times, and of the enormous evils for which a palliative was sought, that there was felt to be advantage in this mode of impressing upon principals and witnesses the awful sanctity of the oath, thus entailing upon them the liability of supporting their asseverations by undergoing the risks of a combat rendered doubly solemn by imposing religious ceremonies.

Various causes were at work to extend the application of the judicial duel to all classes of cases. In the primitive codes of the barbarians, there is no distinction made between civil and criminal law. Bodily punishment being almost unknown, except for slaves, and nearly all infractions of the law being visited with fines, there was no necessity for such niceties, the matter at stake in all cases being simply money or money's worth. Accordingly, we find the wager of battle used indiscriminately, both as a defence against accusations of crime, and as a mode of settling cases of disputed property, real and personal. Yet some of the earlier codes refer to it but seldom. The Salic law, as we have seen, hardly recognizes its existence; the Ripuarian code alludes to it but four times, and that of the

---

[1] L. Burgund. Tit. xlv.—The remedy, however, would seem to have proved insufficient, for a subsequent enactment provides an enormous fine (300 solidi) to be levied on the witnesses of a losing party, by way of making them share in the punishment, "Quo facilius in posterum ne quis audeat propria pravitate mentire."—L. Burgund. Tit. lxxx. § 2. The position of witness in those unceremonious days was indeed an unenviable one.

Capit. Car. Mag. ex Lege Longobard. c. xxxiv. (Baluze).

[3] L. Longobard. Lib. ii. Tit. iv. § 34.

Alamanni but six times. In others, like the Baioarian, it is appealed to on almost every occasion, and among the Burgundians we may assume, from a remark of St. Agobard, that it superseded all evidence and rendered superfluous any attempt to bring forward witnesses.[1] This variation is probably rather apparent than real, and if in any of these bodies of laws there were originally substantial limitations on its use, in time they disappeared, for it was not difficult to find expedients to justify the extension of a custom which accorded so perfectly with the temper of the age. How little reason was requisite to satisfy the belligerent aspirations of justice is shown by a curious provision in the code of one of the Frisian tribes, by which a man unable to disprove an accusation of homicide was allowed to charge the crime on whomsoever he might select, and then the question between them was decided by combat.[2]

The elasticity, in fact, with which the duel lent itself to the advantage of the turbulent and unscrupulous had no little influence in extending its sphere of action. This feature in its history is well exemplified in a document containing the proceedings of an assembly of local magnates, held in the year 888, to decide a contention concerning the patronage of the church of Lessingon. After the testimony on one side had been given, the opposite party commenced in reply, when the leaders of the assembly, seizing their swords, vowed that they would affirm the truth of the first pleader's evidence with their blood before King Arnoul and his court—and the case was decided without more ado.[3] The strong and the bold are apt to be the ruling spirits in all ages, and were emphatically so in those periods of scarcely curbed violence when the jurisprudence of the European commonwealths was slowly developing itself.

It is no wonder, therefore, that means were readily found for extending the jurisdiction of the wager of battle as widely

---

[1] Lib. adversus Legem Gundobadi cap. x.

[2] L. Frision. Tit. xiv. § 4.

[3] Goldast. Antiq. Alaman. chart. lxxxv.

as possible.   One of the most fruitful of these expedients was the custom of challenging witnesses.   The duel was a method of determining questions of perjury, and there was nothing to prevent a suitor, who saw his case going adversely, from accusing an inconvenient witness of false swearing and demanding the "campus" to prove it—a proceeding which adjourned the main case, and likewise decided its result.   This summary process, of course, brought every action within the jurisdiction of force, and deprived the judges of all authority to control the abuse.   That it obtained at a very early period is shown by a form of procedure occurring in the Bavarian law, already referred to, by which the claimant of an estate is directed to fight, not the defendant, but his witness;[1] and in 819 a capitulary of Louis le Débonnaire gives a formal privilege to the accused on a criminal charge to select one of the witnesses against him with whom to decide the question in battle.[2]   It is easy, therefore, to understand the custom, prescribed in some of the codes, by which witnesses were required to come into court armed, and to have their weapons blessed on the altar before giving their testimony.   If defeated they were fined, and were obliged to make good to the opposite party any damage which their testimony, had it been successful, would have caused him.[3]

Nor was this merely a temporary extravagance.   Late in the thirteenth century, after enlightened legislators had been strenuously and not unsuccessfully endeavoring to limit the abuse of the judicial combat, the challenging of witnesses was still the favorite mode of escaping legal condemnation.[4]

---

[1] L. Baioar. Tit. XVI. cap. i. § 2.

[2] Capit. Ludov. Pii ann. 819, cap. xv.

[3] L. Baioar. Tit. XVI. c. 5.

[4] Beaumanoir, Coutumes du Beauvoisis, chap. lxi. § 58.—In the contemporary Italian law, however, there was some limitation on the facility of challenging witnesses—" Ita demum inter contrarios testes fit pugna, si ipsi inter se imponant nam pars testibus non potest pugnam imponere nisi velint." —Odofredi Summa de Pugna, c. i. (Patetta, p. 483).

Even in the fourteenth century, the municipal law of Reims, which allowed the duel between principals only in criminal cases, permitted witnesses to be indiscriminately challenged and forced to fight, affording them the privilege of employing champions only on the ground of physical infirmity or advanced age.[1] A still more bizarre extension of the practice, and one which was most ingeniously adapted to defeat the ends of justice, is found in a provision of the English law of the thirteenth century, allowing a man to challenge his own witnesses. Thus in many classes of crimes, such as theft, forgery, coining, etc., the accused could summon a "warrantor" from whom he professed to have received the articles which formed the basis of the accusation. The warrantor could scarcely give evidence in favor of the accused without assuming the responsibility himself. If he refused, the accused was at liberty to challenge him; if he gave the required evidence, he was liable to a challenge from the accuser.[2] The warrantor was sometimes also employed as a champion, and served for hire, but this service was illegal and when detected involved the penalties of perjury.[3] Another mode extensively used in France about the same time was to accuse the principal witness of some crime rendering him incapable of giving testimony, when he was obliged to dispose of the charge by fighting, either personally or by champion, in order to get his evidence admitted.[4]

[1] Lib. Pract. de Consuetud. Remens. §§ 14, 40 (Archives Législat. de Reims, Pt. I. pp. 37, 40).

[2] Bracton de Legibus Angl. Lib. III. Tract. II. cap. xxxvii. § 5.—Fleta, Lib. I. cap. xxii.

[3] Thus in a case in 1220 involving a stolen mare, the accused gave a warrantor, and on the accuser challenging him to battle he gave a second warrantor. On investigation he was found to have received five marks for the service with a promise of five more, and he was mercifully treated by being condemned only to the loss of a foot—" Sciendum quod misericorditer agitur cum eo per consilium domini regis cum majorem pœnam de jure demeruisset."—Maitland, Select Pleas of the Crown, I. 127.

[4] Beaumanoir, chap. vi. § 16.

11

It is not easy to imagine any cases which might not thus be brought to the decision of the duel; and the evidence of its universality is found in the restriction which prevented the appearance as witnesses of those who could not be compelled to accept the combat. Thus the testimony of women and ecclesiastics was not receivable in lay courts in suits where appeal of battle might arise;[1] and when in the twelfth century special privileges were granted by the kings of France empowering serfs to bear testimony in court, the disability which prevented a serf from fighting with a freeman was declared annulled in such cases, as the evidence was only admissible when the witness was capable of supporting it by arms.[2]

The result of this system was that, in causes subject to such

[1] Beaumanoir, ch. xxxix. §§ 30, 31, 66.—Assises de Jerusalem, cap. 169. A somewhat similar principle is in force in the modern jurisprudence of China. Women, persons over eighty or under ten years of age, and cripples who have lost an eye or a limb are entitled to buy themselves off from punishment, except in a few cases of aggravated crime. They are, therefore, not allowed to appear as accusers, because they are enabled by this privilege to escape the penalties of false witness.—Staunton, Penal Code of China, Sects. 20–22, and 339. In the ancient Brahmanic law also there is a long enumeration of persons who are not receivable as witnesses, including women, children, and men over eighty years of age. In this, however, the exclusion of women would appear to be because they were presumably under tutelage.—Institutes of Vishnu, VIII. 2.

The exclusion of women as witnesses during the mediæval period was also one of the numerous disabilities by which the Church expressed its contempt for the sex which had tempted Adam to his fall. As early as the fourth century Hilary the Deacon, in a tract which long passed current under the name of St. Augustin, says: "Nec docere enim potest, nec testis esse, neque fidem dicere, neque judicare" (Hilari Diac. Quæstt. ex Vet. Testamento, c. xlv.—Migne, T. XXX. p. 2244). And this was carried through Ivo of Chartres (Decreti, P. VIII. c. 85) into the body of the canon law (Gratiani Decr. Caus. XXXIII. Q. v. cap. 17).

[2] The earliest of these charters is a grant from Louis le Gros in 1109 to the serfs of the church of Paris, confirmed by Pope Pascal II. in 1113 (Baluz. et Mansi III. 12, 62). D'Achery (Spicileg. III. 481) gives another from the same monarch in 1128 to the church of Chartres.

appeals, no witness could be forced to testify, by the French law of the thirteenth century, unless his principal entered into bonds to see him harmless in case of challenge, to provide a champion, and to make good all damages in case of defeat;[1] though it is difficult to understand how this could be satisfactorily arranged, since the penalties inflicted on a vanquished witness were severe, being, in civil causes, the loss of a hand and a fine at the pleasure of the suzerain, while in criminal actions "il perderoit le cors avecques."[2] The only limit to this abuse was that witnesses were not liable to challenge in cases concerning matters of less value than five sous and one denier.[3]

If the position of a witness was thus rendered unenviable, that of the judge was little better. As though the duel had not received sufficient extension by the facilities for its employment just described, another mode of appealing to the sword in all cases was invented by which it became competent for the defeated party in any suit to challenge the court itself, and thus obtain a forcible reversal of judgment. It must be borne in mind that this was not quite as absurd a practice as it may seem to us in modern times, for under the feudal system the dispensing of justice was one of the most highly prized attributes of sovereignty; and, except in England, where the royal judges were frequently ecclesiastics, the seignorial courts were presided over by warriors. In Germany, indeed, where the magistrates of the lower tribunals were elective, they were required to be active and vigorous of body.[4] Towards the end of the twelfth century in England we find Glanville acknowledging his uncertainty as to whether or not the court could depute the settlement of such an appeal to a champion, and also as to what, in case of defeat, was the legal position of

---

[1] Beaumanoir, chap. lxi. § 59.   [2] Ibid. chap. lxi. § 57.
[3] Ibid. chap. xl. § 21.
   Jur. Provin. Alaman. cap. lxviii. § 6.

the court thus convicted of injustice.[1] These doubts would seem to indicate that the custom was still of recent introduction in England, and not as yet practised to an extent sufficient to afford a settled basis of precedents for its details. Elsewhere, however, it was firmly established. In 1195, the customs of St. Quentin allow to the disappointed pleader unlimited recourse against his judge.[2] Towards the latter half of the thirteenth century, we find in the *Conseil* of Pierre de Fontaines the custom in its fullest vigor and just on the eve of its decline. No restriction appears to be imposed as to the cases in which appeal by battle was permitted, except that it was not allowed to override the customary law.[3] The suitor selected any one of three judges agreeing in the verdict; he could appeal at any stage of the proceedings when a point was decided against him; if unsuccessful, he was only liable in a pecuniary penalty to the judges for the wrong done them, and the judge, if vanquished, was exposed to no bodily punishment.[4] The villein, however, was not entitled to the privi-

---

[1] "Curia . . . tenetur tamen judicium suum tueri per duellum . . . Sed utrum curia ipsa teneatur per aliquem de curia se defendere, vel per alium extraneum hoc fieri possit, quero" (De Leg. Angliæ Lib. VIII. cap. ix.). The result of a reversal of judgment must probably have been a heavy fine and deprivation of the judicial function, such being the penalty provided for injustice in the laws of Henry I.—"Qui injuste judicabit, cxx sol. reus sit et dignitatem judicandi perdat" (L. Henrici I. Tit. xiii. § 4)—which accords nearly with the French practice in the time of Beaumanoir.

[2] Cited by Marnier in his edition of Pierre de Fontaines.

[3] Car poi profiteroient les costumes el païs, s'il s'en covenoit combatre; ne dépecier ne les puet-om par bataille.—Édition Marnier, chap. XXII. Tit. xxxii.

[4] Chap. XXII. Tit. i. vi. viii. x. xxvii. xxxi.—"Et certes en fausement ne gist ne vie ne menbre de cels qui sont fausé, en quelconques point que li fausemenz soit faiz, et quele que la querele soit" (Ibid. Tit. xix.). If the judge was accused of bribery, however, and was defeated, he was liable to confiscation and banishment (Tit. xxvi.). The increasing severity meted out to careless, ignorant, or corrupt judges manifests the powerful influence of the Roman law, which, aided by the active efforts of legists, was

lege, except by special charter.[1] While the feudal system was supreme, this appeal to arms was the only mode of reversing a judgment, and an appeal in any other form was an innovation introduced by the extension of the royal jurisdiction under St. Louis, who labored so strenuously and so effectually to modify the barbarism of feudal institutions by subordinating them to the principles of the Roman jurisprudence. De Fontaines, indeed, states that he himself conducted the first case ever known in Vermandois of an appeal without battle.[2] At the same time the progress of more rational ideas is manifested by his admission that the combat was not necessary to reverse a judgment manifestly repugnant to the law, and that, on the other hand, the law was not to be set aside by the duel.

Twenty years later, we find in Beaumanoir abundant evidence of the success of St. Louis in setting bounds to the abuses which he was endeavoring to remove. The restrictions which he enumerates are greatly more efficacious than those alluded to by de Fontaines. In capital cases, the appeal did not lie ; while in civil actions, the suzerain before whom the appeal was made could refuse it when the justice of the verdict was self-evident. Some caution, moreover, was requisite in conducting such cases, for the disappointed pleader who did not manage matters rightly might find himself pledged to a combat, single handed, with all his judges at once ; and as the bench consisted of a collection of the neighboring gentry, the result might be the confirmation of the sentence in a manner more emphatic than agreeable. An important change is likewise observable in the severe penalty imposed upon a judge

infiltrating the customary jurisprudence and altering its character everywhere. Thus de Fontaines quotes with approbation the Code, *De pœna judicis* (Lib. VII. Tit. xlix. l. 1) as a thing more to be desired than expected, while in Beaumanoir we already find its provisions rather exceeded than otherwise.

[1] De Fontaines, chap. XXII. Tit. iii.

[2] Ibid. chap. XXII. Tit. xxiii.—Et ce fu li premiers dont je oïsse onques parler qui fust rapelez en Vermendois sanz bataille.

vanquished in such an appeal, being a heavy fine and deprivation of his functions in civil cases, while in criminal ones it
was death and confiscation—" il pert le cors et quanques il a."[1]

The king's court, however, was an exception to the general
rule. No appeals could be taken from its judgments, for there
was no tribunal before which they could be carried.[2] The
judges of the royal court were therefore safe from the necessity
of vindicating their decisions in the field, and they even carried this immunity with them and communicated it to those
with whom they might be acting. De Fontaines accordingly
advises the seigneur justicier who anticipates the appeal of battle in his court to obtain a royal judge to sit with him, and
mentions an instance in which Philip (probably Philip Augustus) sent his whole council to sit in the court of the Abbey of
Corbie, when an appeal was to be entered.[3]

By the German law of the same period, the privilege of reversing a sentence by the sword existed, but accompanied
with regulations which seem evidently designed to embarrass,
by enormous trouble and expense, the gratification of the impulse which disappointed suitors would have to establish their
claims in such manner. Thus, by the Suabian law, it could
only be done in the presence of the sovereign himself, and not
in that of the immediate feudal superior ;[4] while the Saxon code

---

[1] Coutumes du Beauvoisis, chap. lxi. §§ 36, 45, 47, 50, 62.—It should
be borne in mind, however, that Beaumanoir was a royal bailli, and the
difference between the "assise de bailli" and the "assises de chevaliers"
is well pointed out by Beugnot (Les Olim, T. II. pp. xxx. xxxi.). Beaumanoir in many cases evidently describes the law as he would wish it to be.

[2] Et pour ce ne l'en puët fausser, car l'en ne trouveroit mie qui droit en
feist car li rois ne tient de nului fors de Dieu et de luy.—Établissements,
Liv. I. chap. lxxviii.

[3] Conseil, ch. XXII. tit. xxi.

[4] Si contingat ut de justitia sententiæ pugnandum sit, illa pugna debet
institui coram rege (Jur. Provin. Alaman. cap. xcix. § 5—Ed. Schilt.).
In a French version of this code, made probably towards the close of the
fourteenth century, the purport of this passage is entirely changed. "De
chascun iugemant ne puet lan trover leaul ne certain consoil si bien come

requires the extraordinary expedient of a pitched battle, with seven on each side, in the king's presence.   It is not a little singular that the feudal law of the same period has no allusion to the custom, all appeals being regularly carried to and heard in the court of the suzerain.[2]

CHAPTER IV.

CONFIDENCE REPOSED IN THE JUDICIAL DUEL.

Thus carefully moulded in conformity with the popular prejudices or convictions of every age and country, it may readily be imagined how large a part the judicial combat played in the affairs of daily life.   It was so skilfully interwoven throughout the whole system of jurisprudence that no one could feel secure that he might not, at any moment, as plaintiff, defendant, or witness, be called upon to protect his estate or his life either by his own right hand or by the club of some professional and possibly treacherous bravo.   This organized violence assumed for itself the sanction of a religion of love and peace, and human intelligence seemed too much blunted to recognize the contradiction.

There was, in fact, no question which might not be submitted to the arbitrament of the sword or club.   If Charlemagne, in dividing his vast empire, forbade the employment

per le consoil de sages de la cort le roi."—Miroir de Souabe, P. I. c. cxiii. (Ed. Matile, Neufchatel, 1843).   We may hence conclude that by this period the custom of armed appeal was disused, and the extension of the royal jurisdiction was established.

[1] Jur. Provin. Saxon. I. 18; II. 12.—This has been questioned by modern critics, but there seems to be no good reason for doubting its authority. The whole formula for the proceeding is given in the Richstich Landrecht (cap. 41), a manual of procedure of the fourteenth century, adapted to the Saxon code.

[2] Richstich Lehnrecht, cap. xxvii.

of the wager of battle in settling the territorial questions which might arise between his heirs,[1] the prohibition merely shows that it was habitually used in affairs of the highest moment, and the constant reference to it in his laws proves that it was in no way repugnant to his general sense of justice and propriety.

The next century affords ample evidence of the growing favor in which the judicial combat was held. About the year 930, Hugh, King of Provence and Italy, becoming jealous of his uterine brother, Lambert, Duke of Tuscany, asserted him to be a supposititious child, and ordered him in future to claim no relationship between them. Lambert, being " vir . . . bellicosus et ad quodlibet facinus audax," contemptuously denied the aspersion on his birth, and offered to clear all doubts on the subject by the wager of battle. Hugh accordingly selected a warrior named Teudinus as his champion; Lambert was victor in the ensuing combat, and was universally received as the undoubted son of his mother. His triumph, however, was illegally brought to a sudden close, for Hugh soon after succeeded in making him prisoner and deprived him of eyesight.[2] Still, the practice continued to be denounced by some enlightened ecclesiastics, represented by Atto, Bishop of Vercelli, who declared it to be totally inapplicable to churchmen and not to be approved for laymen on account of the uncertainty of its results;[3] but representations of this kind were useless. About the middle of the century, Otho the Great appears, throwing the enormous weight of his influence in its favor. As a magnanimous and warlike prince, the wager of battle appears to have possessed peculiar attraction for his chivalrous instincts, and he extended its application as far as lay in his power. Not only did he force his daughter Liutgarda, in defending herself from a villanous accusation, to

[1] Carol. Mag. Chart. Divisionis ann. 806 cap. xiv.
[2] Liutprandi Antapodos, Lib. III. cap. 46.
[3] De Pressuris Eccles. Pt. II. This was written about 945.

forego the safer modes of purgation, and to submit herself to the perilous decision of a combat,[1] but he also caused the abstract question of representation in the succession of estates to be settled in the same manner; and to this day in Germany the division of a patrimony among children and grandchildren is regulated in accordance with the law enacted by the doughty arms of the champions who fought together nine hundred years ago at Steil.[2] There was no question, indeed, which according to Otho could not be satisfactorily settled in this manner. Thus when, in 963, he was indulging in the bitter recriminations with Pope John XII. which preceded the subjugation of the papacy under the Saxon emperors, he had occasion to send Bishop Liutprand to Rome to repel certain accusations brought against him, and he ordered the armed followers of his ambassador to sustain his assertions by the duel; a proposition promptly declined by the pontiff, skilled though he was in the use of weapons.[3] A duellist, in fact, seems to have been reckoned a necessary adjunct to diplomacy, for when, in 968, the same Liutprand was dispatched by Otho to Constantinople on a matrimonial mission, and during the negotiations for the hand of Theophania a discussion arose as to the circumstances which had led to Otho's conquest of Italy, the warlike prelate offered to prove his veracity by the sword of one of his attendants: a proposition which put a triumphant end to the argument.[4] A more formal assertion of the diplomatic value of the duel was made when in 1177 the conflicting claims of the kings of Castile and Navarre were referred to Henry II. of

---

[1] Dithmari Chron. Lib. II. ann. 950.

[2] Widukind. Rer. Saxon. Lib. II. cap. x.—The honest chronicler considers that it would have been discourteous to the nobility to treat questions relating to them in a plebeian manner. " Rex autem meliori consilio usus, noluit viros nobiles ac senes populi inhoneste tractari, sed magis rem inter gladiatores discerni jussit." In both these cases Otho may be said to have had ancient custom in his favor. See L. Longobard. Lib. I. Tit. xii. § 2.—L. Alamann. cap. LVI., LXXXIV.; Addit. cap. XXII.

[3] Liutprandi Hist. Otton. cap. vii.   [4] Liutprandi Legat. cap. vi.

England for adjudication, and both embassies to the English court were supplied with champions as well as with lawyers, so as to be prepared in case the matter was submitted to the duel for decision.[1]

Nor were these solitary instances of the reference of the mightiest state questions to the chances of the single combat. Allusion has already been made to the challenge which passed between Charles of Anjou and Pedro of Aragon, and not dissimilar was that which resulted from the interview at Ipsch in 1053 between the Emperor Henry III. of Germany and Henry I. of France.[2] A hundred years earlier, in 948, when, at the Synod of Ingelheim, Louis d'Outremer invoked the aid of the Church in his death-struggle with the rising race of Capet, he closed the recital of the wrongs endured at the hands of Hugh le grand by offering to prove the justice of his complaints in single combat with the aggressor.[3] When the battle ordeal was thus thoroughly incorporated in the manners of the age, we need scarcely be surprised that, in a life of St. Matilda, written by command of her son Otho the Great, the author, after describing the desperate struggles of the Saxons against Charlemagne, should gravely inform us that the war was at last concluded by a duel between the Christian hero and his great antagonist Witikind, religion and empire being both staked on the issue as a prize of the victor; nor does the pious chronicler shudder at the thought that the destiny of Christianity was intrusted to the sword of the Frank.[4] His story could not seem improbable to those who witnessed in 1034 the efforts of Conrad the Salic to pacify the Saxon marches. On his inquiring into the causes of the mutual devastations of the neighboring races, the Saxons, who were really the aggressors, offered to prove by the duel that the

---

[1] Benedict. Abbat. Gesta Henrici II. p. 139 (M. R. Series).
[2] Lambert. Hersfeld. ann. 1056.
[3] Conquest. Ludov. in Synod. Ingilheim. ann. 948.
[4] S. Mathild. Regin. Vit. c. 1.

Pagan Luitzes were in fault, trusting that their Christianity would overbalance the injustice of their cause. The defeat of their champion by his heathen adversary was, however, a memorable example of the impartial justice of God, and was received as a strong confirmation of the value of the battle trial.[1]

The second Otho was fully imbued with his father's views, and so completely did he carry them out, that in a gloss on the Lombard law he is actually credited with the introduction of the duel.[2]   In the preceding essay, allusion has been made to his substitution of the judicial combat for the compurgatorial oath in 983, and about the same period he made an exception, in favor of the battle ordeal, to the immemorial policy of the barbarians which permitted to all subject races the enjoyment of their ancestral usages. At the council of Verona, where all the nobles of Italy, secular and ecclesiastical, were assembled, he caused the adoption of a law which forced the Italians in this respect to follow the customs of their conquerors.[3]   Even the church was deprived of any exemption which she might previously have enjoyed, and was only allowed the privilege of appearing by her *advocati* or champions.[4] There were small chances of escape from the stringency of these regulations, for an edict of Otho I. in 971 had decreed the punishment of confiscation against any one who should refuse to undergo the chances of the combat.[5]   It may even be assumed, from the wording of a constitution of the Emperor Henry II., that in the early part of the eleventh century it was no longer necessary that there should be a doubt as to the guilt of the accused to entitle him to the privileges of the combat, and that even the most notorious criminal could have a chance of escape by an appeal to the sword.[6]

---

[1] Wipponis vit. Chunradi Salici.

[2] " Nos belli dono ditat rex maximus Otto."

[3] L. Longobard. Lib. II. Tit. lv. § 38.   [4] Ibid. § 34.

[5] Si non audeat, res suæ infiscentur.—Convent. Papiens. ann. 971.

[6] Qui vero infra treugam, post datum osculum pacis, alium hominem interfecerit, et negare voluerit, pugnam pro se faciat.—L. Longobard. Lib. I. Tit ix. § 38.

Thus it came to pass that nearly every question that could possibly arise was finally deemed liable to the decision of the wager of battle. If Otho the Great employed champions to legislate respecting a disputed point of law, he was not more eccentric than the Spaniards, who settled in the same manner a controversy regarding the canonical observances of religion, when Gregory VII. endeavored to force the introduction of the Roman liturgy into Castile and Leon, in lieu of the national Gothic or Mozarabic rite. With considerable difficulty, some years before, Navarre and Aragon had been led to consent to the change, but the Castilians were doggedly attached to the observances of their ancestors, and stoutly refused compliance. In 1077, Alfonso I. procured the assent of a national council, but the people rebelled, and after repeated negotiations the matter was finally referred to the umpirage of the sword. The champion of the Gothic ritual was victorious, and tradition adds that a second trial was made by the ordeal of fire; a missal of each kind was thrown into the flames, and the national liturgy emerged triumphantly unscathed.[1]

Nearly contemporary with this was the celebrated case of Otho, Duke of Bavaria, perhaps the most noteworthy example of a judicial appeal to the sword. A worthless adven-

[1] Roderici Toletani de Reb. Hispan. VI. xxvi. This story has been called in question by orthodox writers for the reason that Archbishop Roderic, who flourished in the middle of the thirteenth century, is the only authority for it, but there is nothing in the manners of the age to render it incredible, and he mentions that the champion of the Mozarabic rite came from Matanza near the Pisuerga, and that his family still existed.

In 1121, when the Queen-regent Urraca was at Compostella, one of her courtiers informed a gentleman of the Archbishop Diego Gelmirez, that she was plotting to seize him, whereupon he surrounded himself with a guard. This attracted attention and led to discussion in which the archbishop's retainer gave the name of his informant. The latter denied the statement and Urraca, as a matter of course, ordered the duel between them, in which her courtier was defeated and was punished with blinding.—Historia Compostellana, Lib. II. c. xxix. (Florez, España Sagrada, T. XX. p. 312).

turer, named Egeno, accused Otho of conspiring against the
life of Henry IV. In a diet held at Mainz, the duke was
commanded to disprove the charge by doing battle with his
accuser within six weeks. According to some authorities, his
pride revolted at meeting an adversary so far his inferior; according to others, he was prevented from appearing in the lists
only by the refusal of the emperor to grant him a safe conduct. Be this as it may, the appointed term elapsed, his
default of appearance caused judgment to be taken against
him, and his duchy was accordingly confiscated. It was bestowed on Welf, son of Azo d'Este and of Cunigunda, descend-
ant and heiress of the ancient Guelfic Agilolfings; and thus,
on the basis of a judicial duel, was founded the second Bavarian house of Guelf, from which have sprung so many royal
and noble lines, including their Guelfic Majesties of Britain.
Some years later, the emperor himself offered to disprove by
the same means a similar accusation brought against him by a
certain Reginger, of endeavoring to assassinate his rival,
Rodolph of Suabia. Ulric of Cosheim, however, who was
involved in the accusation, insisted on taking his place, and
a day was appointed for the combat, which was prevented only
by the opportune death of Reginger.[1]

Scarcely less impressive in its results, and even more remarkable in itself, as exhibiting the duel invested with legis-
lative as well as judicial functions, is the case wherein the
wager of battle was employed in 1180 to break the overgrown
power of Henry the Lion. That puissant Duke of Saxony
and Bavaria had long divided the power of the empire and
defied the repeated efforts of Frederic Barbarossa to punish
his constantly recurring rebellions. Cited to appear and
answer for his treasons in successive diets, he constantly refused, on the plea that the law required him to have a trial
within his own dominions. At length, in the diet of Würz-

---

[1] Lambert. Hersfeld. ann. 1070, 1073, 1074.—Conrad. Ursperg. ann.
1071.—Bruno de Bello Saxonico.

12

burg, a noble arose and declared himself ready to prove by the single combat that the emperor could legally cite his princes before him at any place that he might select within the limits of the empire.   Of course there was none to take up the challenge, and Frederic was enabled to erect the principle thus asserted into a binding law.   Henry was condemned by default, and his confiscated possessions were shared between those who had arranged and enacted the comedy.[1]

No rank of life in fact procured exemption from the duel between antagonists of equal station.   When in 1002, on the death of Otho III., the German throne was filled by the election of Henry the Lame, Duke of Bavaria, one of his disappointed competitors, Hermann, Duke of Suabia, is said to have demanded that their respective claims should be determined by a judicial combat, and the new king, feeling himself bound to accept the wager of battle, proceeded to the appointed place, and waited in vain for the appearance of his antagonist.[2]   Thus the champion of England, who until 1821 figured in the coronation pageant of Westminster Abbey, was a relic of the times when it was not an idle ceremony for the armed and mounted knight to fling the gauntlet and proclaim aloud that he was ready to do battle with any one who challenged the right of the new monarch to his crown.[3]   A striking example of the liability attaching to even the most exalted rank is afforded by a declaration of the privileges of the Duchy of Austria, granted by Frederic Barbarossa in 1156, and confirmed by Frederic II. in 1245.   These privileges rendered the dukes virtually independent sovereigns, and among them is enumerated the right of employing a champion to represent the reigning duke when summoned to the judicial duel.[4]   Even more instructive is the inference deducible from the For de Morlaas, granted to his subjects by Gaston IV. of

---

[1] Conrad. Ursperg. ann. 1175.   [2] Dithmari Chron. Lib. v.

[3] From the time of Henry I., the office of king's champion was one of honor and dignity.   See Spelman's Glossary.

[4] Constit. Frid. II. ann. 1245 cap. 9 (Goldast. Const. Imp. I. 303).

Béarn about the year 1100.   The privileges contained in it
are guaranteed by a clause providing that, should they be in-
fringed by the prince, the injured subject shall substantiate
his complaint by his simple oath, and shall not be compelled
to prove the illegality of the sovereign's acts by the judicial
combat, thus indicating a pre-existing custom of the duel between the prince and his vassals.[1]

It is not to be supposed, however, from these instances that
the duel was an aristocratic institution, reserved for nobles and
affairs of state.   It was an integral part of the ordinary law,
both civil and criminal, employed habitually for the decision
of the most every-day affairs.   Thus a chronicler happens to
mention that in 1017 the Emperor St. Henry II. coming to
Merseburg hanged a number of robbers who had been convicted in single combat by champions, and then proceeding
to Magdeburg he had all the thieves assembled and treated
them in the same manner.[2]   So much was it a matter of course,
that, by the English law of the thirteenth century, a pleader
was sometimes allowed to alter the record of his preliminary
plea, by producing a man who would offer to prove with his
body that the record was incorrect, the sole excuse for the
absurdity being that it was only allowed in matters which could
not injure the other side;[3] and a malefactor turning king's
evidence was obliged, before receiving his pardon, to pledge
himself to convict all his accomplices, if required, by the duel.[4]

The habitual use of such a method of administering justice
required no little robustness of faith in the expected intervention of God to control the event.   Even in the fifteenth century, when the combat was rapidly becoming obsolete, this faith
is pictorially embodied in an illuminated MS. of Tallhöfer's
Kamprecht, where a miniature represents the victor kneeling

[1] For de Morlaas, Rubr. xxvi.

Dithmari Chron. Lib. VII. c. 36, 37.—" Ibi tunc multi latrones a gladiatoribus in singulari certamine devicti suspendio perierunt."

Bracton. Lib. III. Tract. ii. cap. 37, § 5.

[4] Bracton. Lib. III. Tract. ii. cap. 33, § 2; 34, § 2.

and returning thanks to God, while the vanquished is lying on his back with Satan grasping at his open mouth as though already seizing the soul of the criminal.[1] This robustness of faith was proof against experience and common sense, and sought to explain the frequent miscarriage of justice by any process of reasoning rather than the right one. Thus about the year 1100 a sacrilegious thief named Anselm stole the sacred vessels from the church of Laon and sold them to a merchant, from whom he exacted an oath of secrecy. Frightened at the excommunications fulminated by the authorities of the plundered church, the unhappy trader revealed the name of the robber. Anselm denied the accusation, offered the wager of battle, defeated the unfortunate receiver of stolen goods, and was proclaimed innocent. Encouraged by impunity, he repeated the offence, and after his conviction by the ordeal of cold water he confessed the previous crime. The doubts cast by this event on the efficacy of the judicial combat were, however, happily removed by the suggestion that the merchant had suffered for the violation of the oath which he had sworn to Anselm, and the reputation of the duel remained intact.[2]

The frequent cases of this nature often did not admit of so ingenious an explanation of the criminal's escape, and legal casuists assumed a condition of being, guilty in the sight of God, but not in that of man—a refinement of speculation which even finds place in the German codes of the thirteenth century;[3]

[1] Dreyer, Anmerckung von den ehemaligen Quellgesetzen, p. 156.

[2] Guibert. Noviogent. de Vita sua Lib. III. cap. xvi.—Hermann. de Mirac. S. Mariæ Laudun. Lib. III. cap. 28.—Forsitan, ut multi putarunt, pro fidei violatæ reatu, qua promiserat fidem Anselmo, quod eum non detegeret.

[3] Und diser vor Got schuldig, und vor den luten nit (Jur. Provin. Alamann. cap. ccxix. § 8). This is a provision for cases in which a thief accuses a receiver of having suggested and assisted in the crime. The parties are made to fight, when, if the receiver is worsted, both are hanged; if the thief, he alone, and the receiver escapes though criminal. The French version enlarges somewhat on the principle involved: " Se il puet vancre

and men contented themselves then, as they do still, with predicting future misfortunes and an eternity of punishment. The more direct solution, in cases of unjust condemnation, was very much like that which justified the defeat of Anselm's merchant —that the unfortunate victim, though innocent of the special offence charged, suffered in consequence of other sins. This doctrine was even supported by the infallible authority of the papacy, as enunciated in 1203 by Innocent III. in a case wherein the priory of St. Sergius was unjustly convicted of theft by the judicial duel, and its possessions were consequently seized by the authorities of Spoleto.[1]

An example justifying this theory is found in the case of Henry of Essex in 1163. He was a favorite of Henry II. and one of the most powerful nobles of his day, till he was accused of treason by his kinsman Robert de Montfort for having abandoned his king when in desperate straits in the Welsh war of 1157. A duel ensued, fought on an island of the Thames near Reading, in presence of an immense assemblage. Henry had been a bad neighbor to the Abbey of St. Edmund, and when engaged in the desperate contest he was dismayed at seeing the angry saint hovering in the air and threatening him; nor was this all, for Gilbert de Cerivilla, whom he had unjustly put to death, likewise appeared and menaced him. The inevitable result of this was his defeat; he was left for dead on the field, but at the instance of his powerful kindred his body was allowed Christian burial in the Abbey of Reading. Carried thither he unexpectedly revived and embraced a religious life in the abbey, where years afterwards he related the story of his discomfiture to the veracious chronicler who has handed it down.[2]

lautre il est quites et li autre sera panduz, et sera an colpe anver lo munde et anver dex andui: ce avient a assez de genz, que aucons sunt an colpe anver dex et ne mie anver le seigle" (Miroir de Souabe, P. II. c. vi.).

[1] Innoc. PP. III. Regest. vi. 26 (c. 2 Extra, v. 35)—"Duellum in quo aliis peccatis suis præpedientibus, ceciderunt."

[2] Chron. Jocelini de Brakelonda (Ed. Camden Soc. pp. 50–2).

That the combatants themselves did not always feel implicit confidence in the event, or rely solely upon the righteousness of their cause, is shown by the custom of occasionally bribing Heaven either to assist the right or to defend the wrong. Thus, in the eleventh century, we find the monastery of St. Peter at Bèze in the enjoyment of certain lands bestowed on the Saint by Sir Miles the Stammerer, who in this way endeavored to purchase his assistance in a combat about to take place—a bargain no doubt highly appreciated by the worthy monks.[1] According to the belief of the pious, Heaven might be propitiated by less venal means, for Cæsarius of Heisterbach relates on the authority of an eye-witness that when Henry VI. entered Lombardy in 1196, a castellan was accused before him of oppression and rapine by his neighbors, who produced a champion of enormous size to vindicate their case. The Emperor decreed the battle, when the brother of the accused offered himself for the defence—a slender and most unequal antagonist. He prepared himself for the strife, however, by assiduous confession and prayer, and easily overcame his huge adversary; and thus, exclaims the worthy chronicler, a guilty man escaped the death he had deserved, solely by virtue of the humble confession of his brother.[2] Cæsarius also mentions another case, in a duel decreed by Frederic Barbarossa between a knight and a gigantic champion, where the inequality was more than counterbalanced by the fact that the knight piously took the precaution of receiving the sacrament before entering the lists, and thus was enabled to overcome his adversary.[3]

Less creditable means were sometimes employed, and men did not hesitate, with the unreasoning inconsistency characteristic of superstition, to appeal to God and at the same time

---

[1] Isdem quoque Milo . . . monomachi certaturus pugna, attribuit sancto Petro terram quam habebat in Luco, prope atrium ecclesiæ, quo sibi adjutor in disposito bello existerit.—Chron. Besuense, Chart. de Luco.

[2] Cæsar. Heisterbach. Dial. Mirac. Dist. III. c. xviii.

[3] Ibid. Dist. IX. c. xlviii.

endeavor to influence God's judgment by the use of unlawful expedients. This was not confined to the laity. In 1355 there was an important suit between the Bishop of Salisbury and the Earl of Salisbury respecting the ownership of a castle, in which the combat was adjudged. When the champions entered the lists the customary examination of their arms and accoutrements was made, and the combat was adjourned in consequence, as it was said, of finding in the coat of the episcopal champion certain rolls containing prayers and charms. The case was finally compromised by the bishop paying fifteen hundred marks to the earl for the disputed property.[1] That precautions against such devices were deemed necessary is shown by the oath required of all combatants, whether principals or champions, that they had on them no charms or conjurations to affect the result.[2] A quaint formula for this is the oath of the champion in the case of Low *vs.* Paramore in 1571 —" This hear you justices that I have this day neither eat, drunk, nor have upon me either bone, stone, ne glass or any enchantment, sorcery, or witchcraft where-through the power of the Word of God might be inleased or diminished and the devil's power increased, and that my appeal is true, so help me God and his saints and by this Book."[3]

[1] Neilson's Trial by Combat, p. 152.

[2] Odofredi Summa de Pugna (Patetta, p. 487).—The oath prescribed in the Ordonnance of Philippe le Bel in 1306 is very elaborate—"Par les seremens que j'ay fais je n'entens pourter sur moy ne sur mon cheval paroles, pierres, herbes, charmes, charroiz, ne conjurations, invocations d'ennemis [demons] ne nulle autre chose ou j'aye esperance d'avoir ayde ne à luy nuire. Ne n'ay recours fors que à Dieu et à mon bon droit, par mon corps, par mon cheval et par mes armes. Et sur ce je baise ceste vraye croix et les saincts evangiles, et me tais."—Isambert, Anc. Lois Françaises, II. 843.

[3] Stow's Annals, ann. 1571 (Ed. 1615, p. 669).

CHAPTER V.

LIMITATIONS ON THE WAGER OF BATTLE.

THE right of demanding the wager of battle between principals varied much with the age and race, though as a "bilateral"
ordeal, as a rule, from the earliest times either party was entitled to claim it.[1] When Beaumanoir composed his *Coutumes
du Beauvoisis*, in 1283, the practice may be considered to
have entered upon its decadence; twenty years had elapsed
since the determined efforts of St. Louis to abolish it; substitutes for it in legal processes had been provided; and the
manner in which that enlightened jurist manifests his prefer-
ence for peaceful forms of law shows that he fully appreciated
the civilizing spirit in which the monarch had endeavored to
soften the ferocity of his subjects. When, therefore, we see
in Beaumanoir's treatise how few restrictions existed in his
time, we may comprehend the previous universality of the
custom. In criminal cases, if an accuser offered battle, the
defendant was forced either to accept it or to confess his guilt,
unless he could prove an alibi, or unless the accuser was himself notoriously guilty of the crime in question, and the accusation was evidently a mere device to shift the guilt to the
shoulders of another; or unless, in case of murder, the victim
had disculpated him, when dying, and had named the real
criminals.[2] If, on the other hand, the accused demanded to
wage his battle, the judge could only refuse it when his guilt
was too notorious for question.[3] A serf could not challenge a
freeman, nor a bastard a man of legitimate birth (though an

---

[1] Ll. Frision. Tit. IX. § 3.

[2] Coutumes du Beauvoisis, chap. lxi. § 2; chap. xliii. § 6.

[3] Ibid. chap. lxi. § 2; chap. xxxix. § 12.

appeal of battle might lie between two bastards), nor a leper a sound man.[1]   In civil actions, the battle trial was not allowed in cases relating to dower, to orphans under age,[2] to guardianships, or to the equity of redemption afforded by the feudal laws to kinsmen in the sale of heritable property, or where the matter at stake was of less value than twelve deniers.[3] St. Louis also prohibited the duel between brothers in civil cases, while permitting it in criminal accusations.[4]   The slenderness of these restrictions shows what ample opportunities were afforded to belligerent pleaders.[5]

In Germany, as a general rule, either party had a right to demand the judicial combat,[6] subject, however, in practice, to several important limitations.   Thus, difference of rank between the parties afforded the superior a right to decline a challenge, as we shall see more fully hereafter.[7]   Relationship between the contestants was also an impediment, of which either might avail himself,[8] and even the fact that the defendant was not a native of the territory in which the action was brought gave him the privilege of refusing the appeal.[9]   Still,

---

[1] Coutumes du Beauvoisis, chap. lxiii. §§ 1, 2, 10.

[2] Twenty-one years is the age mentioned by St. Louis as that at which a man was liable to be called upon to fight.—Établissements, Liv. I. chap. lxxiii., cxlii.

[3] Coutumes du Beauvoisis, chap. lxiii. §§ 11, 13, 18.   The denier was the twelfth part of the solidus or sou.

[4] Établissements, Liv. I. chap. clxvii.

[5] In contemporary Italy the great jurist Roffredo gives a long enumeration of the cases in which the duel is admitted covering nearly the whole of the more serious criminal actions and a number of civil suits.—Odofredi Summa de Pugna (Patetta, pp. 480–4).

[6] Jur. Provin. Alaman. cap. clxvi. §§ 13, 27; cap. clxxvii. (Ed. Schilt.). —Jur. Prov. Saxon. Lib. I. clxviii.

[7] This rule was strictly laid down as early as the time of Frederic Barbarossa.—Feudor. Lib. II. Tit. xxvii. § 3.

[8] Jur. Provin. Alaman. cap. ccclxxxvi. § 2 (Ed. Schilteri).—Jur. Provin. Saxon. Lib. I. c. lxiii.—Sachsische Weichbild, xxxv. 6.

[9] Jur. Provin. Alaman. cap. ccxcii. § 2.—Jur. Provin. Saxon. Lib. III. c. xxvi. xxxiii.

we find the principle laid down even in the fourteenth century that cases of homicide could not be determined in any other manner.[1] There were circumstances, indeed, in which the complainant, if he could bring the evidence of seven witnesses in his favor, could decline the duel; but if he choose to prove the charge by the combat, no examination or testimony was admitted. In the same way, if a man was slain while committing theft or robbery, and was prosecuted for the crime, the accuser was not bound to offer the duel if he could produce the evidence of seven witnesses; but if a relative of the dead man offered to vindicate him by combat, this annulled all the evidence, and conviction could not be had without the battle ordeal.[2] A curious provision in the Saxon burgher law allowed a man who had been assaulted to challenge to the duel as many men as he had wounds—but the wounds were required to be of a certain degree of severity—*wunden kampff-baren*.[3] So the contemporary law of Suabia provides that in accusations of personal violence, the duel was not to be allowed, unless the injury inflicted on the complainant had been sufficiently serious to cause permanent maiming,[4] thus showing how thoroughly different in spirit was the judicial combat from the modern code of honor which has been affiliated upon it. Yet a general rule is found expressed to the effect that it was necessary only in cases where no other evidence was obtainable, when the result could be safely left to the judgment of Omniscience.[5]

[1] Sed scias si de perpetrato homicidio agitur, probationem sine duello non procedere.—Richstich Landrecht, cap. xlix.

[2] Jur. Provin. Alaman. cap. ccclxxxvi. §§ 28, 29 (Ed. Schilteri).—Jur. Prov. Saxon. Lib. I. art. 64.—Sachsische Weichbild, art. lxxxvii. lxxxviii.

[3] Sachsische Weichbild, lxxxi. If he accused more than the number of his wounds, they could defend themselves with six compurgators.

[4] Jur. Provin. Alaman. cap. clxxii. § 20 (Ed Senckenberg).

[5] Hinc pervenit dispositio de duello. Quod enim homines non vident Deo nihilominus notum est optime, unde in Deo confidere possumus, eum duellum secundum jus diremturum.—Jur. Provin. Alaman. cap. clxviii. § 19 (Ed. Senckenberg).

In a formula of application for the duel, given by Hermann de Bare (De

In the Latin kingdoms of the East, and among the Armenians, who, curiously enough, adopted the customs of their fellow Christians from the West, it would seem that in both the noble and the roturier courts, in civil as well as in criminal cases, the plaintiff or prosecutor was not obliged personally to fight, but that if one of his witnesses offered battle, the defendant or accused was not permitted to decline the challenge under pain of losing his suit or being condemned. On the other hand, unless the complainant or accuser had a witness who was willing to offer battle, the oath of denial of the other party was sufficient, and in criminal cases the accuser was subjected to the *talio*.[1]

Formandis Libellis, 1535), there is no allusion to defect of evidence; it is a simple assertion of the guilt of the other side with a demand for the duel in case it is desired.—" Domine Judex, etc.   Ego Petrus, etc.   Quod Martinus hic præsens est falsus et proditor, qui perditionaliter rapuit mihi quendam equum pili mauri, stellatum in fronte, quod si ipse confiteatur peto ipsum condemnari super prædicta rapina ut raptorem.   Si autem hoc neget ego per pugnam armis paribus sumtis a me et ab eo faciam eum confiteri palam per os suum in campo nobis per vos assignando, vel reddam eum victum vel mortuum in dicto campo.   Et super dicta pugna pignus meum vel chyıothecas meas hic in medio in præsentia vestra offero et reddo, et promitto me juraturum in introitu campi per vos nobis ad certamen seu ad dictam pugnam assignandi quod ego non habeo herbas nec breves conjuratorias vel alia quæ maleficia vel fascinationes pariant vel parturiant quoquo modo.   Et quod tunc Martinus juret similiter illud.   Item et peto per vos Dominum judicem si Martinus prædictam rapinam neget declarari et judicari pugnam posse et debere esse et fieri ex prædicta causa inter me et eum et ipsum sententialiter condemnari ad subeundam pugnam mecum ex prædicta causa ut super prædicta rapina possit per pugnam veritas inveniri."— Eph. Gerhardi Tract. Jurid. de Judicio duellico, cap. 1, § 5 (Francof. 1735).

[1] Assises d'Antioche, Haute Cour, ch. ix. xi. xii; Assises des Bourgeois, ch. vi. vii. (Venise, 1876).   This code, of which the existence has long been suspected, has recently been discovered in an Armenian version made by Sempad, the Constable of Armenia Minor, in 1265, for the use of his fellow countrymen.   It has been published, with a French translation, by the Mehkitarist Society of St. Lazarus, and gives us the customary law of the Crusaders in an earlier form than the current texts of the Assises de Jerusalem.

By the English law of the thirteenth century, a man accused of crime had, in doubtful cases only, the right of election between trial by jury and the wager of battle. When a violent presumption existed against him, he was obliged to submit to the verdict of a jury ; but in cases of suspected poisoning, as satisfactory evidence was deemed unattainable, the accused had only the choice between confession and the combat.[1] On the other hand, when the appellant demanded the duel, he was obliged to make out a probable case before it was granted.[2] When battle had been gaged, however, no withdrawal was permitted, and any composition between the parties to avoid it was punishable by fine and imprisonment[3] —a regulation, no doubt, intended to prevent pleaders from rashly undertaking it, and to obviate its abuse as a means of extortion. In accusations of treason, indeed, the royal consent alone could prevent the matter from being fought out.[4] Any bodily injury on the part of the plaintiff, tending to render him less capable of defence or aggression, likewise deprived the defendant of the right to the wager of battle, and this led to such nice distinctions that the loss of molar teeth was adjudged not to amount to disqualification, while the absence of incisors was considered sufficient excuse, be-

[1] Bracton. Lib. III. Tract. ii. cap. 18.—Fleta Lib. I. cap. xxxi. §§ 2, 3.

[2] Bracton. Lib. III. Tract. ii. cap. 23, § 1.

[3] Si autem uterque defaltam fecerit, et testatum sit quod concordati fuerunt, uterque capiatur, et ipsi et plegii sui in misericordia.—Ibid.

The custom with regard to this varied greatly according to local usage. Thus, a charter of the Count of Forez in 1270 concedes the right of avoiding battle, even at the last moment, by satisfying the adversary, and paying a fine of sixty sols.—Chart. Raynaldi Com. Forens. c. 4 (Bernard, Hist. du Forez, T. I. Preuves, p. 25). According to the customs of Lorris, in 1155, if a composition was effected after battle had been gaged and before security was given, each party paid a fine of two sous and a half. If after security was pledged, the fine was increased to seven sous and a half.— Chart. Ludov. Junior. ann. 1155, cap. xiv. (Isambert, Anciennes Lois Françaises, I. 155).

[4] Fleta Lib. II. cap. xxi. § 2.

cause they were held to be important weapons of offence.[1]
Notwithstanding these various restrictions, cases of treason
were almost always determined by the judicial duel, according
to both Glanville and Bracton.[2] This was in direct opposition to the custom of Lombardy, where such cases were especially exempted from decision by the sword.[3] These restrictions of the English law, such as they were, did not, however,
extend to the Scottish Marches, where the trial by battle was
the universal resource and no proof by witnesses was admitted.[4]

In Bearn, the duel was permitted at the option of the accuser
in cases of murder and treason, but in civil suits only in
default of testimony.[5] That in such cases it was in common
use is shown by a treaty made, in the latter part of the eleventh
century, between Centulla I. of Bearn and the Viscount of
Soule, in which all doubtful questions arising between their
respective subjects are directed to be settled by the combat,
with the singular proviso that the combatants shall be men
who have never taken part in war.[6] In the thirteenth century,
however, a provision occurs which must have greatly reduced
the number of duels, as it imposed a fine of only sixteen sous
on the party who made default, while, if vanquished, he was
visited with a mulct of sixty sous and the forfeiture of his

---

[1] Bracton. Lib. III. Tract. ii. cap. 24 § 4.—" Hujusmodi vero dentes mul-
tum adjuvant ad devincendum."—Olivier de la Marche tells us (*Traités sur
le Duel*, communicated to me by George Neilson, Esq.) that if the defendant
had lost an eye the appellant must have one correspondingly bandaged.
This device can scarce have been known in England, else it would have
deprived Sir William Dalzell of the £200 forfeit adjudged to him by Richard II. when Sir Piers Courtenay refused to submit to the loss of an eye, to
counterbalance that which Sir William had lost at Otterburn (Neilson,
Trial by Combat, p. 237).

[2] Glanvil. Lib. XIV. cap. i.—Bracton. Lib. III. Tract. ii. cap. 3 § 1.

[3] Feudor. Lib. II. Tit. xxxix.

[4] Neilson, Trial by Combat, p. 128.

[5] For de Morlaas, Rubr. xxxviii. xxxix.

[6] Marca, Hist de Béarn. p. 293 (Mazure et Hatoulet).

13

arms.[1] In the neighboring region of Bigorre an exemption was allowed in favor of the widow whose husband had been slain in war. Until she remarried or her sons were of age to bear arms she was exempt from all legal process—a provision evidently intended to relieve her from the duel in which suits were liable to terminate.[2]

In some regions greater restrictions were imposed on the facility for such appeals to the sword. In Catalonia, for instance, the judge alone had the power of deciding whether they should be permitted,[3] and a similar right was reserved in doubtful cases to the podestà in a code of laws in force at Verona in 1228.[4] This must often have prevented the injustice inherent in the system, and an equally prudent reserve was exhibited in a statute of Montpellier, which required the assent of both parties.[5] On the other hand, in Normandy, at the commencement of the thirteenth century, many cases relating to real estate were examined in the first instance by a jury of twelve men, and, if they failed of an unanimous verdict, the question was decided by the duel, whether the parties were willing or not.[6]

By the criminal procedure in England, at about the same period, the duel was prescribed only for cases of felony or crimes of importance, and it was forbidden in trifling misdemeanors.[7] Appeal of battle could not lie between a vassal and his lord during the existence of the connection, nor between a serf and his master except in cases of treason.[8] It would also seem that the defendant could avoid the duel if he could prove that the motive of the appeal was hatred, for

[1] For de Morlaas, Rubr. iv.

[2] De Lagrèze, Hist. du Droit dans les Pyrénées, Paris, 1867, p. 68.

[3] Libell. Catalan. MS. (Du Cange).

[4] Meo arbitrio determinabo duellum, vel judicium judicabo.—Lib. Juris Civil. Veronæ, cap. 78 (p. 63).

[5] Statut. Montispess. ann. 1204 (Du Cange).

[6] Établissements de Normandie, *passim* (Édition Marnier).

[7] Bracton. Lib. III. Tract. ii. cap. 19 § 6, cf. cap. 23 § 2.

[8] Ibid. cap. 20 § 5. Cf. Maitland, Select Pleas of the Crown, Vol. i. p. 43.

there is a curious case on record in which, when the appellant demanded battle, the accused offered to the king a silver mark for an impartial jury to decide this preliminary question, and it was granted to him.[1]   In Southern Germany a fifteenth century MS. enumerates seven crimes for which the duel could be prescribed—detraction of the emperor or empire, treason, theft, robbery and depredation, rape, arson, and poisoning.[2]

From a very early period, a minimum limit of value was established, below which a pugnacious pleader was not allowed to put the life or limb of his adversary in jeopardy. This varied of course with the race and the period.   Thus, among the Angli and Werini, the lowest sum for which the combat was permitted was two solidi,[3] while the Baioarians established the limit at the value of a cow.[4]   In the tenth century, Otho II. decided that six solidi should be the smallest sum worth fighting for.[5]   The so-called laws of Henry I. of England decreed that in civil cases the appeal of battle should not lie for an amount less than ten solidi.[6]   In France, Louis le Jeune, by an edict of 1168, forbade the duel when the sum in debate was less than five sous,[7] and this remained in force

---

[1] Maitland, p. 48—"Utrum verum sit appellum vel athia" (hate).

[2] Würdinger, Beiträge zur Geschichte des Kampfrechtes in Bayern, p. 7.

[3] L. Anglior. et. Werinor. Tit. xv.   The variations in the coinage are so numerous and uncertain, that to express the values of the solidus or sou, at the different periods and among the different races enumerated, is virtually impossible.   In general terms, it may be remarked that the Carlovingian solidus was the twentieth part of a pound of silver, and according to the researches of Guérard was equivalent in purchasing power to about thirty-six francs of modern money.   The marc was half a pound of silver.

[4] L. Baioar. Tit. VIII. cap. ii. § 5 ; cap. iii.

[5] L. Longobard, Lib. ii. cap. lv. § 37.

[6] L. Henrici I. cap. 59.

[7] Isambert, Anciennes Lois Françaises, I. 162.   This occurs in an edict abolishing sundry vicious customs of the town of Orleans.   It was probably merely a local regulation, though it has been frequently cited as a general law.

for at least a century.[1] The custom of Normandy in the
thirteenth century specifies ten sous as the line of demarcation
between the *lex apparens* and the *lex simplex* in civil suits,[2]
and the same provision retains its place in the Coutumier in
use until the sixteenth century.[3] In the Latin States of the
East founded by the Crusaders, the minimum was a silver
marc in cases of both nobles and roturiers.[4] A law of Aragon,
in 1247, places the limit at ten sous.[5]

As regards the inferior classes of society, innumerable documents attest the right of peasants to decide their quarrels by
the ordeal of battle. By the old Lombard law, slaves were
allowed to defend themselves in this manner ;[6] and they could
even employ the duel to claim their liberty from their masters,
as we may infer from a law of King Grimoald denying this
privilege to those who could be proved to have served the same
master for thirty continuous years.[7] Similarly, among the
Frisians, a *litus* claiming his liberty was allowed to prove it
against his master with arms.[8] The institutions of feudalism
widened the distance between the different classes of society,
and we have already seen that, in the thirteenth century, serfs

---

[1] Livres de Jostice et de Plet, Liv. XIX. Tit. xvii. § 3, Tit. xxii. § 4, Tit.
xxxviii. § 3. See also a coutumier of Anjou of the same period (Anciens
Usages d'Anjou, § 32—Marnier, Paris, 1853).

The " Livre de Jostice et de Plet" was the production of an Orléannais,
which may account for his affixing the limit prescribed by the edict of
Louis le Jeune. The matter was evidently regulated by local custom,
since, as we have already seen, his contemporary, Beaumanoir (cap. lxiii.
§ 11), names twelve deniers, or one sou, as the minimum.

[2] Cod. Leg. Norman. P. II. cap. xxi. § 7 (Ludewig, Reliq. MSS. VII.
307). The judgment of God was frequently styled *Lex apparens* or
paribilis.

[3] Anc. Coutum. de Normandie, cap. 87 (Bourdot de Richebourg, IV. 55).

[4] Assises de Jerusalem, cap. 149.—Assises d'Antioche, Haute Cour. ch.
ix.; Assises des Bourgeois, ch. vi.

[5] Laws of Huescar, by Don Jayme I. (Du Cange. s. v. *Torna*).

[6] L. Longobard. Lib. I. Tit. XXV. § 49.

[7] Ibid. Lib. I. Tit. IX. § 38.   [8] L. Frision. Tit. XI. cap. iii.

were enfranchised in order to enable them to support their testimony by the combat; yet this was only the result of inequality of rank. In the time of Beaumanoir (1283), though an appeal would not lie from a serf to a freeman, it may be safely inferred from the context that a combat could be legally decreed between two serfs if the consent of their masters were obtained,[1] and other contempotary authorities show that a man claimed as a serf could defend his freedom with the sword against his would-be master.[2] Even Jews were held liable to the appeal of battle, as we learn from a decision of 1207, preserved in an ancient register of assizes in Normandy,[3] and they no doubt purchased the exemption, which was granted to them, except in cases of flagrant murder, by Philippe le Long, as a special favor, in 1317.[4]

Difference of condition thus became an impediment to the duel, and formed the subject of many regulations, varying with circumstance and locality. The free mountaineers of Bearn, as has been seen, placed the prince and the subject on an equality before the law, but this was a rare example of independence, and the privileges of station were sometimes exhibited in their most odious form. In France, for instance, while the battle trial could take place between the gentilhomme and the *vilain*, the former was secured by the distinction that if the villein presumed to challenge him, he enjoyed the right of fighting on horseback with knightly weapons, while the challenger was on foot and armed only with shield and staff;

---

[1] Coutumes du Beauvoisis, cap. lxiii. § 1.—The consent of the master was necessary to authorize the risk of loss which he incurred by his serf venturing to engage in the duel. Thus, in a curious case which occurred in 1293, " idem Droetus corpus suum ad duellum in quo perire posset obligare non poterat sine nostra licentia speciali."—Actes du Parlement de Paris, I. 446.

[2] Livres de Jostice et de Plet, Liv. XIX. Tit. 13.—Tabul. Vindocinens. cap. 159 (Du Cange. s. v. *adramire*).

[3] Assises de l'Echiquier de Normandie, p. 174 (Marnier).

[4] Laurière, Table Chron. des Ordonnances, p. 105.

but if the gentleman condescended to challenge the villein, they met on equal terms.[1]   This last regulation was enforced with impartial justice, for Beaumanoir mentions a case in which a gentleman challenged a roturier, and presented himself in the lists mounted and armed with his knightly weapons.   The defendant protested against this illegal advantage, and the judges decided that the gentleman had forfeited his horse and arms, and that if he desired to continue the combat he must do so in the condition in which he was left by the disarmament—in his shirt without armor or weapons, while his adversary should retain coat of mail, target, and club.[2]   The barbarous injustice of the general rule, moreover, was by no means of universal application.   Pierre de Fontaines, for instance, directs that in cases of appeal from a roturier to a gentleman the combat shall take place on foot between champions;[3] and I find a case recorded in 1280, in which a *femme de corps* of Aimeri de Rochechouart accused the Sire de Montricher of burning her houses, and as the duel was adjudged she placed in the lists an armed and mounted knight as her champion, to whom no objection seems to have been made.[4]

Throughout both Northern and Southern Germany, where the minute distinctions of birth were guarded with the most jealous care from a very early period, the codes of the thirteenth century, including even the burgher laws, provided that a difference of rank permitted the superior to decline the challenge of an inferior, while the latter was obliged to accept the appeal of the former.   So thoroughly was this principle carried into practice, that, to compel the appearance of a *Semperfri*, or noble of sixteen quarterings, the appellant was

---

[1] Beaumanoir, op. cit. cap. lxi. §§ 9, 10.—Établissements de S. Louis, Liv. I. chap. lxxxii.

[2] Beaumanoir, cap. lxiv. § 3.

[3] Conseil, ch. XXI. Tit. xiv.

[4] Actes du Parlement de Paris, T. I. No. 2269 A. p. 217.

required to prove himself of equally untarnished descent.[1]   In the same spirit a Jew could not decline the appeal of battle offered by a Christian accuser, though we may safely infer that the Jew could not challenge the Christian.[2]   So, in the Latin kingdom of Jerusalem, the Greek, the Syrian, and the Saracen could not challenge the Frank, but could not, in criminal cases, decline his challenge, though they might do so in civil suits.[3]   In Aragon, no judicial duel was permitted between a Christian and a Jew or a Saracen,[4] while in Castile both combatants had to be gentlemen, quarrels between parties of different ranks being settled by the courts.[5]   On the other hand, in Wales, extreme difference of rank was held to render the duel necessary, as in cases of treason against a lord, for there the lord was plaintiff against his vassal, and as no man could enter into law with his lord, the combat was considered the only mode of prosecution befitting his dignity.[6]

---

[1] Jur. Provin. Saxon. Lib. I. c. 50, 62.   Lib. III. c. 29, 65.—Sachsische Weichbild xxxiii. xxxv.   Jur. Provin. Alamann. cap. ccclxxxv. §§ 14, 15 (Ed. Schilteri).   According to some MSS. of the latter, however, this privilege of declining the challenge of an inferior was not allowed in cases of homicide.—"Ibi enim corpus corpori opponitur"—cap. liii. § 4 (Ed. Senckenberg).   On the other hand, a constitution of Frederic Barbarossa, issued in 1168 and quoted above, forbids the duel in capital cases unless the adversaries are of equal birth.

Tallhöfer's Kamp-recht lays down the rule unconditionally—"Item ist das ain man kempflich angesprochen wirt von ainem der nit als gut is als er, dem mag er mit recht ussgan ob er wil . . . . sprict aber der edler den mindern an zu kempfen so mag der der minder nich absyn."—Dreyer, op. cit. p. 166.

[2] Jur. Prov. Alamann. cap. cclviii. § 20.   (Ed. Schilter.)—We have already seen that the converse of this rule was introduced in England, as regards questions between Frenchmen and Englishmen, by William the Conqueror.

[3] Quia surien et greci in omnibus suis causis, præter quam in criminalibus excusantur a duello.—Assises de Jerusalem, Baisse Court, cap. 269.

[4] Laws of Huescar, ann. 1247 (Du Cange s. v. *Torna*).

[5] Las Siete Partidas, P. VII. Tit. iii. l. 3.

[6] Anomalous Laws, Book XIV. chap. xiv. § 1 (Owen II. 625).

A question of this nature was the remote occasion of the murder of Charles the Good, Count of Flanders, in 1127. Bertulf, Provost of the church of Bruges, was rich and powerful, although in reality his family were villeins of the count. He married his nieces to knights, one of whom, in presence of the count, appealed another knight to battle. The appellee refused on the ground that he was not obliged to notice the challenge of a villein, for according to the law of the land a freeman marrying a serf was reduced to the latter condition after the expiration of a year. The count's attention being thus called to his rights over the family of Bertulf, he proceeded to establish them, when Bertulf set on foot the conspiracy which ended in the assassination of the count.[1]

There were three classes—women, ecclesiastics, and those suffering under physical incapacity—with whom personal appearance in the lists would appear to be impossible. When interested in cases involving the judicial duel they were therefore allowed the privilege of substituting a champion, who took their place and did battle for the justice of their cause. So careful were legislators to prevent any failure in the procedure prescribed by custom, that the North German law provided that the dead when prosecuted could appear in the lists by substitutes,[2] and the Assises de Jerusalem ordered the suzerain to supply the expenses for forty days, when a suitor unable to fight was also too poor to pay for a champion to take his place; and when a murdered man left no relatives to prosecute the murderer, the suzerain was likewise obliged to furnish the champion in any trial that might arise.[3] Equally directed to the same purpose was the German law which provided that when a crippled defendant refused or neglected to procure a substitute, the judge was to seize one-half of his property with which to pay the services of a gladiator, who

[1] Galberti Vit. Caroli Boni, cap. 2, n. 12.
[2] Jur. Provin. Saxon. Lib. I. art. 48.
      Assises de Jerusalem, cap. 266, 267.

could claim nothing more.[1] Guardians of women and minors, moreover, were bound to furnish battle in their behalf.[2]

Women, however, did not always restrict themselves to fighting thus vicariously. The German laws refer to cases in which a woman might demand justice of a man personally in the lists, and not only are instances on record in which this was done, as in a case at Berne in 1228, in which the woman was the victor,[3] but it was of sufficiently frequent occurrence to have an established mode of procedure, which is preserved to us in all its details by illuminated MSS. of the period.[4] The chances between such unequal adversaries were adjusted by placing the man up to the navel in a pit three feet wide, tying his left hand behind his back, and arming him only with a club, while his fair opponent had the free use of her limbs and was furnished with a stone as large as the fist, or weighing from one to five pounds, fastened in a piece of stuff. A curious regulation provided the man with three clubs. If in delivering a blow he touched the earth with hand or arm he forfeited one of the clubs ; if this happened thrice his last weapon was gone, he was adjudged defeated, and the woman could order his execution. On the other hand, the woman was similarly furnished with three weapons. If she struck the man while he was disarmed she forfeited one, and with the loss of the third she was at his mercy, and was liable to be buried alive. According to the customs of Freisingen these combats were reserved for accusations of rape. If the man was vanquished, he was beheaded ; if the woman, she only lost a hand, for the reason that the chances of the fight were against her.[5] In Bohemia, also, women over the age of eighteen

---

[1] Jur. Provin. Alamann. cap. lx. § 5.

[2] Jur. Provin. Saxon. Lib. I. c. 42, 43.

[3] Belitz de Duellis Germanorum, p. 9 (Vitembergæ, 1717).

[4] Jur. Provin. Alamann. cap. ccxxix. § 2. This chapter is omitted in the French version of the Speculum Suevicum.

[5] Ephr. Gerhardi Tract. Jurid. de Judic. Duellico, cap. iii. § 7, et Mantissa.—Dreyer, Anmerckung von den Quellgesetzen, p. 160.—Meyer, Der

had the privilege of the duel; the man was put into a pit as deep as his waist; the woman was armed with sword and buckler, but was not allowed to approach nearer than a circle traced around the mouth of the pit.[1]

Gerichtliche Zweikampf, 1873. Gerhardt gives from a MS. of the fifteenth century in the Grand-ducal Library of Saxe-Gotha a rude representation of the first stage of one of these combats, which is here reduced in facsimile. A MS. at Wolfenbüttel has a miniature virtually the same.   In another repre-

Da ſtatt wie Man vnd Frowen mit ein ander kampffen ſollen. Vnd ſtend hie In dem Anfang

Da ſtatt die frow Fry vnd wil ſchlaben und hat ain ſchin In dem ſchleer wigt vir oder fünf pfund.

So ſtatt er In d. rGruben bis an die Mit hin vnd iſt der Kolb als lang als Ir der ſchleer von der Hand.

sentation of these combats, the antagonists are furnished with curved knives (Würdinger, Beiträge, p. 18).

In many places, however, crimes which a man was forced to disprove by combat were subject to the ordeal of hot iron or water when the accused was a woman.   Thus, by the Spanish law of the thirteenth century, " Muger . . salvese por fierro caliente; e si varon fuere legador . . salvese por lid"—Fuero de Baeça (Villadiego, Fuero Juzgo fol. 317[a]).

[1] Patetta, Le Ordalie, p. 159.

The liability of ecclesiastics to the duel varied with the varying relations between the church and state. As early as the year 819, Louis le Débonnaire, in his additions to the Salic law, directs that, in doubtful cases arising between laymen and ecclesiastics, the duel between chosen witnesses shall be employed, but that when both parties are clerical it shall be forbidden.[1] This restriction was not long observed. A decree of the Emperor Guy, in 892, gives to churchmen the privilege of settling their quarrels either by combat or by witnesses, as they might prefer;[2] and, about the year 945, Atto of Vercelli complains that the tribunals allowed to ecclesiastics no exemption from the prevailing custom.[3] As we have seen (p. 131), Otho II., at the Council of Verona in 983, subjected the churches to the law of the duel, only granting them the privilege of employing champions. Some intricate questions involved in the coexistence of the Lombard and the Roman law arose in a celebrated case between the Abbey of Farfa and that of SS. Cosmo and Damianus of Rome, which was pleaded in 998 and 999 before Otho III. and Popes Gregory V. and Sylvester II. The Abbey of Farfa proved that it lived under the Lombard law, while the other was under the Roman law. It was decided, as the Abbey of Farfa desired, that after hearing testimony the case should be settled by the duel, but the witnesses of the Roman abbey were so manifestly perjured that it was held not to have made out a case justifying an appeal to the combat, and the churches in dispute were adjudged to Farfa.[4]

So far was this liability to the duel from being deemed a hardship by the turbulent spirits of the period, that clerks not infrequently disdained to sustain their rights by the interven-

[1] Capit. Ludov. Pii I. ann. 819, cap. x.

[2] Ughelli, T. II. p. 122 (Du Cange).

[3] Addunt insuper, quoniam si aliquis militum sacerdotes Dei in crimine pulsaverit per pugnam sive singulari certamine esse decernendum.—De Pressuris Eccles.

[4] Muratori Script. Rer. Ital. II. II. 499, 505.

tion of a champion, and boldly entered the lists themselves. In 1080 the Synod of Lillebonne adopted a canon punishing by a fine such belligerent churchmen as indulged in the luxury of duels without having first obtained from their bishops a special license authorizing it.[1] About the same period, Geoffrey, Abbot of Vendôme, in a letter to the Bishop of Saintes, complains of one of his monks who had fought in a judicial duel with a clerk of Saintes[2]. The practice continued, and though forbidden by Pope Innocent II. in 1140,[3] Alexander III. and Clement III. found it necessary to repeat the prohibition before the close of the century.[4] Yet Alexander, when appealed to with respect to a priest of the Campagna who had lost a finger in a duel, decided that neither the offence nor the mutilation debarred him from the exercise of his sacerdotal functions, and only directed him to undergo due penance.[5] The progress of the age, however, was shown when, about thirty years afterwards, Celestin III. pronounced sentence of deposition in a similar case submitted to him;[6] and this was formally and peremptorily confirmed by Innocent III. at the great council of Lateran in 1215.[7]

That the peaceful ministers of Christ should vindicate their rights with the sword, either personally or by proxy, was a sacrilege abhorrent to pious minds. As early as the middle of the ninth century, Nicholas I., who did so much to establish the supremacy of the church, endeavored to emancipate it from this necessity, and declared that the duel was not recognized by ecclesiastical law.[8] The utmost privilege which the

---

[1] Clericus . . . si duellum sine episcopi licentia susceperit . . . aut assultum fecerit, episcopis per pecuniam emendetur.—Orderic. Vital. P. II. Lib. v. c. 5.

[2] Goffrid. Vindocinens. Lib. III. Epist. 39.   [3] Du Cange.

[4] Ut clerici non pugnent in duello, nec pro se pugiles introducent.— Chron. S. Ægid. in Brunswig.—C. 1. Extra, Lib. v. Tit. xiv.

[5] C. 1. Extra, Lib. I. Tit. xx.

[6] C. 2 Extra, Lib. v. Tit. xiv.

[7] Council. Lateran. IV. can. 18.

[8] C. 22 Decret. caus. II. q. v.—Nicolai PP. I. Epist. 148.

secular law accorded the clergy, however, was the right of presenting a champion in the lists, which zealous churchmen naturally resented as an arbitrary injustice.[1] How thoroughly it was carried out in practice, notwithstanding all remonstrances, is shown by a charter granted in 1024 by St. Stephen of Hungary to the monastery of St. Adrian of Zala, by which, among other privileges, the pious king bound himself to supply a champion in all suits against the abbey, in order that the holy meditations of the monks might not be interrupted.[2] Not long after, in 1033, the celebrated abbey of St. Clement at Pescara was involved in a dispute concerning some lands which had been cut off from its possessions by a change in the course of the river Pescara, and had been seized by the lords of the contiguous territory. At an assembly of the magnates of the district it was adjudged that the matter must be settled by the duel. The night before the combat was to take place the holy abbot Guido, after enjoining earnest prayers by all the monks, sallied forth alone to the banks of the stream and stretching forth his staff adjured the waters to repair the evil which they had wrought under the impulsion of the devil. The river forthwith returned to its old channel, and next morning the multitude which assembled to witness the combat were astounded to see the miracle. The godless men who had seized on the possessions of the church humbly sought pardon for their sin, and the abbey remained in quiet enjoyment of its rights.[3]

The scandal of maintaining the claims of the church by carnal weapons and bloodshed was not soon suppressed. In 1112 we find a certain Guillaume Maumarel, in a dispute with the chapter of Paris concerning some feudal rights over the domain of Sucy, appearing in the court of the Bishop of Paris for the purpose of settling the question by the duel, and

[1] Atton. Vercell. De Pressuris Eccles. Pt. I.
[2] Chart. S. Stephani (Batthyani Legg. Eccles. Hung. T. I. p. 384).
[3] Chron. Piscariens. Lib. II. (D'Achery, II. 951).

14

though the matter was finally compromised without combat, there does not seem to have been anything irregular in his proceeding.[1] So, about the same period, in a case between the abbey of St. Aubin in Anjou and a neighboring knight, involving some rights of property, the monks not only challenged their adversary, but the duel was held in the seignorial court of another monastery;[2] and in 1164, we find a duel decreed at Monza, by the Archbishop of Cologne as chancellor of Italy, between an abbey and a layman of the vicinity.[3] That such cases, indeed, were by no means uncommon is shown by their special prohibition in 1195 by Celestin III.[4] Yet, notwithstanding the repeated efforts of the Holy See, it was almost impossible for the church to exempt itself from the universal liability. Though in 1174 Louis VII. granted a special privilege of exemption to the church of Jusiers and its men, on the ground that he was bound to abrogate all improper customs,[5] still no general reform appears to have been practicable. An important step was gained when in 1176 Henry II., as a concession to the papacy, agreed that ecclesiastics should not be forced to the duel,[6] but this did not extend to the Scottish Marches, where by law an ecclesiastic was as liable as a layman to personal appearance in the lists; if he presented a champion he was held in custody till the event of the duel, when, if the champion was defeated, his principal was promptly beheaded. Innocent III. sternly prohibited this in 1216, but ineffectually, as is seen by a complaint of the English clergy, in 1237, in which they mention the case of the Prior of Lide, who had thus recently suffered the penalty. This was equally fruitless, for the *Leges Marchiarum*, enacted in 1249, declare

---

[1] Cartulaire de l'Église de Paris, I. 378.

[2] The charter recording the suit and its results is given by Baluze and Mansi, Miscell. III. 59.

[3] Ibid. p. 134.   [4] C. 1 Extra, Lib. v. Tit. xxxv.

[5] Du Boys, Droit Criminel des Peuples Modernes, II. 187.

[6] Matt. Paris Hist. Angl. ann. 1176 (Ed. 1644, p. 92).

that exemption from battle is confined to the persons of the
kings and of the Bishops of St. Andrews and Durham.[1]

In France, during the thirteenth century, the liability continued. In 1239 a knight of Orleans, Gui de Santillac, testified
before the royal council that the chapter of Saint-Aignan had
appealed him in wager of battle.[2] As late as the year 1245,
some vassals of the chapter of Nôtre Dame at Paris denied
the service due by them, and demanded that the claim of the
chapter should be made good by the wager of battle. That
they had a legal right to do so is shown by the fact that the
churchmen were obliged to implore the intervention of the
pope; and Innocent IV. accordingly granted to the chapter
a special privilege, in which, on the ground that single combats were forbidden by the canons, he declared that the church
of Nôtre Dame should be entitled to prove its rights by witnesses, deeds, and other legitimate proofs, notwithstanding the
custom existing to the contrary.[3] It was probably his interference in this case that led him a few years later, in 1252, to
issue a decretal in which he pointed out the manifest hardship
of forcing the clergy in France, when prosecuting such claims
against their serfs, to have recourse to the duel, and thus,
under the canon law, to forfeit their positions. To remedy
this he proclaimed as a general rule that all verdicts should be
void when obtained against clerks either by means of the duel
or through reason of their refusing the combat;[4] yet in the
following year he was obliged to intervene to protect the Archbishop of Sens, who complained that in these cases he was
obliged to make good his claims by battle.[5] In this, Innocent
was consistent, for one of the accusations which he had brought
against the Emperor Frederic II. when the latter was deposed

---

[1] Neilson, Trial by Combat, pp. 122–7.

[2] Actés du Parlement de Paris, T. I. p. cccvii.

[3] Contraria consuetudine non obstante.—Cart. de l'Église de Paris, II.
393–4.

[4] Archives Administratives de Reims, T. I. p. 733.

[5] Berger, Registres d'Innocent IV. n. 6184 (T. III. p. 148).

at the Council of Lyons in 1245 was that he had forced
ecclesiastics to undergo the duel, to the confusion of all distinctions between clerk and layman.[1]   Even in Italy about 1220
the podestà of Florence ordered the duel to decide a suit
concerning certain property between some citizens and the
church of the Apostles; the latter invoked the intervention
of Honorius III., who commanded the matter to be settled
by regular judicial process, boldly alleging that the duel
was unheard of in such matters,[2] but in spite of this and
the repeated prohibitions of the popes, trial by combat was
still towards the close of the thirteenth century regarded
as the only mode of settling disputed questions between
churches when the genuineness of a charter was impugned.[3]
Yet at the same period the doctors of canon law held that
an ecclesiastic appearing in the lists, either personally or
by a champion, was subject to deposition; it was better,
they said, to lose lands and fiefs than to incur mortal
sin.   Unfortunately this was scarce more than a mere *brutum
fulmen,* for a dispensation could always be had from bishop
or pope.[4]   Custom was stubborn, moreover, and half a century
later, when the judicial duel was going out of fashion, a bishop
of Liége so vexed the burghers of Louvain, by repeated citations to the combat to settle disputed questions, that John III.
Duke of Brabant was obliged to appeal to the Emperor Charles
IV., who accordingly wrote to the bishops of Trèves, Cam-
brai, and Verdun desiring them to find some means of putting
an end to the bellicose tendencies of their episcopal brother.[5]

These sporadic cases only show how difficult it was through-

---

[1] Harduin. Concil. VII. 384.

[2] Compilat. V. Lib. v. Tit. vii. (Ed. Friedberg, p. 184). " Rem hactenus
inauditam et tam juri scripto quam æquitati contrariam."

[3] Fit pugna si ecclesia contra ecclesiam habet controversiam vel contra
privatum et instrumentum dicatur falsum.—Odofredi Summa de Pugna
(Patetta, p. 483).

[4] Joh. Friburgens. Summæ Confessorum Lib. II. Tit. iii. Q. 3, 5, 6.—Cf.
Baptist. de Saulis Summam Rosellam s. v. *Dispensatio,* § 7.

[5] Proost, Législation des Jugements de Dieu, p. 19.

out the whole extent of Christendom to eradicate a custom so deeply rooted in ancestral modes of thought. By the middle of the thirteenth century the church had succeeded in virtually establishing the claim, for which it had long striven, that ecclesiastics were not subject to secular law in either civil or criminal matters. This exemption of course released them from liability to the duel and placed them exclusively under spiritual jurisdiction, in which the strongly marked papal aversion to the duel had full opportunity of making itself effective.[1]

Another phase of the relations between the church and the duel is to be seen in the extensive secular jurisdiction of its prelates in their capacity as temporal seigneurs. In this they were accustomed to award the duel as freely as any other form of legal procedure. To do this was not only one of the privileges which marked the feudal superior, but was also a source of revenue from the fees and penalties thence accruing, and these rights were as eagerly sought and as jealously guarded by the spiritual lords as by the warlike barons. It would scarce be necessary to multiply instances, but I may mention a charter granted by Fulk Nera, Count of Anjou, about the year 1010, bestowing these rights on the abbey of Beaulieu in Touraine,[2] and one by the Emperor Henry III., in 1052, to the bishop and church of Volterra in Italy.[3] The

---

[1] It is not easy to understand the remark of Olivier de la Marche, in the latter half of the fifteenth century (Traités du Duel Judiciaire, p. 44, communicated to me by George Neilson, Esq.), warning judges that they cannot condemn clerks to the duel except in cases of *lèse majesté* and those affecting the faith. At that time the faith was exclusively in the hands of the Inquisition, and the canons admit of no exception to clerical immunity in cases of treason. In both matters torture had long before proved itself vastly more efficient than the clumsy and doubtful ordeals.

[2] Du Cange, s. v. *Bellum.*

[3] Muratori, Antiq. Ital. Dissert. 39.—Among various other examples given by the same author is one of the year 1010, in which the court of the bishop of Aretino grants the combat to decide a case between a monastery and a layman.

first authentic evidence of the existence of the battle trial in Scotland is a charter of Alexander I. in 1124 to the Abbey of Scone, in which he bestows on the abbot and monks the right to grant the duel and ordeal in their jurisdiction; and his brother, St. David I., conferred the same rights on the Abbey of Holyrood.[1] Some conscientious churchmen objected to a practice so antagonistic to all the teachings of the religion of which they were professors, and lifted up their voices to check the abuse. Thus, about the close of the eleventh century, we find the celebrated canonist, St. Ivo of Chartres, rebuking the Bishop of Orleans for ordering the combat to decide an important suit in his court.[2] Ivo even carried out his principles to the sacrifice of the jurisdiction usually so dear to the prelates of his day, for in another case he refused to give judgment because it necessarily involved a trial by battle, and he eluded the responsibility by transferring the cause to the court of the Countess of Chartres.[3] A century later Peter Cantor declared that as a priest he would in no case furnish relics on which the preliminary oaths were to be taken, for churchmen were prohibited from being concerned in bloodshed.[4] These precepts and examples were equally unavailing. Churchmen continued to award the wager of battle, and resolutely resisted any invasion of their privileges. In 1150 the statutes of the chapter of Lausanne direct that all duels shall be fought before the provost—and the provost was Arducius, Bishop of Geneva.[5] In 1201 we see the Abbot of St. Alban's and the Abbot of Westminster pleading as to their rights over the manor of Aldenham, including that of the duel.[6] Even in the thirteenth century, in the archbishop's court or officiality of Reims, the duel was a matter of course;[7] and a case is recorded, occur-

---

[1] Neilson, Trial by Combat, pp. 76, 81.

[2] Ivon. Epist. cxlviii.   [3] Ivon. Epist. ccxlvii.

[4] Pet. Cantor. Verb. Abbreviat. cap. lxxviii.

[5] Migne's Patrologia, T. 188, p. 1287.

[6] Baildon, Select Civil Pleas, I. 43.

[7] Lib. Pract. de Consuetud. Remens. *passim* (Archives Législatives de Reims).

ring in 1224, in a dispute about the ownership of a house, which was decided by a duel in the court of the abbey of St. Remy, where the abbot presided over the lists and they were guarded by the royal officials.[1] In 1239 the Bishop of Orleans contested with the king as to the right of the former to the jurisdiction of the duel in his diocese;[2] and in a judgment rendered in 1269, concerning a combat waged within the limits of the chapter of Nôtre Dame of Paris, we find that the first blows of the fight, usually known as *ictus regis* or *les cous lou roi*, are alluded to as *ictus capituli*.[3] How eagerly these rights were maintained is apparent from numerous decisions concerning contested cases. Thus, an agreement of 1193, between the Countess of St. Quentin and the chapter of Nôtre Dame, respecting the disputed jurisdiction of the town of Viry, gives the official of the chapter the right to decree duels, but places the lists under the supervision of both parties, and divides the spoils equally between each.[4] A charter of 1199, concerning the village of Marne, shows that the sergeant, or officer of the chapter, had the cognizance of causes up to the gaging of battle, after which further proceedings were reserved for the court of the bishop himself.[5] In 1219 the commune of Novara arrogated to itself the right of decreeing the duel, but the bishop resisted this invasion of his privileges, and on the matter being referred for arbitration to the Bishop of Turin he decided in favor of his episcopal brother. The Bishop of Modena had a long and expensive suit with his city on the same question, which ended in 1227

[1] Archives Adminst. de Reims, T. I. p. 822.

[2] Actes du Parlement de Paris, T. I. p. cccvii.

[3] Cartulaire de l'Église de Paris, III. 433. After the first blows the parties could be separated on payment of a fine to the court, from the recipient of which the name is evidently derived. Apparently the good canons drew a distinction between awarding the duel and engaging in it, for we have already seen (p. 159) that twenty-four years before they had obtained from Innocent IV. a special privilege exempting them from the necessity of maintaining their rights by battle.

[4] Cartulaire de l'Église de Paris, I. 234.   [5] Ibid. I. 79–80.

with a compromise by which he abandoned the right; the Bishops of Vercelli were more fortunate, for they maintained it until the beginning of the fourteenth century, when judicial duels were going out of fashion.[1] In 1257, while St. Louis was exerting himself with so much energy to restrict the custom, an abbey is found engaged in a suit with the crown to prove its rights to decree the duel, and to enjoy the fees and mulcts thence arising;[2] and in 1277 a similar suit on the part of the abbey of St. Vaast d'Arras was decided in its favor.[3] From a verdict given in 1293, the right of the chapter of Soissons to decree the judicial combat appears to be undoubted, as well as the earnestness of the worthy ecclesiastics to exercise the privilege.[4] Even more significant is a declaration of the authorities of Metz, as late as 1299, by which the granting of all wagers of battle is expressly admitted by the civil magistrates of the city to appertain to the court of the archbishop;[5] and even in 1311 a bishop of St. Brieuc ordered a duel between two squires pleading in his court, in consequence of high words between them. From some cause the combat did not take place, and the Christian prelate seized the arms and horses of the parties as his mulct. They appealed to the Parlement of Paris, which ordered the restoration of the confiscated articles, and fined the bishop for his disregard of the royal edicts prohibiting the single combat.[6] Not long before, Beaumanoir had definitely asserted that the church could not be concerned in cases which involved the judicial duel, or the infliction of death or mutilation;[7] but the church was not disposed to admit this limitation on its jurisdiction, and in spite of the attempted suppression of the wager of battle by the

[1] Patetta, Le Ordalie, p. 437. [2] Les Olim, I. 24.

[3] Actes du Parl. de Paris. T. I. No. 2122, C. p. 197.

[4] Actes du Parl. de Paris, T. I. p. 446.

[5] Du Cange, s. v. *Arramiatio*. [6] Les Olim, III. 679.

[7] Voirs est que tuit li cas où il pot avoir gages de bataille ou peril de perdre vie ou membre, doivent estre justicié par le laie justice; ne ne s'en doit sainte Église meller.—Coutumes du Beauvoisis, cap. xi. art. 30.

crown it continued in its multifarious capacity of seigneur to execute the cruel laws of the period with undiminished activity.[1]

In other lands, where the duel had not experienced as in France the hostility of the supreme power, prelates continued to decree it, regardless of the papal anathemas. It was to no purpose that canon lawyers proved that they thereby incurred mortal sin, and that if death ensued they became "irregular" and incompetent to perform divine service. To all this they turned a deaf ear, and John of Freiburg, towards the close of the thirteenth century, is reduced to wishing that preachers would expound these principles in the pulpit and make them understood by the people at large.[2]

There was one jurisdiction which held itself more carefully aloof from the prevailing influence of barbarism—that of the Admiralty Courts, which covered a large portion of practical mercantile law. This is a fact easily explicable, not only from the character of the parties and of the transactions for which those courts were erected, but from the direct descent of the maritime codes from the Roman law, less modified by trans-mission than any other portions of mediæval jurisprudence. These codes, though compiled at a period when the wager of battle flourished in full luxuriance, have no reference to it whatever, and the Assises de Jerusalem expressly allude to the Admiralty Courts as not admitting the judicial duel in proof,[3] while an English document of 12 Edward III. attests the same principle.[4] When, however, the case was one implying an accusation of theft or deception, as in denying the receipt of cargo, the matter entered into the province of criminal law, and the battle trial might be legitimately ordered.[5]

[1] See the Registre Criminel de la Justice de St. Martin-des-Champs (Paris, 1877).

[2] Joh. Friburgens. Summæ Confessorum Lib. II. Tit. iii. Q. 5.

[3] En la cort de la mer na point de bataille por prueve ne por demande de celuy veage.—Assises de Jerusalem, cap. xliii.

[4] Pardessus, Us et Coutumes de la Mer.

[5] Livres de Jostice et de Plet, Liv. VII. Tit. iv. § 2.

CHAPTER VI.

REGULATIONS OF THE JUDICIAL COMBAT.

THE forms and ceremonies employed in the judicial duel may furnish an interesting subject of investigation for the admirers of chivalry, but they teach in their details little concerning the habits and modes of thought of the Middle Ages, and for the most part are therefore interesting only to the pure archæologist. Although minute directions have come down to us in the manuals compiled for the guidance of judges of the lists, to enumerate them in their varying fashions would hardly be worth the necessary space. Yet there are some details which are of interest as illustrating both the theory and practice of the duel in its legal aspect. Thus the general principle on which the combat was conducted was the absolute assertion by each party of the justice of his cause, confirmed by a solemn oath on the Gospels, or on a relic of approved sanctity, before the conflict commenced.[1] Defeat was thus not

---

[1] According to Bracton, the appellant in criminal cases appears always obliged to swear to his own personal knowledge, *visu ac auditu*, of the crime alleged. This, however, was not the case elsewhere. Among the glossators on the Lombard law there were warm disputes as to the propriety, in certain cases, of forcing one of the contestants to commit perjury. The matter will be found treated at some length in Savigny's Geschichte d. Rom. Recht. B. IV. pp. 159 sqq. Cf. Odofredi Summa de Pugna (Patetta, pp. 485-7).

The formula of the oath as given in the Fleta is as follows: The parties take each other by the hand and first the appellee swears, " Hoc audis, homo quem per manum teneo, qui A. te facis appellari per nomen baptismi tui, quod ego C. fratrem tuum, vel alium parentem vel dominum non occidi, vel plagam ei feci ullo genere armorum per quod remotior esse debuit a vita et morti propinquior; sic me Deus adjuvet et hæc Sancta, etc." Then the appellant responds: " Hoc audis homo quem per manum teneo, qui te R.

merely the loss of the suit, but was also a conviction of perjury, to be punished as such; and in criminal cases it was also a conviction of malicious prosecution on the part of a worsted appellant. That it was regarded as much more serious than the simple loss of a suit is shown by the provisions of the custom of Normandy, whereby a vanquished combatant was classed with perjurers, false witnesses, and other infamous persons, as incapable thenceforth of giving evidence in courts, or of serving on a jury.[1] Accordingly, we find the vanquished party, whether plaintiff or defendant, subjected to penalties more or less severe, varying with time and place.

This was a primeval custom, even in civil cases. In the ancient laws of the Alamanni, when there was controversy as to the ownership of land, the contestants brought to the court of the district some earth and branches of trees from the disputed property. These were wrapped and sealed and placed in the lists, where the combatants touched the bundle with their swords and called upon God to grant victory to the right; the land passed to the victor and the defeated party was fined twelve sous for having made an unjust claim.[2] The tendency, as civilization advanced, was to render the penalty more severe. Thus, in 819, Louis le Débonnaire decreed that, in cases where testimony was evenly balanced, one of the witnesses

facis appellari per nomen baptismi tui, quod tu es perjurus et ideo perjurus quia tali anno, tali die, tali hora et tali loco nequiter et in felonia occidisti C. fratrum meum tali genere armorum, unde obiit infra triduum; sic me Deus, etc."—Lib. I. cap. xxxii. §§ 28, 29.—Bracton, Lib. III. Tract ii. c. 21, § 2.

In the German law the oath was simpler, but quite as absolute.—Jur. Prov. Saxon, Lib. I. cap. lxii.—Sachsische Weichbild, xxxv. 8.

By the ordonnance of Philippe le Bel in 1306 each party was obliged to take three solemn oaths on relics before a priest, asserting his good cause in the most positive manner and his reliance on the judgment of God.—Isambert, Anc. Lois Françaises, II. 840.

[1] Cod. Leg. Normann. P. I. c. lxiv. (Ludewig. Reliq. MSS. T. VII. p. 270).—Anc. Cout. de Normandie (Bourdot de Richebourg, IV. 29).

[2] Leg. Alamann. Tit. 84.

from each side should be chosen to fight it out, the defeated champion suffering the usual penalty of perjury—the loss of a hand ; while the remaining witnesses on the losing side were allowed the privilege of redeeming their forfeited members at the regular legal rate.[1]   William the Conqueror imposed a fine of forty sous on the losing side impartially ;[2] this was increased to sixty sous by the compilation known as the laws of Henry I. ;[3] and the same regulation is stated by Glanville, with the addition that the defeated person was forever disqualified as a witness or champion ;[4] but in practice the amount seems to have been indefinite, for in the Pipe Rolls the fines levied for *recreantise* vary from one mark to a hundred.[5]   In a case occurring in 1221 where the defendant was victorious the record simply states that the appellant was ordered into custody ;[6] while in the time of Edward II. the loser, except in cases of felony, paid to the victor forty sous besides a small gratification under the name of *ruaille*, in addition to the loss of the suit.[7]   By the Lombard customs, early in the eleventh century, the appellant, if vanquished, had the privilege of redeeming his hand ; the defendant, if defeated, lost his hand, and was of course subject in addition to the penalties of the crime of which he was proved guilty.[8]   About the same time the Béarnese legislation is more merciful, a fine of sixty-six

[1] Capit. Ludov. Pii ann. 819, cap. x.   A somewhat similar provision occurs in the L. Burgund. Tit. xlv. et lxxx.

[2] L. Guillelmi Conquest. iii. xii. (Thorpe, I. 493).—A previous law, however, had assessed a Norman appellant sixty sous when defeated (Ibid. ii. ii.).

[3] L. Henrici I. cap. lix. § 15.

[4] Glanvil. de Leg. Angl. Lib. ii. cap. iii.

[5] Pipe Roll Society, I. 21 ; II. 31, 46, 59 ; III. 10.

[6] Maitland, Select Pleas of the Crown, I. 108.

[7] Solement ceux vainqus sont quittes ou lour clients pur eux rendre aux combattants vanquishours 40 sous en nosme de recreantise et ruaille peur la bourse a mettre eins ses deniers oustre le jugement sur le principall.— Horne's Myrror of Justice, cap. iii. sect. 23.

[8] Formul. Vetus in L. Longobard. (Georgisch, p. 1276).

sous Morlaas being imposed impartially on the losing party.[1]
In process of time this system was abandoned in some countries.   The English law of the thirteenth century admitted the
justice of the *lex talionis* in principle, but did not put it in
practice, a vanquished appellant in capital cases being merely
imprisoned as a calumniator, while the defendant, if defeated,
was executed and his property confiscated.[2]   The same distinction is to be found in the contemporary custom of Normandy.[3]   So, by the code in force in Verona in 1228, the
Podestà in criminal cases had the power of ordering the duel,
and of punishing at his pleasure the accuser if vanquished—
the accused when convicted of course undergoing the penalty
of his crime.[4]   Towards the end of the thirteenth century,
however, there were some sceptics in Italy who argued that
conviction by the duel ought not to entail the same punishment as conviction by witnesses " quia pugna est incertum Dei
judicium." This struck directly at the root of the whole system,
and Roffredo insists that the legal penalty is to be enforced.[5]

Mediæval legislation was not usually lenient to a worsted
appellant.   The application of the *lex talionis* to the man
who brought a false charge, thus adjudging to him the penalty
which was incurred by the defendant if convicted, was widely
current during the Middle Ages.   This principle is to be found
enunciated in the broadest and most decided manner in the
ecclesiastical law,[6] and it was naturally brought into play in
regulating the fate of those engaged in the wager of battle.

---

[1] For d'Oloron, Art. 21.

[2] Bracton, Lib. III. Tract. ii. cap. 18, § 4.   In another passage, Bracton
gives a reason for this clemency—" Si autem victus sit in campo . . .
quamvis ad gaolam mittendus sit, tamen sit ei aliquando gratia de misericordia, quia pugnat pro pace" (Ibid. cap. 21, § 7).   See also the Fleta,
Lib. I. cap. xxxii. § 32.

[3] Étab. de Normandie, Tit. " De prandre fame à force" (Marnier).

[4] Lib. Juris Civilis Veronæ, cap. 78 (p. 63).

[5] Odofredi Summa de Pugna c. xii. (Patetta, p. 491–2).

[6] Qui calumniam illatam non probat, pœnam debet incurrere quam si
probasset reus utique sustineret.—C. 2 Decret. Caus. v. q. vi.

15

Thus Guillaume le Breton states that when Philip Augustus, in 1203, wrested Normandy from the feeble grasp of John Lackland, one of the few changes which he ventured to introduce in the local laws of the duchy was to substitute this rule of confiscation, mutilation, or death, according to the degree of criminality involved in the accusation, for the comparatively light pecuniary mulct and loss of legal status previously incurred by a worsted appellant.[1] The same system is followed throughout the legislation of St. Louis, whether the punishment be light or capital, of an equal responsibility on both parties.[2] In capital cases, when champions were employed, the principals were held in prison with the cord around them with which the defeated party was to be hanged; and if one were a woman, for the cord was substituted the spade wherewith she was to be buried alive.[3] The same principle of equal responsibility prevailed throughout the Frankish kingdoms of the East, where, in an appeal of murder, as we have seen, the appellant fought by means of one of his witnesses, and the defendant personally. In civil cases, in the Bourgeois Court, the party defeated, including the plaintiff, if his side was the loser, was forever debarred from giving testimony, and had no future standing in court; while in serious criminal cases, in

[1] . . . ad poenas exigat æquas,
   Victus ut appellans sive appellatus, eadem
   Lege ligaretur mutilari aut perdere vitam.
   Moris enim extiterit apud illos hactenus, ut si
   Appellans victus in causa sanguinis esset,
   Sex solidos decies cum nummo solveret uno
   Et sic impunis, amissa lege, maneret:
   Quod si appellatum vinci contigeret, omni
   Re privaretur et turpi morte periret.
                    Guillielmi Brito. Phillippidos Lib. VIII.
It will be observed that the pre-existing Norman custom here described is precisely that indicated above by Glanville.

[2] *E. g.* Établissements Lib. I. cap. 27 and 91.—" Cil qui seroit vaincus seroit pendus" (cap. 82).

[3] Beaumanoir, chap. lxiv. § 10.

both upper and lower courts, either side, when defeated, was hanged with the utmost impartiality;[1] and it finally established itself in England, where in the fourteenth century we find it positively declared as an imperative regulation by Thomas, Duke of Gloucester, in an elaborate treatise on the rules of single combat printed by Spelman.[2]

In Germany the custom was not uniform. In the Sachsenspiegel, and in one text of the Schwabenspiegel, the principle is laid down that a defeated appellant escaped with a fine to the judge and to his adversary, while the defendant, if vanquished, was visited with the punishment due to his crime, or even with a heavier penalty;[3] while the Saxon burgher law and another text of the Suabian code direct that whichever party be defeated should lose a hand, or be executed, according to the gravity of the crime alleged.[4] An exceptional case, moreover, was provided for, in which both antagonists might suffer the penalty; thus, when a convicted thief accused a receiver of stolen goods of having suggested the crime, the latter was bound to defend himself by the duel, and if defeated, both combatants were hanged without further ceremony.[5] That these penalties were not merely nominal is shown by a case which occurred at Frankfort in 1369, when the divine interference was requisite, not to determine the victor, but to evade the enforcement of the law. Two knights, Zierkin von Vola and Adolf Hanche, who had married two sisters, quarrelled over the inheritance of a deceased brother-in-law, and agreed to settle their difference by the duel.

[1] Assises d'Antioche, Haute Cour, ch. xi.; Assises des Bourgeois, ch. vi. vii. See also Assises de Jerusalem, cap. 317.

[2] Recta fides et æquitas et jus armorum volunt ut appellans eandem incurrat pœnam quam defendens, si is victus fuerit et subactus.—Formula Duelli, apud Spelman. Glossar. s. v. *Campus.*

[3] Jur. Provin. Saxon, Lib. I. c. 63.—Jur. Provin. Alamann. cap. ccclxxxvi. §§ 19, 20 (Ed. Schilter.).

[4] Sachsische Weichbild, 82.—Jur. Provin. Alamann. cap. clxviii. § 20; clxxii. § 18 (Ed Senckenberg.).

[5] Ibid. cap. ccxix. § 6 (Ed. Schilter.).

When the appointed day came, October 12, they entered the lists on their chargers, prepared to do battle to the death, while their pious wives were earnestly praying God to soften their hearts and incline them to peace. These prayers were heard. With a mutual impulse the two warriors leaped from their horses, throwing themselves into each other's arms and exclaiming, "Brother, I confess myself vanquished." The chief magistrate of the city, who presided over the combat, was not disposed to deprive the spectators of their promised entertainment, and indignantly declared that the law of the duel did not permit both antagonists to depart unhurt, for the one who yielded must be put to death; and he confirmed this sentence by a solemn oath that one or the other should die before he would taste food. Then an affecting contest arose between the late antagonists, each one proclaiming himself the vanquished and demanding the penalty on his own head, when suddenly divine vengeance visited the bloody and remorseless judge, who fell dead, thus fulfilling his impious vow that he would not eat until he had a victim.[1]

It was probably as an impressive symbol of the penalties affixed by law to defeat in these combats that in some places the suggestive custom was in force of placing in the lists two biers in readiness for their ghastly occupants. In a duel which occurred at Augsburg in 1409, between two men named Marschalck and Hachsenacker, the former threw his adversary on the ground, and then asked him what he would have done had he been the victor. Hachsenacker grimly replied that he would have slain his foe, whereupon Marschalck despatched him, and placing himself in his bier caused himself to be carried to the church of St. Ulric, where he returned thanks for his victory.[2]

The most hideous exaggeration of the system, however, was found in the Frankish kingdoms of the East, which reserved a special atrocity for women—one of the numerous instances

---

[1] Chron. Cornel. Zantfliet ann. 1369 (Mart. Ampl. Coll. V. 293–4).

[2] Chron. Augustan. (Pistor. III. 684, Ed. 1726).

to be observed in mediæval law of the injustice applied habitually to the weaker sex. When a woman appeared, either as appellant or defendant, in the lists by her champion, if he was defeated she was promptly burnt, no matter what was the crime for which the duel occurred—and as many accusations could only be determined by the wager of battle, she had no choice but to undergo the chance of the most dreadful of deaths.[1]

It was not customary to order the combat to take place immediately, but to allow a certain interval for the parties to put their affairs in order and to undergo the necessary training. In Southern Germany this delay was for nobles from four to six weeks, and for others a fortnight, and during this period any assault by one on the other was a capital offence.[2] They were required to give security for their due appearance at the appointed time, various fines and punishments being inflicted on defaulters. By the law of both Northern and Southern Germany, when default was made by the defendant he was held guilty of the crime charged upon him: and if he was allowed the privilege of redeeming hand or life either as defendant or appellant, he was declared infamous, and deprived of the protection of the law. According to some MSS., indeed, all the possessions of a defaulter were forfeited, either to his heirs or to his feudal superior.[3] In a case occurring in the twelfth century in Hainault, between a seigneur and a man whom he claimed as a serf, the latter demanded the duel, which was allowed, but on the appointed day he failed to appear by nine o'clock. His adversary had waited for him since daybreak, and claimed the verdict which was awarded him by the council of Hainault. At this moment the missing man pre-

---

[1] Assis. Hierosol. Alta Corte cap. cv. (Canciani, V. 208).

[2] Würdinger, Beiträge zur Geschichte des Kampfrechtes in Bayern, p. 8.

[3] Jur. Provin. Saxon. Lib. 1. c. 63, 65.—Sachsische Weichbild, xxxv. —Jur. Provin Alamann. cap. ccclxxxvi. § 31 (Ed. Schilter.) ; cap. clxxviii. §§ 7, 8 (Ed. Senckenb.).   See Würdinger, p. 11, for the solemn sentence placing the defaulter under the ban.

sented himself, but was adjudged to be too late, and was de-
livered to his claimant as a serf.   According to the custom of
Flanders, indeed, the combatant who failed to appear suffered
banishment, with confiscation of all his possessions.[1]   This
extreme rigor, however, did not obtain universally.   Among
the Béarnese, for instance, the forfeiture for a default was only
sixteen sous Morlaas.[2]   By the English law, the defaulter was
declared infamous, and was also liable to a fine to the king,
for which there was apparently no fixed amount.[3]   The Scan-
dinavians punished him popularly by erecting a "nithstong"—
pertica execrationis—a post inscribed with defamatory runes,
and so flagrant was this insult considered, that finally it was
prohibited by law under pain of exile.[4]   Perhaps the most
emphatic assertion, however, of the obligation to appear is
the rule in the law of the Scottish Marches in 1249, that if
the accused should die before the appointed day his body
must be brought to the lists, "for no man can essoin himself
by death."[5]

The bail, of course, was liable for all legal penalties incurred by a defaulter, and occasionally, indeed, was made to
share the fate of his principal, when the latter appeared and
was defeated.   In the law of Southern Germany, according
to one text, the bail under these circumstances was liable to
the loss of a hand, which, however, he could redeem, while
another version makes him suffer the penalty incurred by his
principal.[6]   This latter rule is announced in a miracle play of
the fourteenth century, where a stranger knight at the court of

---

[1] Proost, Législation des Jugements de Dieu, pp. 18, 21.

[2] For de Morlaas, Rubr. IV. art. 5.

[3] Horne's Myrror of Justice, cap. iv. sect. 13.—Pipe Roll Society, I. 65.

[4] Schlegel Comment. ad Gragas § 31.—Gragas sect. VIII. cap. 105.   A
fanciful etymologist might trace to this custom the modern phrase of "post-
ing a coward."

[5] Neilson, Trial by Combat, p. 128.

[6] Jur. Provin. Alamann. cap. ccclxxxvi. § 32 (Ed. Schilter.); cap. clxxiii.
§ 13 (Ed. Senckenberg.).

Paris, compelled to fight in defence of the honor of the king's daughter, is unable to find security.   The queen and princess offer themselves as hostages and are accepted, but the king warns them—

> Dame, par Dieu le roy celestre !
> Bien vous recevray pour hostage ;
> Mais de tant vous fas-je bien sage,
> Se le dessus en peut avoir
> 'Ardré, je vous feray ardoir.
> Et mettre en cendre.[1]

Poverty on the part of one of the combatants, rendering him unable to equip himself properly for the combat, was not allowed to interfere with the course of justice.   In such cases, under the law of Northern Germany, the judge was required to provide him with the requisite weapons.[2]   In England, where the royal jurisdiction embraced all criminal cases, the king furnished the weapons and paid all expenses, and when the combatant was an "approver," or criminal who had turned state's evidence, he was supported until his duty was accomplished of fighting all whom he accused as accomplices. Thus in the accounts of the sheriff of Lincolnshire for 1190, there is an entry of 15s. 10d. for the approver Adam Godechap from Pask until Michaelmas at one penny per diem ; also 6s. for his armor in three duels, and 38s. 6d. for carts to convey prisoners, sureties, and probators from Lincoln to London and

---

[1] Un Miracle de Notre-Dame d'Amis et d'Amille (Monmerqué et Michel, Theat. Français au Moyen-Age, p. 238).

Another passage in the same play signifies the equality of punishment for appellant and defendant in cases of defeat :—

> —Mais quant il seront
> En champ, jamais n'en ysteront
> Sans combatre, soiez-en fis,
> Tant que l'un en soit desconfis ;
> Et celui qui vaincu sera,
> Je vous promet, pendu sera :
> N'en doubte nulz.

[2] Jur Provin. Saxon, I. 63.

elsewhere.[1] The crown likewise paid the expenses of administering the other ordeals: in 1166 a single entry in the Exchequer accounts shows payment for thirty-four ordeals and five battles.[2]

As regards the choice of weapons, much curious anecdote could be gathered from the pages of Brantôme and others learned in punctilio, without throwing additional light upon mediæval customs. It may be briefly observed, however, that when champions were employed on both sides, the law appears generally to have restricted them to the club and buckler, and to have prescribed perfect equality between the combatants.[3] An ordonnance of Philip Augustus, in 1215, directs that the club shall not exceed three feet in length.[4] In England the club or battoon was rendered more efficient with a " crook," usually of horn, but sometimes of iron, giving to the weapon the truly formidable aspect of a pickaxe or tomahawk.[5] When the principals appeared personally, it would seem that in early times the appellant had the choice of weapons, which not only gave him an enormous advantage, but enabled him to indulge any whims which his taste or fancy might suggest, as in the case of a Gascon knight in the thirteenth century, who stipulated that each combatant should be crowned with a wreath of roses. As every detail of equipment was thus subject to the caprice of the challenger,

---

[1] Venables, Lincolnshire Notes and Queries, Vol. I. p. 195 (1889). So an entry in the Pipe Roll for 1158-9 " Et in conductu Rad. Shirloc. 6s. 8d. Et pro apparatu ejusdem Rad. et socii ejus ad duellum 16s. 4d.—Pipe Roll Society, I. 2.

[2] Neilson, Trial by Combat. p. 42.

[3] E. g. Constit. Sicular. Lib. II. Tit. xxxvii. § 1. This was also the case in Bohemia (Patetta, Le Ordalie, p. 159).

[4] Laurière, Table des Ordonn. p. 10.

[5] See facsimile of a record of a duel between Walter Blowberme and Hamo le Stare, where in the background the latter unlucky defendant is represented as hanging on a gallows (Maitland's Select Pleas of the Crown, Vol. I.). It had already been engraved in Bysshe's notes to Upton's De Studio Militari, p. 37.

those who were wealthy sometimes forced their poorer adversaries to lavish immense sums on horses and armor.[1] When, however, the spirit of legislation became hostile to the wager of battle, this advantage was taken from the appellant. Frederic II. appears to have been the first to promulgate this rational idea, and, in decreeing that in future the choice of arms shall rest with the defendant, he stigmatizes the previous custom as utterly iniquitous and unreasonable.[2] In this, as in so many other matters, he was in advance of his age, and the general rule was that neither antagonist should have any advantage over the other, except the fearful inequality, to which allusion has already been made, when a roturier dared to challenge a gentleman.[3] In the law of Northern Germany care was taken that the advantage of the sun was equally divided between the combatants; they fought on foot, with bare heads and feet, clad in tunics with sleeves reaching only to the elbow, simple gloves, and no defensive armor except a wooden target covered with hide, and bearing only an iron boss; each carried a drawn sword, but either might have as many more as he pleased in his belt.[4] Even when nobles were concerned, who fought on horseback, it was the rule that they should have no defensive armor save a leather-covered wooden shield and a glove to cover the thumb; the weapons allowed were lance, sword, and dagger, and they fought bare-headed and clad in linen tunics.[5] According to Upton, in the fifteenth century, the judges were bound to see that the arms were equal, but he admits that on many points there were no settled or definite rules.[6] In Wales, an extraordinary custom violated all the principles of equality. Under the Welsh law, twins were considered as one person, and as they were entitled to but one share in the patrimony of the family, so they were allowed to

---

[1] Revue Historique de Droit, 1861, p. 514.

[2] Constit. Sicular. Lib. II. Tit. xxxvii. § 4.

[3] This, moreover, was not permitted by Frederic (*Ubi sup.*).

[4] Jur. Provin. Saxon. I. 63.   [5] Würdinger, Beiträge, p. 22.

[6] De Militari Officio Lib. II. cap. viii.

come into the field of combat as one man.[1]   In Russia, each combatant followed his own pleasure; and a traveller in the sixteenth century relates that the Muscovites were in the habit of embarrassing themselves with defensive armor to an extent which rendered them almost helpless, so that in combats with Poles, Lithuanians, and Germans they were habitually worsted, until judicial duels between natives and foreigners were at length prohibited on this account.[2]

As a general rule the combat ended at sunset or when the stars became visible, and in such case if it was a drawn battle the case was decided in favor of the defendant, because the prosecutor had not proved his charge.   Yet a charter of 961 recites that two gentlemen, Bernard and Gerbert, appeared before Count Raymond, each claiming the church of St. Médard and its appurtenances, which had been bequeathed by the late owner Ricaud, for the repose of his soul, to the Abbey of St. Peter of Beaulieu.   The count granted them the trial by battle.   At two o'clock their champions entered the lists and fought without result until sunset.   Then the count declared the battle ended and adjudged the church to the abbey; the contestants acquiesced and signed the charter confirming its rights.[3]   In Italy, however, the duel was fought to an end; if stopped by darkness the judge was instructed to note carefully the respective positions of the combatants and replace them exactly the next morning, so that neither might derive advantage from the adjournment.[4]

The issue at stake being death or dishonor, with severe penalties hanging over the vanquished, whether principal or champion, no chivalric courtesy was to be expected in these combats.   They were fought to the bitter end with persistent and brutal ferocity, resembling the desperate encounters of wild beasts.   A fairly illustrative example is furnished in an inci-

---

[1] Book of Cynog, chap. xi. § 34 (Owen, II. 211).

[2] Du Boys, op. cit. I. 611.

[3] D'Achery Spicilegium, T. III. p. 376.

[4] Odofredi Summa de Pugna, vii. xi. (Patetta, pp. 490, 491).

dent which followed the assassination of Charles the Good of Flanders in 1127. One of the accomplices, a knight named Guy, was challenged for complicity by another named Herman. Both were renowned warriors, but Herman was speedily unhorsed by his adversary, who with his lance frustrated all his attempts to remount. Then Herman disabled the horse of his opponent and the combat was renewed on foot with swords. Equally skilful in fence they continued the struggle till fatigue compelled them to drop sword and shield and they wrestled for the mastery. Guy threw his antagonist, fell on him and beat him in the face with his gauntlets till he seemed to be motionless, but Herman quietly slipped his hand below the other's coat of mail, grasped his testicles and with a mighty effort wrenched them away. Guy fell over and expired; he we adjudged guilty and his body, after exposure in the pillory, was hung on the top of a mast along with that of the leader of the conspiracy who had been executed the same day, the two corpses being made to embrace each other, as though conferring about the plot.[1] Ghastly details such as these serve to emphasize the difference between the judicial combat and the modern duel.

CHAPTER VII.

CHAMPIONS.

ALLUSIONS have occurred above to the employment of champions, a peculiarity of these combats which received an application sufficiently extended to deserve some special notice.[2]

[1] Galfridi Vit. Caroli Boni, cap. xiii. n. 94.

Similar persistence was exhibited in a combat before Richard II. in 1380. Katrington, the defeated defendant died the next day in delirium caused by exhaustion.—Neilson's Trial by Combat, p. 172.

[2] It is perhaps worthy of remark that in India, where the judicial duel was unknown, in the other ordeals one of the ancient lawgivers, Katyayana, allows, and in some cases prescribes, the use of champions.—Patetta, Le Ordalie, p. 110.

It has been seen that those unable to wield the sword or club were not therefore exempted from the duel, and even the scantiest measure of justice would require that they should have the right to delegate their vindication to some more competent vehicle of the Divine decision. This would seem originally to have been the office of some member of the family, as in the cognate procedure of sacramental purgation. Among the Alamanni, for instance, a woman when accused could be defended by a kinsman *cum tracta spata;*[1] the same rule is prescribed by the Lombard law,[2] and by that of the Angli and Werini;[3] while the universal principle of family unity renders the presumption fair that it prevailed throughout the other races in whose codes it is not specifically indicated. Restricted to cases of disability, the use of champions was a necessity to the battle ordeal; but at a very early period the practice received a remarkable extension, which was directly in conflict with the original principles of the judicial duel, in permitting able-bodied antagonists to put forward substitutes, whether connected with them or not by ties of blood, who fought the battle for their principals. With regard to this there appears to have been a considerable diversity of practice among the races of primitive barbarians. The earliest Frisian laws not only grant unlimited permission for their employment, but even allow them to be hired for money.[4] The laws of the Franks, of the Alamanni, and of the Saxons make no allusion to such a privilege, and apparently expect the principal to defend his rights himself, and yet an instance occurs in 590, where, in a duel fought by order of Gontran, the defendant was allowed to intrust his cause to his nephew, though, as he was accused of killing a stag in the king's forest,

[1] L. Alamann. Add. cap. xxi.

[2] L. Longobard. Lib. i. Tit. iii. § 6, and Lib. ii. Tit. lv. § 12.

[3] L. Anglior. et Werinor. Tit. xiv.

[4] Licet unicuique pro se campionem mercede conducere si eum invenire potuerit.—Ll. Frision. Tit. xiv. c. iv.

physical infirmity could hardly have been pleaded.[1] From some expressions made use of by St. Agobard, in his onslaught on the ordeal of battle, we may fairly presume that, under Louis le Débonnaire, the employment of champions, in the Burgundian law, was, if not forbidden, at least unusual as respects the defendant, even in cases where age or debility unfitted him for the combat, while it was allowed as a matter of course to the appellant.[2] On the other hand, the Baioarian law, which favored the duel more than any of the other cognate codes, alludes to the employment of champions in every reference to it, and with the Lombards the judicial combat and the champion seem to have been likewise convertible terms even with regard to defendants.[3] In a charter of the latter half of the tenth century in France, recording a judicial duel to decide a contest concerning property, the judge, in ordering the combat, calls upon the antagonists to produce skilled champions to defend their claims at the time and place indicated, which would show that the principals were not expected to appear personally.[4] Under the North German law it rested with the appellant to demand the duel either with or without champions. If the defendant were crippled, and was on that account obliged to appear by a hired champion, then the appellant could put forward another to meet him. A defendant, moreover, who had suffered a previous conviction for theft or rapine was always obliged to appear personally. When the duel was decreed by the court, and not demanded

[1] Greg. Turon. Hist. Lib. x. cap. x.   In this case, both combatants perished, when the accused was promptly put to death, showing that such a result was regarded as proving the truth of the offence alleged.

[2] Horum enim causa accidit ut non solum valentes viribus, sed etiam infirmi et senes lacessantur ad certamen et pugnam etiam pro vilissimis rebus (Lib. adv. Legem Gundobadi cap. vii.).   Mitte unum de tuis, qui congrediatur mecum singulari certamine, ut probat me reum tibi esse, si occiderit (Lib. contra Judicium Dei cap i.).

[3] Liceat ei per campionem, id est per pugnam, crimen ipsum de super se si potuerit ejicere.—L. Longobard. Lib. i. Tit. i. § 8.

[4] Proost, Législation des Jugements de Dieu, p. 82.

16

by the appellant, then the accused could decline it if he could prove that the prosecutor had hired a champion.[1] The practical spirit of the Italians led to the universal substitution of champions for the principals; they were selected by the magistrates and were paid by the state when the parties were too poor to bear the expense.[2]

In all these provisions for the putting forward of substitutes in the duel there is something so repugnant to the fierce and self-relying spirit in which the wager of battle found its origin, and the use of a professional gladiator is so inconsistent with the pious reference to the judgment of God, which was the ostensible excuse for the duel, that some external reason is required to account for its introduction. This reason is doubtless to be found in the liberty allowed of challenging witnesses, to which allusion has already been made (p. 121). The prevalence of this throughout Western Europe readily enabled parties, unwilling themselves to encounter the risks of a mortal struggle, to put forward some truculent bravo who swore unscrupulously, and whose evidence would require him to be forced out of court at the sword's point.

This becomes very evident as early as we have detailed regulations of procedure in the books of the twelfth and thirteenth centuries. In England, for instance, until the first statute of Westminster, issued by Edward I., in 1275, the hired champion of the defendant, in a suit concerning real estate, was obliged to assume the position of a witness, by swearing that he had been personally present and had seen seizin given of the land, or that his father when dying had enjoined him by his filial duty to maintain the defendant's

[1] Jur. Provin. Saxon. Lib. I. art. 39, 48.—Sachsische Weichbild, art. xxxv. 2. 4; art. lxxxii. 2.

[2] Patetta, Le Ordalie, pp. 427–9. Roffredo, after carefully enumerating six cases in which champions were allowed by the law, adds: "Hodie tamen de consuetudine permittitur cuilibet campionem dare."—Odofredi Summa de Pugna (Patetta, p. 485).

title as though he had been present.[1]   This legal fiction was
common also to the Norman jurisprudence of the period,
where in such cases the champion of the plaintiff was obliged
to swear that he had heard and seen the matters alleged in
support of the claim, while the opposing champion swore that
they were false.[2]   In a similar spirit, an earlier code of
Normandy prescribes that champions shall be taken to see the
lands and buildings in dispute, before receiving the oath of
battle, in the same manner as a jury of view.[3]   We have seen
that in the Assises d'Antioche it was requisite for a prosecutor
or a plaintiff to have a witness who was ready to offer battle,
in default of which the unsupported oath of the other party
was sufficient to secure a verdict.[4]   It necessarily follows that
this witness must in most cases have been a hired champion,
and this connection between the two functions is further
shown in the regulation of the Assises de Jerusalem and of the
Sicilian constitutions, which directed that the champion should
swear on the field of battle as to his belief in the justice of the
quarrel which he was about to defend,[5] a practice which is
also found in the Scottish law of the thirteenth century.[6]   An
English legal treatise of the period, indeed, assumes that the
principals can put forward only witnesses as substitutes, and
gives as a reason why combats in civil suits were always conducted by champions, that in such cases the principals could
not act as witnesses for themselves.[7]   In a similar spirit, if on
the field of battle one of the parties presented a champion who

---

[1] Glanvil. de Leg. Angl. Lib. II. iii.   Thus in a suit over a knight's fee
in 1201, the plaintiffs offer a champion, Walter Wider, "qui idem optulit ut
de visu suo et auditu."—Baildon, Select Civil Pleas, I. 33.

[2] Cod. Leg. Norman. P. II. cap. lxiv. (Ludewig Reliq. MSS. VII. 416).

[3] Étab. de Normandie, p. 21 (Marnier).

[4] Assises d'Antioche, Haute Cour, ch. ix. xi. xii.; Assises des Bourgeois,
ch. vi. vii.

[5] Assis. Hierosol. Bassa Corte, cap. ccxxxviii. (Canciani, II. 534).—
Constit. Sicular. Lib. II. Tit. xxxvii. § 2.

[6] Neilson's Trial by Combat, pp. 88, 90–1.

[7] Horne's Myrror of Justice, cap. iii. § 23.

was not receivable as a witness and had not been accepted by the court, the case could be decided against him by default.[1]

Looking on the profession of a champion in this light, as that of a witness swearing for hire, we can find a justification for the heavy penalties to which he was subjected in case of defeat—penalties of which the real purport presumably was to insure his fidelity to his principal. Thus, in the Norman coutumier above referred to, in civil suits as to disputed landed possessions, the champion swearing to the truth of his principal's claim was, if defeated, visited with a heavy fine and was declared infamous, being thenceforth incapable of appearing in court either as plaintiff or as witness, while the penalty of the principal was merely the loss of the property in dispute;[2] and a similar principle was recognized in the English law of the period.[3] In criminal cases, from a very early period, while the principal perhaps escaped with fine or imprisonment, the hired ruffian was hanged, or at best lost a hand or foot, the immemorial punishment for perjury;[4] while the laws of the Kingdom of Jerusalem prescribe that in combats between champions, the defeated one shall be promptly hanged, whether dead or alive.[5] The Assises d'Antioche are somewhat more reasonable, for they provide merely that the

[1] Myrror of Justice, cap. iv. § 11.

[2] Cod. Leg. Norman. P. II. cap. lxiv. § 18 (Ludewig VII. 417).

[3] Among the crimes entailing infamy is enumerated that of " ceux qui combatent mortelment pur loyer qui sont vanquish en combate joyné per jugement."—Horne's Myrror of Justice, cap. iv. sect. 13.

[4] Et campioni qui victus fuerit, propter perjuriam quod ante pugnam commisit, dextra manus amputetur (Capit. Ludov. Pii ann. 819, § x.).—Victus vero in duello centum solidos et obolum reddere tenebitur. Pugil vero conductitius, si victus fuerit, pugno vel pede privabitur (Charta ann. 1203—Du Cange).—Also Beaumanoir, Cout. du Beauv., cap. lxvii. § 10 (Du Cange seems to me to have misinterpreted this passage).—See also Monteil's admirable " Histoire des Français des divers États," XVe Siècle, Hist. XIII.

[5] Assis. Hierosol. Bassa Corte, cap. ccxxxviii. Alta Corte, cap. cv. (Canciani II. 534; V. 208).

vanquished champion and his principal shall suffer the same
penalty, whether simply a forfeiture of civil rights in civil
cases, or hanging as in accusations of homicide or other
serious crime.[1] That, in the later periods, at least, the object
of this severity was to prevent the champion from betraying
his employer's cause was freely admitted. Beaumanoir thus
defends it on the ground of the liability of champions to be
bought over by the adverse party, which rendered the gentle
stimulus of prospective mutilation necessary to prevent them
from being purchased by the adversary;[2] and it is probably
owing to this that the full severity of the punishment is shown
to be still in existence by a charter of so late a date as 1372,
when the use of the judicial duel had fully entered on its decline.[3] In the same spirit, the Emperor Frederic II. prohibited champions from bargaining with each other not to use
teeth and hands. He commanded them to inflict all the
injury possible on their adversaries, and decreed that they
should, in case of defeat, share the punishment incurred by
the principal, if the judge of the combat should consider that
through cowardice or treachery they had not conducted the
duel with proper energy and perseverance.[4]

With such risks to be encountered, it is no wonder that the
trade of the champion offered few attractions to honest men,
who could keep body and soul together in any other way.
In primitive times, the solidarity of the family no doubt
caused the champion in most cases to be drawn from among
the kindred; at a later period he might generally be procured

---

[1] Assises d'Antioche, Haute Cour, ch. xi.; Assises des Bourgeois, ch.
vi. vii.

[2] Et li campions vaincus a le poing copé; car se n'estoit por le mehaing
qu'il emporte, aucuns, par barat, se porroit faindre par loier et se clameroit
vaincus, par quoi ses mestres emporteroit le damace et le vilonie, et cil
emporteroit l'argent; et por ce est bons li jugemens du mehaing (Cout.
du Beauv., cap. lxi. § 14).

[3] Isambert, Anciennes Lois Françaises V. 387.

[4] Constit. Sicular. Lib. ii. Tit. xxxvii. § 3.

from among the freedmen or clients of the principal, and an expression in the Lombard law justifies the assumption that this was habitual, among that race at least.[1] In the palmy days of chivalry, it was perhaps not uncommon for the generous knight to throw himself bodily into the lists in defence of persecuted and friendless innocence, as he was bound to do by the tenor of his oath of knighthood.[2] Even as late as the fifteenth century, indeed, in a collection of Welsh laws, among the modes by which a stranger acquired the rights of kindred is enumerated the act of voluntarily undergoing the duel in the place of a principal unable or unwilling to appear for himself.[3] A vast proportion of pleaders, however, would necessarily be destitute of these chances to avoid the personal appearance in the arena for which they might be unfitted or disinclined, and thus there arose the regular profession of the paid gladiator. Reckless desperadoes, skilled at quarter-staff, or those whose familiarity with sword and dagger, gained by a life spent in ceaseless brawls, gave them confidence in their own ability, might undertake it as an occupation which exposed them to little risk beyond what they habitually incurred, and of such was the profession generally composed. This evil must have made itself apparent early, for we find Charlemagne endeavoring to oppose it by decreeing that no robber should be allowed to appear in the lists as a champion, and the order needed to be frequently repeated.[4]

[1] Et post illam inquisitionem, tradat manum ipse camphio in manu parentis aut conliberti sui ante judicem.—L. Longobard. Lib. II. Tit. lv. § 11.

[2] Thus the oath administered by the papal legate to William of Holland, on his receiving knighthood previous to his coronation as King of the Romans in 1247, contains the clause "pro liberatione cujuslibet innocentis duellum inire.' —Goldast. Constit. Imp. T. III. p. 400.

[3] Anomalous Laws, Book x. chap. ii. § 9 (Owen, II. 315). The position thus acquired was that of brother or nephew in sharing and paying *wer-gild.*

[4] Ut nemo furem camphium mancipiis aut de qualibet causa recipere præsumat, sicut sæpius dominus imperator commendavit.—Capit. Carol. Mag. ex L. Longobard. cap. xxxv. (Baluze).

When the Roman law commenced to exercise its powerful influence in moulding the feudal customs into a regular body of procedure, and admiring jurists lost no opportunity of making use of the newly-discovered treasures of legal lore, whether applicable or not, it is easy to understand that the contempt and the civil disabilities lavished by the Imperial jurisprudence on the gladiator of antiquity came to be transferred to the mediæval champion ; although the latter, by the theory of the law, stood forth to defend the innocent, while the former ignobly exposed his life for the gratification of an imbruted populace. This legacy of shame is clearly traceable in Pierre de Fontaines. To be a gladiator or an actor was, by the Roman law, a competent cause for disinheritance.[1] One of the texts prescribing it is translated bodily by de Fontaines, the *arenarius* of the Roman becoming the *champions* of the Frenchman ;[2] and in another similar transcription from the Digest, the *athleta* of the original is transformed into a "champion."[3] By the thirteenth century, the occupation of champion had thus become infamous. Its professors were classed with the vilest criminals, and with the unhappy females who exposed their charms for sale, as the champion did his skill and courage.[4] They were held incapable of appearing as witnesses, and the extraordinary anomaly was exhibited of seeking to learn the truth in affairs of the highest moment by a solemn appeal to God, through the instrumentality of those who were already considered as convicts of the worst kind, or

[1] Novel. cxv. cap. iii. § 10—more fully set forth in Lib. III. Cod. Tit. xxvii. l. 11.

[2] Conseil. chap. xxxiii. tit. 32.

[3] Ibid. chap. xv. tit. 87, which is a translation of Lib. IV. Dig. Tit. ii. l. 23, § 2.

[4] Percutiat si quis hominem infamem, hoc est lusorem vel pugilem, aut mulierem publicam, etc.—Sachsische Weichbild, Art. cxxix. " Plusieurs larrons, ravisseurs de femmes, violleurs d'églises, batteurs à loyer," etc.— Ordonn. de Charles VII. ann. 1447, also Anciennes Coutumes de Bretagne (Monteil, *ubi sup.*).

who, by the very act, were branded with infamy if successful in justifying innocence, and if defeated were mutilated or hanged.[1] By the codes in force throughout Germany in the thirteenth and fourteenth centuries, they were not only, in common with bastards, actors, and jugglers, deprived of all legal privileges, such as succeeding to property, bearing witness, etc., but even their children were visited with the same disabilities.[2] The utter contempt in which they were held was moreover quaintly symbolized in the same codes by the provisions of a tariff of damages to be assessed for blows and other personal injuries. A graduated list of fines is given for such insults offered to nobles, merchants, peasants, etc., in compensation of their wounded honor; below the serf come the mountebank and juggler, who could only cuff the assailant's shadow projected on the wall; and last of all are rated the champion and his children, whose only redress was a glance of sunshine cast upon them by the offender from a duelling shield. Deemed by law incapable of receiving an insult, the satisfaction awarded was as illusory as the honor to be repaired.[3] That this poetical justice was long in vogue is proved by the commentary upon it in the Richstich Landrecht, of which the

---

[1] Johen de Beaumont dit que chanpions loiez, prové de tel chose, ne puet home apelier á gage de bataille an nul quas, si n'est por chanpion loiez por sa deffansse; car la poine de sa mauvese vie le doit bien en ce punir.—Livres de Jostice et de Plet, Liv. XIX. Tit. ii. § 4.

[2] Campiones et eorum liberi (ita nati) et omnes qui illegitime nati sunt, et omnes qui furti aut pleni latrocinii nomine satisfecere, aut fustigationem sustinuere, hi omnes juris beneficiis carent.—Jur. Provin. Alaman. cap. xxxvi. § 2 (Ed. Schilter.).—Jur. Provin. Saxon. Lib. III. c. xlv.

[3] Campionibus et ipsorum liberis emendæ loco datur fulgur ex clypeo nitido, qui soli obvertitur, ortum; hoc is qui eis satisfactionem debet loco emendæ præstare tenetur (Jur. Prov. Alaman. cap. cccv. § 15.—Jur. Provin. Saxon. Lib. III. art. xlv.). In the French version of the Speculum Suevicum, these emblematic measures of damage are followed by the remark "cestes emandes furent establies an la vieillie loy per les roys" (P. II. c. lxxxvi.), which would appear to show that they were disused in the territories for which the translation was made.

date is shown to be not earlier than the close of the fourteenth century, by an allusion in the same chapter to accidental deaths arising from the use of firearms.[1]

The Italians, however, took a more sensible and practical view of the matter. Accepting as a necessity the existence of champions as a class, they were disposed rather to elevate than to degrade the profession. The law required that they should not be criminals or infamous, and the fact that they fought for hire did not render them so.[2] In the Veronese code of 1228, they appear as an established institution, consisting of individuals selected and appointed by the magistrates, who did not allow them to receive more than one hundred sous for the performance of their office.[3]

It is evident that the evils attendant upon the employment of champions were generally recognized, and it is not singular that efforts were occasionally made to abrogate or limit the practice. Otho II., whose laws did so much to give respectability to the duel, decreed that champions should be permitted only to counts, ecclesiastics, women, boys, old men, and cripples.[4] That this rule was strictly enforced in some places we may infer from the pleadings of a case occurring in 1010 before the Bishop of Arezzo, concerning a disputed property, wherein a crippled right hand is alleged as the reason for allowing a champion to one of the parties.[5] In other parts of Italy, however, the regulation must have been speedily disregarded, for about the same period Henry II. found it necessary to promulgate a law forbidding the employment of substitutes to able-bodied defendants in cases of parricide or of aggravated murder;[6] and when, two hundred years later, Frederic II. almost abolished the judicial combat in his

---

[1] Richstich Landrecht, Lib. II. cap. xxv.

[2] Odofredi Summa de Pugna c. v. (Patetta, p. 489).

[3] Lib. Juris Civilis Veron. cap. 125, 126 (Veronæ, 1728, p. 95).

[4] L. Longobard. Lib. II. Tit. lv. §§ 38, 40.

[5] Muratori, Antiq. Ital. Dissert. 39.

[6] L. Longobard. Lib. I. Tit. ix. § 37; Tit. x. § 4.

Neapolitan dominions, we may fairly presume from one of his remarks that champions were universally employed.[1] Indeed, he made provision for supplying them at the public expense to widows, orphans, and paupers who might be unable to secure for themselves such assistance.[2] In Germany, early in the eleventh century, it would seem that champions were a matter of course, from the expressions made use of in describing the execution of a number of robbers convicted in this manner at Merseburg in 1017.[3] At a later period, it seems probable, from a comparison of two chapters of the Suabian laws, that efforts were made to prevent the hiring of professional gladiators,[4] and in the Saxon burgher laws a man could refuse the duel if he could prove that his antagonist was a champion serving for pay.[5] That these efforts to restrict the practice, however, were attended with little success may be inferred from the disabilities which were so copiously showered on the class by the same laws.

In England, where, as we have seen, the identity of champions and witnesses was clearly asserted, there were prolonged efforts to suppress their hiring. In 1150, Henry II. strictly prohibited the wager of battle with hired champions in his Norman territories;[6] although the Norman custom not only admitted them but required the principal to pay the full sum agreed upon to his champion whether defeated or not.[7] We learn from Glanville that a champion suspected of serving for money might be objected to by the opposite party, whence arose a secondary combat to determine his fitness for the

---

[1] Vix enim aut nunquam duo pugiles inveniri poterunt sic æquales, etc.—Constit. Sicular. Lib. II. Tit. xxxiii.

[2] Ibid. Lib. I. Tit. xxxiii.

[3] Ibi tunc multi latrones a gladiatoribus singulari certamine devicti, suspendio perierunt.—Dithmari. Chron. Lib. VII.

[4] Jur. Provin. Alaman. cap. xxxvi. § 2; cap. lx. § 1.

[5] Sachsische Weichbild, c. lxxxii. § 3.

[6] Concil. Eccles. Rotomag. p. 128 (Du Cange).

[7] Cod. Leg. Norman. P. II. c. lxiv. § 19 (Ludewig. VII. 416).

primary one.[1]   Bracton, moreover, develops this by asserting as a rule that a witness suspected of being a hired champion was not allowed to proceed to the combat, but was tried for the attempt by a jury, and if convicted suffered the penalty of perjury in the loss of a hand or a foot,[2] and in another passage he states that hired champions were not permitted.[3]   How far these rules were enforced it would now be difficult to determine.   Records show that a frequent defence against an adverse witness was an offer to prove that he was a hired champion.[4]   On the other hand, the payment of champions was frequent and no concealment seems to have been thought necessary concerning it.   Towards the close of the twelfth century, by a charter Stephen de Nerbana grants two *virgata* of land to William son of Ralph " propter duellum quod fecit pro me."[5]   In another charter of Bracton's date John " quondam porcarius de Coldingham" grants to the Priory of Coldingham a tract of land which he had received from Adam de Riston in payment for victoriously fighting a duel for him.[6]

[1] De Leg. Angliæ Lib. II. cap. iii.

[2] Bracton, Lib. III. Tract. ii. cap. 32 § 7.

[3] Ibid. c. 18 § 4.

[4] See a case in which Ralph Rusdike, a witness, offers battle against Elias of Dumbleton—" et Elias defendit totum versus eum ut versus campionem conductitium et villanus."   Then Ralph shows that he has an interest in the matter which warrants his acting as appellor and battle is gaged. —Maitland's Select Pleas of the Crown, Vol. I. p. 80.   Also another case in 1220 in which the appellant offers a silver mark to the king for opportunity to prove that an adverse witness is a hired champion.—Ib. p. 124. Another case in 1220 (p. 137) shows how customary it was to impugn an adverse witness as a hired champion.

[5] Neilson's Trial by Combat, p. 49.

[6] This charter, which has recently been found among the records of Durham Cathedral, is printed in the London *Athenæum* of November 10th, 1866.   It is not dated, but the names of the subscribing witnesses show that it must have been executed about the year 1260.

I owe to James Clephan, Esq., of Newcastle-on-Tyne, the interesting fact that the Sherburn Hospital, Durham, is still in possession of the vill of Garmondsway which was bestowed upon it in the latter ha.f of the twelfth

Even more significant are the formal agreements with champions, such as that by which in 1276 Bishop Swinefeld declares to all men that he has appointed Thomas of Brydges his champion, on a salary of 6s. 8d. per annum, so long as he shall be able to fight, with extra compensation in case he is called upon to perform his functions.[1] Eventually, as we have seen (p. 183), in civil cases, both parties were compelled by law to employ champions, which presupposes, as a matter of course, that in a great majority of instances the substitutes must have been hired.[2] In criminal cases there seems to have been a compromise; in felonies, the defendant was obliged to appear personally, while in accusations of less moment he was at liberty to put forward a witness as champion;[3] and when the appellant, from sex or other disability, or the defendant from age, was unable to undergo the combat personally, it was forbidden, and the case was decided by a jury.[4] By the Scottish law of the thirteenth century, it is evident that champions were not allowed in any case, since those disabled by age or wounds were forced to undergo the ordeal in order to escape the duel.[5] This strictness became relaxed in time, though the practice of employing champions seems never to have received much encouragement. By a law of Alexander II., about the

century by Ralph, son of Paulinus of York, who had obtained it as the result of a judicial combat between his champion and that of the opposing claimants.

[1] Neilson, Trial by Combat, p. 51.

[2] Lord Eldon, in his speech advocating the abolition of trial by battle, in 1819, stated, "In these the parties were not suffered to fight *in propria persona*—they were compelled to confide their interests to champions, on the principle that if one of the parties were slain, the suit would abate."—Campbell's Lives of the Chancellors, VII. 279.

[3] Pur felony ne poit nul combattre pur autre; en personal actions nequidant venials, list aux actors de faire les battailes per lour corps ou per loyal tesmoigne come en droit reals sont les combats.—Horne's Myrror of Justice, cap. iii. sect. 23.

[4] Bracton. Lib. III. Tract. ii. cap. 21, §§ 11, 12.—Ibid. cap. 24.

[5] Regiam Majestatem, Lib. IV. cap. iii.

year 1250, it appears that a noble had the privilege of putting forward a substitute ; but if a peasant challenged a noble, he was obliged to appear personally, unless his lord undertook the quarrel for him and presented the champion as from himself.[1]

The tendency exhibited by the English law in distinguishing between civil and criminal cases is also manifested elsewhere. Thus, in France and the Frankish kingdoms of the East, there were limitations placed by law on the employment of champions in prosecutions for crime,[2] while in civil actions there appear to have been, at least in France, no restrictions whatever.[3] This distinction between civil and criminal practice is very clearly enunciated by Pierre de Fontaines, who states that in appeal of judgment the appellant in criminal cases is bound to show satisfactory cause for employing a champion, while in civil affairs the right to do so requires no argument.[4] In practice, however, it is doubtful whether there was any effectual bar to their use in any case, for the Monk of St. Denis, in praising St. Louis for suppressing the battle-trial, gives as one of the benefits of its abrogation, the removal of the abuse by which a rich man could buy all the champions of the vicinity, so that a poorer antagonist had no resource to avoid the loss of life or heritage.[5] This hiring of champions, moreover, was legally recognized as a necessity attendant upon the privilege of employing them.[6]   High rank, or a marked differ-

---

[1] Neilson's Trial by Combat, p. 115.   By the Burgher laws of Scotland, a man who was incapacitated by reason of age from appearing in the field, was allowed to defend himself with twelve conjurators.—L. Burgor. cap. xxiv. §§ 1, 2.

[2] Assises de Jerusalem, Baisse Court, cap. 145, 146.—Beaumanoir, cap. lxi. § 6; cap. lxii. § 4.

[3] Beaumanoir, cap. lxi. § 14.   [4] Conseil, chap. XXII. Tit. xiii.

[5] Grandes Chroniques T. IV. p. 427.

[6] Il est usage que se aucun demende la cort de bataille qui est juege par champions loées, il la tendra le jor maimes, et si ele est par le cors des quereléors il metra jor avenant à la tenir autre que celui.—Coutumes d'Anjou, XIII.ᵉ Siècle, § 74.

ence between the station of parties to an action, was also admitted as justifying the superior in putting forward a champion in his place.[1] Local variations, however, are observable
in the customs regulating these matters. Thus the municipal
laws of Reims, in the fourteenth century, not only restrict
the admission of champions in criminal matters to cases in
which age or physical disability may incapacitate the principals from personally taking part in the combat, but also require the accused to swear that the impediment has supervened
since the date of the alleged offence; and even this was of
no avail if the prosecutor had included in his appeal of battle
an assertion that such disability had existed at the time specified.[2] Witnesses obliged to support their testimony by the
duel were not only subject to the same restrictions, but in
substituting a hired gladiator were obliged to swear that they
had vainly sought among their friends for some one to assume
the office voluntarily.[3] The whole tenor of these provisions,
indeed, manifests a decided intention to surround the employment of champions with every practicable impediment. In
Béarn, again, the appellant in cases of treason had a right to
decide whether the defendant should be allowed to put forward a substitute, and from the expressions in the text it may
be inferred that in the selection of champions there was an
endeavor to secure equality of age, size, and strength.[4] This
equalization of chances was thoroughly carried out in Italy,
where the law required them to be selected with that view.[5]

[1] Kar haute persone doit bien metre por lui, à deffendre soi, home,
honeste persone, se l'an l'apele, ou s'il apele autre.—Livres de Jostice et
de Plet, Liv. II. Tit. xviii.

[2] Lib. Pract. de Consuet. Remens. § 40 (Archives Législ. de Reims,
Pt. I. p. 40).

[3] Ibid. § 14; p. 37.

[4] For de Morlaas, Rubr. liii. art. 188.

[5] Quando pugna debet fieri per campionem debet fieri eorum equa dis-
tributio . . . et etiam jure longobardo cavetur quod pugna debet fieri per
similes campiones.—Odofredi Summa de Pugna c. iv. (Patetta, p. 488).

Thus in the Veronese code of 1228, where, as has been seen, the champions were a recognized body, regulated and controlled by the state, no one could engage a champion before a duel had been judicially decreed.   Then the magistrate was bound to choose gladiators of equal prowess, and the choice between them was given to the defendant; an arrangement which rendered the mutilation inflicted on the vanquished combatant only justifiable on the score of suspected treachery.[1] A Bolognese regulation of the thirteenth century was even fairer, and reduced the combat to an affair of chance in which the judgment of God had the fullest scope, for when the champions were in the lists a child placed inside of the garments of each a card bearing the name of his principal, and until the combat was ended no one knew which of them represented the plaintiff and which the defendant.[2] In Bigorre, the only restriction seems to have been that champions should be natives and not foreigners, and their payment was recognized as a matter of course.[3] By the Spanish law of the thirteenth century, the employment of champions was so restricted as to show an evident desire on the part of the legislator to discourage it as far as possible.   The defendant had the right to send a substitute into the field, but the appellant could do so only by consent of his adversary.   The champion was required to be of birth equal to his principal, which rendered the hiring of champions almost impossible, and not superior to him in force and vigor.   Women and minors appeared by their next of kin, and ecclesiastics by their advocates.[4] In Russia, until the sixteenth century, champions were never employed, contestants being always obliged to appear in person.   In 1550,

---

[1] L. Jur. Civilis Veronæ cap. 125, 126 (p. 95).

[2] Patetta, Le Ordalie, pp. 427-9.

[3] Pugiles in Bigorra non nisi indigenæ recipiantur (Lagrèze, Hist. du Droit dans les Pyrénées, p. 251). By the same code, the tariff of payment to the champion was 20 sous, with 12 for his shield and 6 for training— "pro præparatione."

[4] Las Siete Partidas, Pt. VII. Tit. iv. l. 3.

the code known as the Sudebtnick at length permitted the employment of champions in certain cases.[1]

There were two classes of pleaders, however, with whom the hiring of champions was a necessity, and who could not be bound by the limitations imposed on ordinary litigants. While the sexagenary, the infant, and the crippled might possibly find a representative among their kindred, and while the woman might appear by her husband or next of kin, the ecclesiastical foundations and chartered towns had no such resource. Thus, in a suit for taxes, in 1164, before the court of Verona, Bonuszeno of Soavo proved that the village of Soavo had exempted his father Petrobatalla from all local imposts for having served as champion in a duel between it and a neighboring community, and his claim to the reversion of the exemption was allowed.[2] So a charter of 1104 relates how the monks of Noailles were harassed by the seizure of some mills belonging to their abbey, claimed by an official of William Duke of Aquitaine, until at length the duke agreed to allow the matter to be decided by the duel, when the champion of the church was victorious and the disputed property was confirmed to the abbey.[3] At length the frequent necessity for this species of service led to the employment of regularly appointed champions, who fought the battles of their principals for an annual stipend, or for some other advantages bestowed in payment. Du Cange, for instance, gives the text of an agreement by which one Geoffry Blondel, in 1256, bound himself to the town of Beauvais as its champion for a yearly salary of twenty sous Parisis, with extra gratifications of ten livres Tournois every time that he appeared in arms to defend its cause, fifty livres if blows were exchanged, and a hundred livres if the combat were carried to a triumphant issue. It is

---

[1] Du Boys, Droit Criminel des Peuples Modernes, I. 611–13.

[2] Campagnola, Lib. Juris Civ. Veronæ (Veronæ, 1728, p. xviii).

[3] Polyptichum Irminonis, App. No. 33 (Paris, 1836, p. 372).

a little singular that Beaumanoir, in digesting the customs of Beauvais but a few years later, speaks of this practice as an ancient and obsolete one, of which he had only heard through tradition.[1] That it continued to be in vogue until long after, is shown by Monteil, who alludes to several documents of the kind, bearing date as late as the fifteenth century.[2]

As a rule, ecclesiastical communities were likewise under the necessity of employing champions to defend their rights. Sometimes, as we have seen, these were hired, and were of no better character than those of common pleaders. They seem to have been well paid if we may judge from an agreement of 1258 between the Abbey of Glastonbury and Henry de Fernbureg, by which the latter bound himself to defend by battle the rights of the abbey to certain manors against the Bishop of Bath and Wells, for which he is to receive thirty sterling marks, of which ten are to be paid when battle is gaged, five when he is shaved for the combat, and on the day of the duel fifteen are to be placed in the hands of a third party to be paid over to him if he strikes a single blow.[3] Sometimes, however, gentlemen did not disdain to serve God by fighting for the Church in special cases, as when, so late as the middle of the fourteenth century, the priory of Tynemouth had a suit with a troublesome neighbor, Gerard de Widdrington, over the manor of Hawkshaw, and Sir Thomas Colville, who had won great renown in the French wars, appeared in court as its champion and offered the combat. No one could be found hardy enough to accept his challenge

[1] Une malvese coustume souloit courre anciemment, si comme nos avons entendu des seigneurs de lois.—Cout. du Beauvoisis, cap. xxxviii. § 15.

[2] Hist. des Français, XVe Siècle, Hist. xiii.—The tariff of rewards paid to Blondel, and Beaumanoir's argument in favor of mutilating a defeated champion, offer a strong practical commentary on the fundamental principles upon which the whole system of appeals to the judgment of God was based—that success was an evidence of right.

[3] Bysshe's notes to Upton's De Studio Militari, p. 36.

and the manor was adjudged to the priory.[1] There was, moreover, another class of champions of the Church who occupied a distinguished position, and were bound to defend the interests of their clients in the field as well as in the court and in the lists; they also led the armed retainers of the church when summoned by the suzerain to national war. The office was honorable and lucrative, and was eagerly sought by gentlemen of station, who turned to account the opportunities of aggrandizement which it afforded; and many a noble family traced its prosperity to the increase of ancestral property thus obtained, directly or indirectly, by espousing the cause of fat abbeys and wealthy bishoprics, as when, in the ninth century, the Abbot of Figeac, near Cahors, bestowed on a neighboring lord sixty churches and five hundred mansi on condition of his fighting the battles of the abbey.[2] The influence of feudalism early made itself felt, and the office of *Vidame* or *Avoué* became generally hereditary, after which its possessors, for the most part, rendered themselves independent of their benefactors, their exactions and spoliations becoming a favorite theme of objurgation among churchmen, who regarded them as the worst enemies of the foundations which they had sworn to protect.[3] In many instances the position was a consideration obtained for donations bestowed upon churches, so that in some countries, and particularly in England, the title of *advocatus* became gradually recognized as synonymous with patron. Thus, one of the worst abuses of the Anglican Church is derived from this source, and the forgotten wrongs of the Middle Ages are perpetuated, etymologically at least, in the advowson which renders the cure of souls too often a matter of bargain and sale.

[1] Neilson's Trial by Combat, p. 150.

[2] Hist. Monast. Figeacens. (Baluz. et Mansi IV. p. 1).

[3] Abbonis Floriac. Collect. Canon. can. ii.—Histor. Trevirens. (D'Achery Spicileg. II. 223).—Gerohi Reichersperg. de Ædificio Dei cap. VI.

CHAPTER VIII.

DECLINE OF THE JUDICIAL COMBAT.

So many influences were at work in favor of the judicial duel, and it was so thoroughly engrafted in the convictions and prejudices of Europe, that centuries were requisite for its extirpation.   Curiously enough, the earliest decisive action against it took place in Iceland, where it was formally interdicted as a judicial proceeding in 1011 ;[1] and though the assumption that this was owing to the introduction of Christianity has been disproved, still, the fact that both events were contemporaneous allows us to conclude that some influence may have been exercised by even so imperfect a religion as that taught to the new converts, though the immediate cause was a *holmgang* between two skalds of distinction, Gunnlaug Ormstunga and Skald-Rafn.[2]   Norway was not long in following the example, for about the same period the Jarls Erik and Sven Hakonsen abolished the *holmgang*, while paganism was as yet widely prevalent.[3]   Denmark was almost equally prompt : indeed Saxo Grammaticus

---

[1] Schlegel Comment. ad Grágás, p. xxii.—Dasent, in his Icelandic Chronology (Burnt Njal, I. cciii.), places this in 1006, and Keyser (Religion of the Northmen, Pennock's Trans. p. 258) in 1000.

[2] The kind of Christianity introduced may be estimated by the character of the Apostle of Iceland.   Deacon Thangbrand was the son of Willibald Count of Saxony, and even after he had taken orders continued to ply his old vocation of viking or sea robbing.   To get rid of him and to punish him, King Olaf Tryggvesson of Norway imposed upon him the task of converting Iceland, which he accomplished with the sword in one hand and the Bible in the other.—See Dasent, Burnt Njal, II. 361.—Olaf Tryggvesson's Saga c. lxxx. (Laing's Heimskringla, I. 441).

[3] Keyser, op. cit. p. 258.

in one passage attributes to it the priority, asserting that when Poppo, in 965, converted Harold Blaatand by the ordeal of red-hot iron, it produced so powerful an effect as to induce the substitution of that mode of trial for the previously existing wager of battle.[1] Yet it evidently was not abolished for a century later, for when Harold the Simple, son of Sven Estrith, ascended the throne in 1074, among the legal innovations which he introduced was the substitution of the purgatorial oath for all other forms of defence, which, as Saxo specifically states, put an end to the wager of battle, and opened the door to great abuses.[2]

Fiercer tribes than these in Europe there were none, and their abrogation of the battle trial at this early age is an inexplicable anomaly. It was an exceptional movement, however, without results beyond their own narrow boundaries. Other causes had to work slowly and painfully for ages before man could throw off the bonds of ancestral prejudice. One of the most powerful of these causes was the gradual rise of the Tiers-État to consideration and importance. The sturdy bourgeois, though ready enough with morion and pike to defend their privileges, were usually addicted to a more peaceful mode of settling private quarrels. Devoted to the arts of peace, seeing their interest in the pursuits of industry and commerce, enjoying the advantage of settled and permanent tribunals, and exposed to all the humanizing and civilizing influences of close association in communities, they speedily acquired ideas of progress very different from those of the savage feudal nobles living isolated in their fastnesses, or of the wretched serfs who crouched for protection around the castles of their masters. Accordingly, the desire to escape from the necessity of purgation by battle is almost coeval with the founding of the first communes. The earliest instance of this tendency that I have met with is contained in the charter granted to Pisa by the Emperor Henry IV. in 1081, by which

---

[1] Saxon. Grammat. Hist. Dan. Lib. x.   [2] Ibid. Lib. xi.

he agrees that any accusations which he may bring against
citizens can be tried without battle by the oaths of twelve
compurgators, except when the penalties of death or mutilation
are involved ; and in questions concerning land, the duel is
forbidden when competent testimony can be procured.[1] Limited
as these concessions may seem, they were an immense innovation on the prejudices of the age, and are important as affording the earliest indication of the direction which the new
civilization was assuming.   More comprehensive was the
privilege granted soon afterwards by Henry I. to the citizens
of London, by which he released them wholly from the duel,
and this was followed by similar exemptions during the twelfth
century bestowed on one town after another; but it was not
till near the end of the century that in Scotland William the
Lion granted the first charter of this kind to Inverness.[2]
About the year 1105, the citizens of Amiens received a charter
from their bishop, St. Godfrey, in which the duel is subjected
to some restriction—not enough in itself, perhaps, to effect
much reform, yet clearly showing the tendency which existed.
According to the terms of this charter no duel could be decreed concerning any agreement entered into before two or
three magistrates if they could bear witness to its terms.[3]
One of the earliest instances of absolute freedom from the
judicial combat occurs in a charter granted to the town of
Ypres, in 1116 by Baldwin VII. of Flanders, when he substituted the oath with four conjurators in all cases where the
duel or the ordeal was previously in use.[4] This was followed
by a similar grant to the inhabitants of Bari by Roger, King

---

[1] Lünig Cod. Diplom. Ital. I. 2455.—The liberal terms of this charter
show the enlightenment of the Emperor, and explain the fidelity manifested
for him by the imperial cities in his desperate struggles with his rebellious
nobles and an implacable papacy.

[2] Neilson's Trial by Combat, pp. 33, 65, 97.

[3] Chart. Commun. Ambianens. c. 44 (Migne's Patrolog. T. 162, p. 750).

[4] The charter is given by Proost, op. cit. p. 96.

of Naples, in 1132.[1] Curiously enough, almost contemporary
with this is a similar exemption bestowed on the rude mountaineers of the Pyrenees.   Centulla I. of Bigorre, who died in
1138, in the Privileges of Lourdes, authorizes the inhabitants
to prosecute their claims without the duel;[2] and his desire to
discourage the custom is further shown by a clause permitting
the pleader who has gaged his battle to withdraw on payment
of a fine of only five sous to the seigneur, in addition to what
the authorities of the town may levy.[3] Still more decided
was a provision of the laws of Soest in Westphalia, somewhat
earlier than this, by which the citizens were absolutely prohibited from appealing each other in battle;[4] and this is also
to be found in a charter granted to the town of Tournay by
Philip Augustus in 1187, though in the latter the cold water
ordeal is prescribed for cases of murder and of wounding by
night.[5] In the laws of Ghent, granted by Philip of Alsace in
1178, there is no allusion to any species of ordeal, and all
proceedings seem to be based on the ordinary processes of law,
while in the charter of Nieuport, bestowed by the same prince
in 1163, although the ordeal of red-hot iron and compurgatorial
oaths are freely alluded to as means of rebutting accusations,
there is no reference whatever to the battle trial, showing that
it must then have been no longer in use.[6] The charters
granted to Medina de Pomar in 1219 by Fernando III. of
Castile, and to Treviño by Alfonso X. in 1254, provide that

[1] Ferrum, cacavum, pugnam, aquam, vobis non judicabit vel judicari
faciet (Muratori, Antiq. Ital. Dissert. 38).

[2] Priviléges de Lourdes, cap. ii. (Lagrèze, op. cit. p. 482).

[3] Ibid., cap. xiii. (Lagrèze p. 484).   These privileges were confirmed at
various epochs, until 1407.

[4] Statuta Susatensia, No. 41 (Hæberlin Analect. Med. Ævi. p. 513).
This is retained in the subsequent recension of the law, in the thirteenth
century (Op. cit. p. 526).

[5] Consuetud. Tornacens. ann. 1187, §§ ii. iii. xxi (D'Achery Spicileg. III.
552).

[6] Oudegherst, Annales de Flandre ed. Lesbroussart. T. I. pp. 426 sqq.;
T. II. not. ad. fin.

there shall be no trial by single combat.[1]   Louis VIII. in the
charter of Crespy, granted in 1223, promised that neither
himself nor his officials should in future have the right to demand the wager of battle from its inhabitants;[2] and shortly
after, the laws of Arques, conceded by the abbey of St. Bertin
in 1231, provided that the duel could only be decreed between
two citizens of that commune when both parties should assent
to it.[3]   In the same spirit the laws of Riom, granted by
Alphonse de Poitiers, the son of St. Louis, in 1270, declared
that no inhabitant of the town should be forced to submit to
the wager of battle.[4]   In the customs of Maubourguet, granted
in 1309, by Bernard VI. of Armagnac, privileges similar to
those of Lourdes, alluded to above, were included, rendering
the duel a purely voluntary matter.[5]   Even in Scotland, partial
exemptions of the same kind in favor of towns are found as
early as the twelfth century.   A stranger could not force a
burgher to fight, except on an accusation of treachery or theft,
while, if a burgher desired to compel a stranger to the duel,
he was obliged to go beyond the confines of the town.   A
special privilege was granted to the royal burghs, for their
citizens could not be challenged by the burghers of nobles or
prelates, while they had the right to offer battle to the latter.[6]
Much more efficient was the clause of the third *Keure* of
Bruges, granted in 1304 by Philip son of Count Guy of
Flanders, which strictly prohibited the duel.   Any one who

[1] Coleccion de Cédulas, etc., Madrid, 1830, Tom. VI. p. 142.—Memorial
Histórico Español, Madrid, 1850, T. I. p. 47.

[2] Statuta Commun. apud Crispiacum (D'Achery Spicileg. III. 595).

[3] Legg. Villæ de Arkes ⚹ xxxi. (Ibid. p. 608).

[4] Libertates Villæ Ricomag. § 6 (Ibid. p. 671).

[5] E sobre ayso que dam e autreyam als borges de la vielle de Maubourguet que totz los embars pusquen provar sens batalhe, etc.—Coutumes de
Maubourguet, cap. v. That this, however, was not expected to do away
entirely with the battle trial is shown by the regulation prescribed in cap.
xxxvii. (Lagrèze, op. cit. pp. 470, 474).

[6] L. Burgorum, c. 14, 15 (Skene).

gave or received a wager of battle was fined sixty sols, one-half for the benefit of the town, and the other for the count.[1]

The special influence exercised by the practical spirit of trade in rendering the duel obsolete is well illustrated by the privilege granted, in 1127, by William Clito, to the merchants of St. Omer, declaring that they should be free from all appeals to single combat in all the markets of Flanders.[2] In a similar spirit, when Frederic Barbarossa, in 1173, was desirous of attracting to the markets of Aix-la-Chapelle and Duisbourg the traders of Flanders, in the code which he established for the protection of such as might come, he specially enacted that they should enjoy immunity from the duel.[3] Even Russia found it advantageous to extend the same exemption to foreign merchants, and in the treaty which Mstislas Davidovich made in 1228 with the Hanse-town of Riga, he granted to the Germans who might seek his dominions immunity from liability to the red-hot iron ordeal and wager of battle.[4]

Germany seems to have been somewhat later than France or Italy in the movement, yet her burghers evidently regarded it with favor.   Frederic II., who recorded his disapproval of the duel in his Sicilian Constitutions, was ready to encourage them in this tendency, and in his charters to Ratisbon and Vienna he authorized their citizens to decline the duel and clear themselves by compurgation,[5] while as early as 1219 he exempted the Nürnbergers from the appeal of battle throughout the empire.[6] The burgher law of Northern Germany alludes to the judicial combat only in criminal charges, such

---

[1] Warnkönig, Hist. de la Flandre, IV. 129.

[2] In omni mercato Flandriæ si quis clamorem adversus eos suscitaverit, judicium scabinorum de omni clamore sine duello subeant; ab duello vero ulterius liberi sint.—Warnkönig. Hist. de la Flandre, II. 411.

[3] Nemo mercatorem de Flandria duello provocabit (Ibid. II. 426).

[4] Traité de 1228, art. 3 (Esneaux, Hist. de Russie, II. 272).

[5] Belitz de Duellis Germanorum, p. 9.   Vitembergæ, 1717.

[6] Constit. Frid II. de Jur. Norimb. § 4 (Goldast. Constit. Imp. I. 291).

as violence, homicide, housebreaking, and theft;[1] and this is limited in the statutes of Eisenach, of 1283, which provide that no duel shall be adjudged in the town, except in cases of homicide, and then only when the hand of the murdered man shall be produced in court at the trial.[2] In 1291, Rodolph of Hapsburg issued a constitution declaring that the burghers of the free imperial cities should not be liable to the duel outside of the limits of their individual towns,[3] and in the Kayser-Recht this privilege is extended by declaring the burghers exempt from all challenge to combat, except in a suit brought by a fellow-citizen.[4] Notwithstanding this, special immunities continued to be granted, showing that these general laws were of little effect unless supported by the temper of the people. Thus Louis IV. in 1332 gave such a privilege to Dortmund, and so late as 1355 Charles IV. bestowed it on the citizens of Worms.[5]

A somewhat noteworthy exception to this tendency on the part of the municipalities is to be found in Moravia. There, under the laws of Ottokar Premizlas, in 1229 the duel was forbidden between natives and only allowed when one of the parties was a foreigner. Yet his son Wenceslas, some years later, confirmed the customs of the town of Iglau, in which the duel was a recognized feature enforced by an ascending scale of fines. If the accused compounded with the prosecutor before the duel was ordered he paid the judge one mark; after it was adjudged, two marks; after the lists were entered, three marks;

---

[1] Sachsische Weichbild, Art. xxxv. lxxii. lxxxi.–lxxxiv. lxxxix. xc. xcii. cxiv.

[2] Henke, Gesch. des Deut. Peinlichen Rechts I. 192 (Du Boys, op. cit. II. 590).

[3] Goldast. op. cit. I. 314.

[4] Jur. Cæsar. P. iv. cap. i. (Senckenberg Corp. Jur. German. I. 118). This portion of the Kayser-Recht is probably therefore posterior to the rise of the Hapsburg dynasty.

[5] Belitz de Duel. German. p. 11.

18

after weapons were taken, four marks; and if he waited till the weapons were drawn he had to pay five marks.[1]

All these were local regulations which had no direct bearing on general legislation, except in so far as they might assist in softening the manners of their generation and aiding in the general spread of civilization.   A more efficient cause was to be found in the opposition of the Church.   From Liutprand the Lombard to Frederic II., a period of five centuries, no secular lawgiver, south of Denmark, seems to have thought of abolishing the judicial combat as a measure of general policy, and those whose influence was largest were the most conspicuous in fostering it.   During the whole of this period the Church was consistently engaged in discrediting it, notwithstanding that the local interests or pride of individual prelates might lead them to defend the vested privileges connected with it in their jurisdictions.

When King Gundobald gave form and shape to the battle ordeal in digesting the Burgundian laws, Avitus, Bishop of Vienne, remonstrated loudly against the practice as unjust and unchristian.   A new controversy arose on the occasion of the duel between the Counts Bera and Sanila, to which allusion has already been made as one of the important events in the reign of Louis le Débonnaire.   St. Agobard, Archbishop of Lyons, took advantage of the opportunity to address to the Emperor a treatise in which he strongly deprecated the settlement of judicial questions by the sword ; and he subsequently wrote another tract against ordeals in general, consisting principally of scriptural texts with a running commentary, proving the incompatibility of Christian doctrines with these unchristian practices.[2]   Some thirty-five years later the Council of

[1] Jura Primæva Moraviæ, Brunæ, 1781, pp. 33, 102.

[2] " Liber adversus Legem Gundobadi" and " Liber contra Judicium Dei" (Agobardi Opp. Ed. Baluz I. 107, 301).   Both of these works display marked ability, and a spirit of enlightened piety, mingled with frequent absurdities which show that Agobard could not in all things rise

Valence, in 855, denounced the wager of battle in the most decided terms, praying the Emperor Lothair to abolish it throughout his dominions, and adopting a canon which not only excommunicated the victor in such contests, but refused the rights of Christian sepulture to the victim.[1] By this time the forces of the church were becoming consolidated in the papacy, and the Vicegerent of God was beginning to make his voice heard authoritatively throughout Europe. The popes accordingly were not long in protesting energetically against the custom. Nicholas I. denounced it vigorously as a tempting of God, unauthorized by divine law,[2] and his successors consistently endeavored, as we have already seen, to discredit it. In the latter half of the twelfth century, Peter Cantor argues that a champion undertaking the combat relies either on his superior strength and skill, which is manifest injustice; or on the justice of his cause, which is presumption; or on a special miracle, which is a devilish tempting of God.[3] Alexander III. decided that a cleric engaging in a duel, whether willingly or unwillingly, whether victor or vanquished, was subject to deposition, but that his bishop could grant him a dispensation provided there had been loss of neither life nor limb.[4] Towards the close of the century Celestine III. went further, and in the case of a priest who had put forward a champion who had slain his antagonist he decided that both principal and champion were guilty of homicide and the priest could no longer perform his functions, though he might have a dispensation to hold his benefice.[5] These cases suggest one of the reasons why the repeated papal prohibitions were so ineffective. The all-pervading venality of the Church of the period found in the dis-

superior to his age. One of his favorite arguments is that the battle ordeal was approved by the Arian heretic Gundobald, whom he stigmatizes as " quidam superbus ac stultus hæreticus Gundobadus Burgundionum rex."

[1] Concil. Valentin. ann. 855 can. 12.

[2] C. 22 Decreti caus. II. q. v.

[3] Pet. Cantor. Verb. Abbrev. cap. LXXVIII.

[4] C. 1 Extra Lib. v. Tit. xiv.   [5] C. 2 Ibid.

pensing power an exhaustless source of profit, and dispensations for "irregularities" of all kinds were so habitually issued that the threatened punishments lost their terrors, and as Rome gradually absorbed the episcopal jurisdiction, offenders of all kinds knew that relief from the operation of the canons could always be had there. Some reason for setting them aside was never hard to find. In 1208 a canon of Bourges was elected prior; his disappointed competitor claimed that he was ineligible because he had once served as judge in a duel in which there was effusion of blood. Innocent III. was appealed to, who decided that the canon was capable of promotion to any dignity, and the chief reason alleged was that the evil custom of the duel was so universal in some regions that ecclesiastics of all classes from the lowest to the highest were habitually concerned in them.[1]

Innocent III., however, took care that the great council of Lateran in 1215 should confirm all the previous prohibitions of the practice.[2] It was probably this papal influence that led Simon de Montfort, the special champion of the church, to limit the use of the duel in the territories which he won in his crusade against the Count of Toulouse. In a charter given December 1, 1212, he forbids its use in all the seignorial courts in his dominions, except in cases of treason, theft, robbery, and murder.[3] De Montfort's dependence on Rome, however, was exceptional, and Christendom at large was not as yet prepared to appreciate the reformatory efforts of the popes. The most that the Council of Paris, held in 1212 for the reformation of the church by the cardinal-legate Robert de Curzon,

---

[1] Innocent. PP. III. Regest. XI. 64—Verum quoniam hujusmodi duellorum judicia juxta pravam quarundam consuetudinem regionum non solum a laicis seu clericis in minoribus ordinibus constitutis, sed etiam a majoribus ecclesiarum prælatis consueverunt, prout multorum assertione didicimus, exerceri.

[2] Concil. Lateranens. IV. can. 18.

[3] Consuetud. S. Montisfortis (Contre le Franc-Alleu sans Tiltre, p. 229).

could do was to order the bishops not to permit the duel in cemeteries or other sacred places.[1]

The opposition of the church as represented by its worthiest and most authoritative spokesmen continued. St. Ramon de Peñafort, the leading canonist of his time, about 1240, asserts uncompromisingly that all concerned in judicial combats are guilty of mortal sin ; the sin is somewhat lightened indeed when the pleader is obliged to accept the combat by order of the judge, but the judge himself, the assessors who counsel it, and the priest who gives the benediction all sin most gravely ; if death occurs they are all homicides and are rendered "irregular."[2]   About the same time Alexander Hales ingeniously argued away the precedent of David and Goliath by showing that it was simply a prefiguration of the Passion, in which Christ triumphed over Satan as in a duel.[3]   With the development, moreover, of the subtilties of scholastic theology the doctors found that the duel was less objectionable than the other forms of ordeal, because, as Thomas Aquinas remarks, the hot iron or boiling water is a direct tempting of God, while the duel is only a matter of chance, for no one expects miraculous interposition unless the champions are very unequal in age or strength.[4]   This struck at the very root of the faith on which confidence in the battle ordeal was based, yet in spite of it the persistence of ecclesiastical belief in the divine interposition is fairly illustrated by a case, related with great triumph by monkish chroniclers, as late as the fourteenth century, when a duel was undertaken by direction of the Virgin Mary herself.   In 1325, according to the story, a French Jew feigned conversion to Christianity in order to gratify his spleen by mutilating the images in the churches, and at length he committed the sacrilege of carrying off the holy wafer to aid

[1] Concil. Parisiens. ann. 1212, P. IV. c. xv. (Harduin. VI. II. 2017).

[2] S. Raymundi Summæ Lib. II. Tit. iii.—Cardinal Henry of Susa is equally uncompromising— Hostiensis Aureæ Summæ Lib. v. Tit. *De Cler. pugnant.*

[3] Alexandri de Ales Summæ P. III. Q. xlvi. Membr. 3.

[4] Sec. Sec. Q. 95 art. 8.

in the hideous rites of his fellows. The patience of the Virgin being at last exhausted, she appeared in a vision to a certain smith, commanding him to summon the impious Israelite to the field. A second and a third time was the vision repeated without effect, till at last the smith, on entering a church, was confronted by the Virgin in person, scolded for his remissness, promised an easy victory, and forbidden to pass the church door until his duty should be accomplished. He obeyed and sought the authorities. The duel was decreed, and the unhappy Hebrew, on being brought into the lists, yielded without a blow, falling on his knees, confessing his unpardonable sins, and crying that he could not resist the thousands of armed men who appeared around his adversary with threatening weapons. He was accordingly promptly burned, to the great satisfaction of all believers.[1]

Evidently the clergy at large did not second the reformatory efforts of their pontiffs. There was not only the ancestral belief implanted in the minds of those from among whom they were drawn, but the seignorial rights enjoyed by prelates and abbeys were not to be willingly abandoned. The progress of enlightenment was slow and the teachings of the papacy can only be enumerated as one of the factors at work to discredit the judicial duel.[2] We can estimate how deeply rooted were the

[1] Wilhelmi Fgmond. Chron. (Matthæi Analect. IV. 231). Proost (Législation des Jugements de Dieu, p. 16) gives this story, with some variations, as occurring at Mons, and states that the duel was authorized by no less a personage than Pope John XXII. Cornelius Zantfliet in his Chronicle (Martene Ampl. Collect. V. 182) locates it at Cambron in Hainault, and states that the Jew was a favorite of William Count of Hainault. Mr. Neilson informs me that Olivier de la Marche likewise adopts Cambron as the scene of the occurrence. The tale apparently was one which obtained wide currency.

[2] In 1374 Gregory XI. when condemning the Sachsenspiegel laid especial stress on the passages in which the judicial duel was prescribed (Sachsenspiegel, ed. Ludovici, 1720, p. 619). As late as 1492, the Synod of Schwerin promulgated a canon prohibiting Christian burial to those who fell in the duel or in tournaments.—Synod. Swerin. ann. 1492, Can. xxiv. (Hartzheim Concil. German. V. 647).

prejudices to be overcome when we find Dante seriously arguing that property acquired by the duel is justly acquired ; that
God may be relied upon to render the just cause triumphant ;
that it is wicked to doubt it, while it is folly to believe that a
champion can be the weaker when God strengthens him.[1]

In its endeavors to suppress the judicial duel the Church had
to weigh opposing difficulties.   It could, as we have seen (p.
156), enjoin its members from taking part in such combats and
from adjudging them in their jurisdictions; it could decree
that priests became "irregular" if death ensued in duels where
they gave the benediction, or perhaps even where they had
only brought relics on which the combatants took the oaths.
But over the secular courts it had only the power of persuasion,
or at most of moral coercion, and among the canon doctors
there was considerable discussion as to the extent to which it
could pronounce participation in the duel a mortal sin, entailing excommunication and denial of the rites of sepulture.
When a man sought the duel, when he demanded it of the
judge and provoked his adversary to it, he could be pronounced
guilty of homicide if death ensued.   It was otherwise where
an innocent man was accused of a mortal crime and would be
hanged if he refused the duel adjudged to him by court.   It
was argued that the Church was a harsh mother if she forced
her children thus to submit to death and infamy for a scruple
of recent origin, raised merely by papal command, though
the more rigid casuists insisted even on this.   All agreed, however, that in civil cases a man ought rather to undergo the loss of
his property than to imperil his soul and disobey the Church.[2]

Perhaps the most powerful cause at work was the revival of
the Roman jurisprudence, which in the thirteenth century com-

---

[1] " Et si Deus adest nonne nefas est habendo justitiam succumbere posse ?
. . . Et si justitia in duello succumbere nequit, nonne de jure acquiritur
quod per duellum acquiritur ? . . . stultum enim est valde vires quas Deo
comfortat inferiores in pugile suspicari."—De Monarchia II. 10 (Patetta,
Le Ordalie, p. 415).

[2] Joh. Friburgens. Summæ Confessorum Lib. II. Tit. iii. Q. 3–5.

menced to undermine all the institutions of feudalism. Its
theory of royal supremacy was most agreeable to sovereigns
whose authority over powerful vassals was scarcely more than
nominal ; its perfection of equity between man and man could
not fail to render it enticing to clear-minded jurists, wearied
with the complicated and fantastic privileges of ecclesiastical,
feudal, and customary law. Thus recommended, its progress
was rapid. Monarchs lost no opportunity of inculcating respect for that which served their purpose so well, and the civil
lawyers, who were their most useful instruments, speedily rose
to be a power in the state. Of course the struggle was long,
for feudalism had arisen from the necessities of the age, and
a system on which were based all the existing institutions of
Europe could only be attacked in detail, and could only be
destroyed when the advance of civilization and the general
diffusion of enlightenment had finally rendered it obsolete.
The French Revolution was the final battle-field, and that
terrible upheaval was requisite to obliterate a form of society
whose existence had numbered nine hundred years.

The wager of battle was not long in experiencing the first
assaults of the new power. The earliest efficient steps towards
its abolition were taken in 1231 by the Emperor Frederic II.
in his Neapolitan code. He pronounces it to be in no sense a
legal proof, but only a species of divination, incompatible with
every notion of equity and justice ; and he prohibits it for the
future, except in cases of poisoning or secret murder and
treason where other proof is unattainable ; and even in these
it is placed at the option of the accuser alone ; moreover, if
the accuser commences by offering proof and fails he cannot
then have recourse to combat ; the accused must be acquitted.[1]
The German Imperial code, known as the Kayser-Recht, which
was probably compiled about the same time, contains a similar denunciation of the uncertainty of the duel, but does not

---

[1] Constit. Sicular. Lib. II. Tit. xxxii. xxxiii.—" Non tam vera probatio
quam quædam divinatio . . . quæ naturæ non consonans, a jure communi
deviat, æquitatis rationibus non consentit." Cf. Lib. I. Tit. xxi. cap. 2.

venture on a prohibition, merely renouncing all responsibility for it, while recognizing it as a settled custom.[1] In the portion, however, devoted to municipal law, which is probably somewhat later in date, the prohibition is much more stringently expressed, manifesting the influences at work ;[2] but even this is contradicted by a passage almost immediately preceding it. How little influence these wise counsels had, in a state so intensely feudal and aristocratic, is exemplified in the Suabian and Saxon codes, where the duel plays so important a part. Yet the desire to escape it was not altogether confined to the honest burghers of the cities, for in 1277 Rodolph of Hapsburg, even before he granted immunity to the imperial towns, gave a charter to the duchy of Styria, securing to the Styrians their privileges and rights, and in this he forbade the duel in all cases where sufficient testimony could be otherwise obtained; while the general tenor of the document shows that this was regarded as a favor.[3] The Emperor Albert I. was no less desirous of restricting the duel, and in ordinary criminal cases endeavored to substitute compurgation.[4]

Still, as late as 1487, the Inquisitor Sprenger, in discountenancing the red-hot iron ordeal in witch-trials, feels himself obliged to meet the arguments of those who urged the lawfulness of the duel as a reason for permitting the cognate appeal to the ordeal. To this he naïvely replies, as Thomas Aquinas had done, that they are essentially different, as the champions in a duel are about equally matched, and the killing of one of them is a simple affair, while the iron ordeal, or that of drinking boiling water, is a tempting of God by

---

[1] Cum viderit innocentes in duello succubuisse, et sontes contra in sua iniustitia nihilominus victoriam obtinuisse. Et ideo in jura imperii scriptum est, ubi duo ex more in duellum procedunt, hoc non pertinet ad imperium.—Jur. Cæsar. P. ii. c. 70 (Senckenberg I. 54).

[2] Quilibet sciat imperatorem jussisse ut nemo alterum ad duellum provòcet. . . . Nemo enim unquam fortiores provocari vidit, sed semper debiliores, et fortiores semper triumpharunt.—Ibid. P. iv. cap. 19.

[3] Rudolphi I. Privileg. (Ludewig. Reliq. MSS. T. IV. p. 260).

[4] Goldast. Constitt. Imp. III. 446.

requiring a miracle.[1] This shows at the same time how thoroughly the judicial combat had degenerated from its original theory, and that the appeal to the God of battles had become a mere question of chance, or of the comparative strength and skill of a couple of professional bravos.

In Spain the influence of Roman institutions, transmitted through the Wisigothic laws, had allowed to the judicial duel less foothold than in other mediæval lands, and the process of suppressing it began early. In Aragon the chivalrous Jayme I., *el Conquistador*, in the franchises granted to Majorca, on its conquest in 1230, prohibited the judicial combat in both civil and criminal cases.[2] Within forty years from this, Alfonso the Wise of Castile issued the code generally known as Las Siete Partidas. In this he evidently desired to curb the practice as far as possible, stigmatizing it as a custom peculiar to the military class (*por lid de caballeros ò de peones*), and as reprehensible both as a tempting of God and as a source of perpetual injustice.[3] Accordingly, he subjected it to very important limitations. The wager of battle could only be granted by the king himself; it could only take place between gentlemen, and in personal actions alone which savored of treachery, such as murder, blows, or other dishonor, inflicted without warning or by surprise. Offences committed against property, burning, forcible seizure, and other wrongs, even without defiance, were specifically declared not subject to its decision, the body of the plaintiff being its only recognized justification.[4] Even in this limited sphere, the consent of both

[1] Malleus Maleficar. Francof. 1580, pp. 527–9.

[2] Villanueva, Viage Literario, XXII. 288.

[3] Los sabios antiguos que ficieron las leyes non lo tovieron por derecha prueba; ed esto por dos razones; la una porque muchas vegadas acaesce que en tales lides pierde la verdat e vence la mentira; la otra porque aquel que ha voluntad de se adventurar á esta prueba semeja que quiere tentar á Dios nuestro señor.—Partidas, P. III. Tit. xiv. l. 8.

[4] Ibid. P. VII. Tit. iii. l. 2, 3. According to Montalvo's edition of the Partidas (Sevilla, 1491), these laws were still in force under Ferdinand and Isabella.

parties was requisite, for the appellant could prosecute in the ordinary legal manner, and the defendant, if challenged to battle, could elect to have the case tried by witnesses or inquest, nor could the king himself refuse him the right to do so.[1] When to this is added that a preliminary trial was requisite to decide whether the alleged offence was treacherous in its character or not, it will be seen that the combat was hedged around with such difficulties as rendered its presence on the statute book scarcely more than an unmeaning concession to popular prejudice ; and if anything were wanting to prove the utter contempt of the legislator for the decisions of the battle-trial, it is to be found in the regulation that if the accused was killed on the field, without confessing the imputed crime, he was to be pronounced innocent, as one who had fallen in vindicating the truth.[2] The same desire to restrict the duel within the narrowest possible limits is shown in the rules concerning the employment of champions, which have been already alluded to. Although the Partidas as a scheme of legislation was not confirmed until the cortes of 1348 these provisions were lasting and produced the effect designed. It is true that in 1342 we hear of a combat ordered by Alfonso XI. between Pay Rodriguez de Ambia and Ruy Paez de Biedma, who mutually accused each other of treason. It was fought before the king and lasted for three days without either party obtaining the victory, till, on the evening of the third day, the king entered the lists and pacified the quarrel, saying that both antagonists could serve him better by fighting the Moors, with whom he was at war, than by killing each other.[3] Not long

[1] Tres dias débese acordar al reptado para escoger una de las tres maneras que desuso dixiemos, qual mas quisiere porque se libre el pleyto. . . . ca el re nin su corte non han de mandar lidiar por riepto.—Ibid. P. VII. Tit. iii. l. 4. Some changes were introduced in these details by subsequent ordinances.

[2] Muera quito del riepto ; ca razon es que sea quito quien defendiendo la verdad recibió muerte.—Ibid. P. VII. Tit. iv. l. 4.

[3] Crónica de Alfonso el Onceno, cap. CCLXII.

afterwards Alfonso in the Ordenamiento de Alcalá, issued in 1348, repeated the restrictions of the Partidas, but in a very cursory manner, and rather incidently than directly, showing that the judicial combat was then a matter of little importance.[1] In fact, the jurisprudence of Spain was derived so directly from the Roman law through the Wisigothic code and its Romance recension, the Fuero Juzgo, that the wager of battle could never have become so deeply rooted in the national faith as among the more purely barbarian races. It was therefore more readily eradicated, and yet, as late as the sixteenth century, a case occurred in which the judicial duel was prescribed by Charles V., in whose presence the combat took place.[2]

The varying phases of the struggle between progress and centralization on the one side, and chivalry and feudalism on the other, were exceedingly well marked in France, and as the materials for tracing them are abundant, a more detailed account of the gradual reform may perhaps have interest, as illustrating the long and painful strife which has been necessary to evoke order and civilization out of the incongruous elements from which modern European society has sprung. The sagacity of St. Louis, so rarely at fault in the details of civil administration, saw in the duel not only an unchristian and unrighteous practice, but a symbol of the disorganizing feudalism which he so energetically labored to suppress. His temper led him rather to adopt pacific measures, in sapping by the forms of law the foundations of the feudal power, than to break it down by force of arms as his predecessors had attempted. The centralization of the Roman polity might well appear to him and his advisers the ideal of a well-ordered state, and the royal supremacy had by this time advanced to a point where the gradual extension of the judicial prerogatives of the crown might prove the surest mode of humbling eventually the haughty vassals who had so often bearded the

---

[1] Ordenamiento de Alcalá, Tit. XXXII. ll. vii.–xi. See also the Ordenanzas Reales of 1480, Lib. IV. Tit. IX.

[2] Meyer, Institutions Judiciaires, I. 337.

sovereign. No legal procedure was more closely connected with feudalism, or embodied its spirit more thoroughly, than the wager of battle, and Louis accordingly did all that lay in his power to abrogate the custom. The royal authority was strictly circumscribed, however, and though, in his celebrated Ordonnance of 1260, he formally prohibited the battle trial in the territory subject to his jurisdiction,[1] he was obliged to admit that he had no power to control the courts of his barons beyond the domains of the crown.[2] Even within this comparatively limited sphere, we may fairly assume from some passages in the Établissements, compiled about the year 1270, that he was unable to do away entirely with the practice. It is to be found permitted in some cases both civil and criminal, of peculiarly knotty character, admitting of no other apparent

[1] Nous deffendons à tous les batailles par tout nostre demengne, més nous n'ostons mie les clains, les respons, les convenants, etc. . . . fors que nous ostons les batailles, et en lieu des batailles nous meton prueves de tesmoins, et si n'oston pas les autres bones prueves et loyaux, qui ont esté en court laye siques à ore.—Isambert, I. 284.

Laurière (Tabl. des Ordonn. p. 17) alludes to an edict to the same purport, under date of 1240, of which I can nowhere else find a trace. There is no reference to it in the Tables des Ordonnances of Pardessus (Paris, 1847).

It is a curious illustration of the fluctuating policy of the contest that in his struggle to enforce the supremacy of the royal jurisdiction as against the prelates of the province of Reims, one of the complaints of the bishops at the Council of Saint-Quentin in 1235 is that he forced ecclesiastics in his court to prove by the duel their rights over their serfs—"Item, supplicat concilium quod dominus rex non compellat personas ecclesiasticas probare per duellum in curia sua homines quos dicunt suos esse de corpore suo" (Harduin. VII. 259).

[2] Se ce est hors l'obeissance le Roy, gage de bataille (Étab. de St. Louis, Liv. II. chap. xi. xxix. xxxviii.). Beaumanoir repeats it, a quarter of a century later, in the most precise terms, "Car tout cil qui ont justice en le conté poent maintenir lor cort, s'il lor plest, selonc l'ancienne coustume; et s'il lor plest il le poent tenir selonc l'establissement le Roy" (Cout. du Beauv. cap xxxix. § 21). And again, "Car quant li rois Loïs les osta de sa cort il ne les osta pas des cours à ses barons" (Cap. LXI. § 15).

19

solution.[1] It seems, indeed, remarkable that he should even have authorized personal combat between brothers, in criminal accusations, only restricting them in civil suits to fighting by champions,[2] when the German law of nearly the same period forbids the duel, like marriage, between relations in the fifth degree, and states that previously it had been prohibited to those connected in the seventh degree.[3]

Even this qualified reform provoked determined opposition. Every motive of pride and interest prompted resistance. The prejudices of birth, the strength of the feudal principle, the force of chivalric superstition, the pride of self-reliance gave keener edge to the apprehension of losing an assured source of revenue. The right of granting the wager of battle was one of those appertaining to the *hauts-justiciers*, and so highly was it esteemed that paintings of champions fighting frequently adorned their halls as emblems of their prerogatives; Loysel, indeed, deduces from it a maxim, "The pillory, the gibbet, the iron collar, and paintings of champions engaged, are marks of high jurisdiction."[4] This right had a considerable money value, for the seigneur at whose court an appeal of battle was tried received from the defeated party a fine of sixty livres if he was a gentleman, and sixty sous if a roturier, besides a

---

[1] Liv. I. chap. xxvii. xci. cxiii. etc. This is so entirely at variance with the general belief, and militates so strongly with the opening assertion of the Établissements (Ordonn. of 1260) that I should observe that in the chapters referred to the direction for the combat is absolute; no alternative is provided, and there is no allusion to any difference of practice prevailing in the royal courts and in those of the barons, such as may be seen in other passages (Liv. I. chap. xxxviii. lxxxi. cxi. etc.). Yet in a charter of 1263, Louis alludes to his having interdicted the duel in the domains of the crown in the most absolute manner.—"Sed quia duellum perpetuo de nostris domaniis duximus amovendum" (Actes du Parlement de Paris No. 818 A. T. I. p. 75, Paris, 1863).

[2] Établissements Liv. I. chap. clxvii.

[3] Jur. Provin. Alamann. cap. CLXXI. §§ 10, 11, 12.

[4] Pilori, échelle, carquant, et peintures de champions combattans sont marques de haute justice.—Instit. Coutum Liv. II. Tit. ii. Règle 47.

perquisite of the horses and arms employed, and heavy mulcts for any delays which might be asked,[1] besides fines from those who withdrew after the combat was decreed.[2] Nor was this all, for during the centuries of its existence there had grown and clustered around the custom an immeasurable mass of rights and privileges which struggled lustily against destruction. Thus, hardly had the ordonnance of prohibition been issued when, in 1260, a knight named Mathieu le Voyer actually brought suit against the king for the loss it inflicted upon him. He dolefully set forth that he enjoyed the privilege of guarding the lists in all duels adjudged in the royal court at Corbon, for which he was entitled to receive a fee of five sous in each case; and, as his occupation thus was gone, he claimed compensation, modestly suggesting that he be allowed the same tax on all inquests held under the new law.[3] How closely all such sources of revenue were watched is illustrated by a case occurring in 1286, when Philippe le Bel remitted the fines accruing to him from a duel between two squires adjudged in

---

[1] Beaumanoir, op. cit. chap. LXI. §§ 11, 12, 13.

In Normandy, these advantages were enjoyed by all seigneurs justiciers. "Tuit chevalier et tuit sergent ont en leurs terres leur justice de bataille en cause citeaine; et quant li champions sera vaincuz, il auront LX sols et I denier de la récréandise."—Etab. de Normandie (Ed. Marnier, p. 30). These minutely subdivided and parcelled out jurisdictions were one of the most prolific causes of debate during the middle ages, not only on account of the power and influence, but also from the profits derived from them. That the privilege of decreeing duels was not the least remunerative of these rights is well manifested by the decision of an inquest held during the reign of Philip Augustus to determine the conflicting jurisdictions of the ducal court of Normandy and of the seigneurs of Vernon. It will be found quoted in full by Beugnot in his notes on the Olim, T. I. p. 969. See also Coutumes d'Auzon (Chassaing, Spicilegium Brivatense, p. 95).

[2] See Coutume de Saint-Bonnet, cap. 13 (Meyer, Recueil d'Anciens Textes, Paris, 1874, I. 175).

[3] Les Olim, I. 491. It is perhaps needless to add that Mathieu's suit was fruitless. There are many cases recorded in the Olim showing the questions which arose and perplexed the lawyers, and the strenuous efforts made by the petty seigneurs to preserve their privileges.

the royal court of Tours. The seneschal of Anjou and Touraine brought suit before the Parlement of Paris to recover one-
third of the amount, as he was entitled to that proportion of
all dues arising from combats held within his jurisdiction, and
he argued that the liberality of the king was not to be exercised
to his disadvantage. His claim was pronounced just, and a
verdict was rendered in his favor.[1]

But the loss of money was less important than the curtail-
ment of privilege and the threatened absorption of power of
which this reform was the precursor. Every step in advancing
the influence of peaceful justice, as expounded by the jurists
of the royal courts, was a heavy blow to the independence of
the feudatories. They felt their ancestral rights assailed at
the weakest point, and they instinctively recognized that, as
the jurisdiction of the royal bailiffs became extended, and as
appeals to the court of the Parlement of Paris became more
frequent, their importance was diminished, and their means of
exercising a petty tyranny over those around them were
abridged. Entangled in the mazes of a code in which the
unwonted maxims of Roman law were daily quoted with increasing veneration, the impetuous seigneur found himself the
prey of those whom he despised, and he saw that subtle lawyers
were busily undoing the work at which his ancestors had
labored for centuries. These feelings are well portrayed in a
song of the period, exhumed not long since by Le Roux de
Lincy. Written apparently by one of the sufferers, it gives so
truthful a view of the conservative ideas of the thirteenth
century that a translation of the first stanza may not be
amiss :—

> Gent de France, mult estes esbahis !
> Je di à touz ceus qui sont nez des fiez, etc.[2]

> Ye men of France, dismayed and sore
> Ye well may be. In sooth, I swear,

---

[1] Actes du Parlement de Paris, I. 407.

[2] Recueil de Chants Historiques Français, I. 218. It is not unreasonable to conjecture that these lines may have been occasioned by the cele-

Gentles, so help me God, no more
  Are ye the freemen that ye were!
Where is your freedom?   Ye are brought
  To trust your rights to inquest law,
Where tricks and quibbles set at naught
  The sword your fathers wont to draw.
Land of the Franks!—no more that name
  Is thine—a land of slaves art thou,
Of bondsmen, wittols, who to shame
  And wrong must bend submissive now!

Even legists—de Fontaines, whose admiration of the Digest led him on all occasions to seek an incongruous alliance between the customary and imperial law, and Beaumanoir, who in most things was far in advance of his age, and who assisted so energetically in the work of centralization—even these enlightened lawyers hesitate to object to the principles involved in the battle trial, and while disapproving of the custom, express their views in language which contrasts strongly with the vigorous denunciations of Frederic II. half a century earlier.[1]

How powerful were the influences thus brought to bear against the innovation is shown by the fact that when the

brated trial of Enguerrand de Coucy in 1256. On the plea of baronage, he demanded trial by the Court of Peers, and claimed to defend himself by the wager of battle. St. Louis proved that the lands held by Enguerrand were not baronial, and resisted with the utmost firmness the pressure of the nobles who made common cause with the culprit. On the condemnation of de Coucy, the Count of Britanny bitterly reproached the king with the degradation inflicted on his order by subjecting its members to inquest.—Beugnot, Olim I. 954.—Grandes Chroniques ann. 1256.

[1] Et se li uns et li autres est si enreués, qu'il n'en demandent nul amesurement entrer pueent par folie en périll de gages (Conseil, chap. xv. Tit. xxvii.). Car bataille n'a mie leu ou justise a mesure (Ibid. Tit. xxviii.). Mult a de perix en plet qui est de gages de bataille, et mult es grans mestiers c'on voist sagement avant en tel cas (Cout. du Beauv. chap. lxiv. § 1). Car ce n'est pas coze selonc Diu de soufrir gages en petite querele de meubles ou d'eritages; mais coustume les suefre ès vilains cas de crieme (Ibid. chap. vi. § 31).

mild but firm hand of St. Louis no longer grasped the sceptre, his son and successor could not maintain his father's laws. In 1280 there is a record of a duel adjudged in the king's court between Jeanne de la Valete and the Sire of Montricher on an accusation of arson;[1] and about 1283 Philippe even allowed himself to preside at a judicial duel, scarcely more than twenty years after the promulgation of the ordonnance of prohibition.[2] The next monarch, Philippe le Bel, was at first guilty of the same weakness, for when in 1293 the Count of Armagnac accused Raymond Bernard of Foix of treason, a duel between them was decreed, and they were compelled to fight before the king at Gisors; though Robert d'Artois interfered after the combat had commenced, and induced Philippe to separate the antagonists.[3]   Philippe, however, was too astute not to see that his interests lay in humbling feudalism in all its forms; while the rapid extension of the jurisdiction of the crown, and the limitations on the seignorial courts, so successfully invented and asserted by the lawyers, acting by means of the Parlement through the royal bailiffs, gave him power to carry his views into effect such as had been enjoyed by none of his predecessors.   Able and unscrupulous, he took full advantage of his opportunities in every way, and the wager of battle was not long in experiencing the effect of his encroachments.   Still, he proceeded step by step, and the vacillation of his legislation shows how obstinate was the spirit with which he had to deal. In 1296 he prohibited the judicial duel in time of war, and in 1303 he was obliged to repeat the prohibition.[4]   It was probably not long after this that he interdicted the duel wholly[5]—possibly impelled thereto by a case occurring in 1303,

[1] Actes du Parlement de Paris, T. I. No. 2269 A. p. 217.

[2] Beaumanoir, op. cit. chap. lxi. § 63.

[3] Grandes Chroniques, T. IV. p. 104.

[4] Isambert, II. 702, 806.

[5] I have not been able to find this Ordonnance.   Laurière alludes to it (Tabl. dés Ordonn. p. 59), but the passage of Du Cange which he cites refers only to prohibition of tournaments.   The catalogue of Pardessus and

in which he is described as forced to grant the combat between two nobles, on an accusation of murder, very greatly against his wishes, and in spite of all his efforts to dissuade the appellant.[1]

In thus abrogating the wager of battle, Philippe le Bel was in advance of his age. Before three years were over he was forced to abandon the position he had assumed; and though he gave as a reason for the restoration of the duel that its absence had proved a fruitful source of encouragement for crime and villany,[2] yet at the same time he took care to place on record the assertion of his own conviction that it was worthless as a means of seeking justice.[3] In thus legalizing it by the Ordonnance of 1306, however, he by no means replaced it on its former footing. It was restricted to criminal cases involving the death penalty, excepting theft, and it was

the collection of Isambert contain nothing of the kind, but that some legislation of this nature actually occurred is evident from the preamble to the Ordonnance of 1306—"Savoir faisons que comme ça en arrière, pour le commun prouffit de nostre royaume, nous eussions defendu généraument à tous noz subgez toutes manieres de guerres et tous gaiges de batailles, etc." It is worthy of note that these ordonnances of Philippe were no longer confined to the domain of the crown, but purported to regulate the customs of the whole kingdom.

[1] Willelmi Egmond. Chron. (Matthæi Analect. IV. 135-7).

[2] Dont pluseurs malfaicteurs se sont avancez par la force de leurs corps et faulx engins à faire homicides, traysons et tous autres maléfices, griefz et excez, pource que quant ilz les avoient fais couvertement et en repost, ilz ne povoient estre convaincuz par aucuns tesmoings dont par ainsi le maléfice se tenoit.—Ordonnance de 1306 (Éd. Crapelet, p. 2).

[3] Car entre tous les périlz qui sont, est celui que on doit plus craindre et doubter, dont maint noble s'est trouvé déceu ayant bon droit ou non, par trop confier en leurs engins et en leurs forces ou par leurs ires oultrecuidées (Ibid. p. 34). A few lines further on, however, the Ordonnance makes a concession to the popular superstition of the time in expressing a conviction that those who address themselves to the combat simply to obtain justice may expect a special interposition of Providence in their favor—"Et se l'intéressé, sans orgueil ne maltalent, pour son bon droit seulement, requiert bataille, ne doit doubter engin ne force, car le vray juge sera pour lui."

only permitted when the crime was notorious, the guilt of the accused probable, and no other evidence attainable.[1] The ceremonies prescribed, moreover, were fearfully expensive, and put it out of the reach of all except the wealthiest pleaders. As the ordonnance, which is very carefully drawn, only refers to appeals made by the prosecutor, it may fairly be assumed that the defendant could merely accept the challenge and had no right to offer it.

Even with these limitations, Philippe was not disposed to sanction the practice within the domains of the crown, for, the next year (1307), we find him commanding the seneschal of Toulouse to allow no duel to be adjudged in his court, but to send all cases in which the combat might arise to the Parlement of Paris for decision.[2] This was equivalent to a formal prohibition. During the whole of the period under considera- tion, numerous causes came before the Parlement concerning challenges to battle, on appeals from various jurisdictions throughout the country, and it is interesting to observe how uniformly some valid reason was found for its refusal. In the public register of decisions, extending from 1254 to 1318, scarcely a single example of its permission is to be found.[3] One doubtful instance which I have observed is a curious case occurring in 1292, wherein a man accused a woman of homicide in the court of the Chapter of Soissons, and the royal officers interfered on the ground that the plaintiff was a bastard. As by the local custom he thus was in some sort a serf of the crown, they assumed that he could not risk his body without the express permission of the king. The Chapter contended for the appellant's legitimacy, and the case became so much obscured by the loss of the record of examination made, that the Parlement finally shuffled it out of court without any definite decision.[4]

---

[1] Ordonnance de 1306, cap. i.   [2] Isambert, II. 850.

[3] See Les Olim, *passim*.

[4] Actes du Parlement de Paris, I. 446.

Two decisions, in 1309, show that the Ordonnance of 1306 was in force, for while they admit that the duel was legally possible, the cases are settled by inquest as capable of proof by investigation.   One of these was an incident in the old quarrel between the Counts of Foix and Armagnac, and its decision shows how great a stride had been made since their duel of 1293.   Raymond de Cardone, a kinsman of Foix, gaged his battle in the king's court against Armagnac; Armagnac did the same against Foix and claimed that his challenge had priority over that of Raymond, while Bernard de Comminges also demanded battle of Foix.   All these challenges arose out of predatory border incursions between these nobles, and in its verdict the Parlement refuses to grant the combat in any of them, orders all the parties to swear peace and give bail to keep it, and moreover condemns Foix in heavy damages to his adversaries and to the king, whose territories he had invaded in one of his forays.   The Count of Foix made some objection to submitting to the sentence, but a short imprisonment brought him to his senses.[1]   A more thorough vindication of the royal jurisdiction over powerful feudatories could scarcely be imagined, and the work of the civil lawyers seemed to be perfectly accomplished.   It was the same with all the variety of cases involving the duel which were brought to the cognizance of the Parlement.   Some ingenious excuse was always found for refusing it, whether by denying the jurisdiction of the court which had granted it, or by alleging other reasons more or less frivolous, the evident intention of all the *arrêts* being to restrict the custom, as allowed under the ordonnance, within limits so narrow as to render it practically a nullity.   The astute lawyers who composed the royal court knew too well the work committed to them to hesitate as to their conclusions, while Philippe's distaste for the duel probably received a stimulus when, at the Council of

[1] Les Olim, III. 381-7.—Vaissette, Hist. Gén. de Languedoc, T. IV., Preuves, 140-44.

Vienne in 1312 he endeavored to obtain the condemnation of the memory of Boniface VIII., and two Catalan knights offered to prove by the single combat that the late pope had been legitimately elected and had not been a heretic.[1]

In spite of these efforts, the progress of reform was slow. On the breaking out afresh of the perennial contest with Flanders, Philippe found himself, in 1314, obliged to repeat his order of 1296, forbidding all judicial combats during the war, and holding suspended such as were in progress.[2] As these duels could have little real importance in crippling his military resources, it is evident that he seized such occasions to accomplish under the war power what his peaceful prerogative was unable to effect, and it is a striking manifestation of his zeal in the cause, that he could turn aside to give attention to it amid the preoccupations of the exhausting struggle with the Flemings. Yet how little impression he made, and how instinctively the popular mind still turned to the battle ordeal, as the surest resource in all cases of doubt, is well illustrated by a passage in a rhyming chronicle of the day. When the close of Philippe's long and prosperous reign was darkened by the terrible scandal of his three daughters-in-law, and two of them were convicted of adultery, Godefroy de Paris makes the third, Jeanne, wife of Philippe le Long, offer at once to prove her innocence by the combat :—

> Gentil roy, je vous requier, sire,
> Que vous m'oiez en deffendant.
> Se nul ou nule demandant
> Me vait chose de mauvestie,
> Mon cuer sens si pur, si haitie,
> Que bonement me deffendrai,
> Ou tel champion baillerai,
> Qui bien saura mon droit deffendre,
> S'il vous plest à mon gage prendre.[3]

---

[1] Wadding. Annal. Minor. ann. 1312 No. 2.

[2] Isambert, III. 40.   [3] Chronique Métrique, I. 6375.

The iron hand of Philippe was no sooner withdrawn than the nobles made desperate efforts to throw off the yoke which he had so skilfully and relentlessly imposed on them. His son, Louis Hutin, not yet firmly seated on the throne, was constrained to yield a portion of the newly-acquired prerogative. The nobles of Burgundy, for instance, in their formal list of grievances, demanded the restoration of the wager of battle as a right of the accused in criminal cases, and Louis was obliged to promise that they should enjoy it according to ancient custom.[1] Those of Amiens and Vermandois were equally clamorous, and for their benefit he re-enacted the Ordonnance of 1306, permitting the duel in criminal prosecutions where other evidence was deficient, with an important extension authorizing its application to cases of theft, in opposition to previous usage.[2] A legal record, compiled about 1325 to illustrate the customs of Picardy, shows by a group of cases that it was still quite common, and that indeed it was the ordinary defence in accusations of homicide.[3] The nobles of Champagne demanded similar privileges, but Louis, by the right of his mother, Jeanne de Champagne, was Count of Champagne, and his authority was less open to dispute. He did not venture on a decided refusal, but an evasive answer, which was tantamount to a denial of the request,[4] showed that his previous concessions were extorted, and not willingly granted. Not content with this, the Champenois repeated their demand, and received the dry response, that the existing edicts on the subject must be observed.[5]

[1] Et quant au gage de bataille, nous voullons que il en usent, si comme l'en fesoit anciennement.—Ordonn. Avril 1315, cap. 1 (Isambert, III. 62).

[2] Nous voullons et octroions que en cas de murtre, de larrecin, de rapte, de trahison et de roberie, gage de bataille soit ouvert, se les cas ne pouvoient estre prouvez par tesmoings—Ordonn. 15 Mai 1315 (Isambert, III. 74).

[3] Ancien Coutumier inédit de Picardie, p. 48 (Marnier, Paris, 1840).

[4] Ordonn. Mai 1315, P. I. chap. 13 (Isambert, III. 90).

[5] Ibid. P. II. chap. 8 (Isambert, III. 95).

The threatened disturbances were avoided, and during the succeeding years the centralization of jurisdiction in the royal courts made rapid progress. It is a striking evidence of the successful working of the plans of St. Louis and Philippe le Bel that several ordonnances and charters granted by Philippe le Long in 1318 and 1319, while promising reforms in the procedures of the bailiffs and seneschals, and in the manner of holding inquests, are wholly silent on the subject of the duel, affording a fair inference that complaints on that score were no longer made.[1] Philip of Valois was especially energetic in maintaining the royal jurisdiction, and when in 1330 he was obliged to restrict the abusive use of appeals from the local courts to the Parlement,[2] it is evident that the question of granting or withholding the wager of battle had become practically a prerogative of the crown. That the challenging of witnesses must ere long have fallen into desuetude is shown by an edict of Charles VI., issued in 1396, by which he ordered that the testimony of women should be received in evidence in all the courts throughout his kingdom.[3]

Though the duel was thus deprived, in France, of its importance as an ordinary legal procedure, yet it was by no means extinguished, nor had it lost its hold upon the confidence of the people. An instructive illustration of this is afforded by the well-known story of the Dog of Montargis. Though the learned Bullet[4] has demonstrated the fabulous nature of this legend, and has traced its paternity up to the Carlovingian romances, still, the fact is indubitable that it was long believed to have occurred in 1371, under the reign of Charles le Sage, and that authors nearly contemporary with that period recount the combat of the dog and the knight as an unquestionable fact, admiring greatly the sagacity of the animal, and regarding as a matter of course both the extra-

[1] Isambert, III. 196–221.
[2] Ordonn. 9 Mai 1330 (Isambert, IV. 369).
[3] Neron, Récueil d'Édits, I. 16.
[4] Dissertations sur la Mythologie Française.

ordinary judicial proceedings and the righteous judgment of God which gave the victory to the greyhound.

In 1371 there was battle gaged between Sir Thomas Felton, Seneschal of Aquitaine, and Raymond de Caussade, Seigneur de Puycornet. Apparently they felt that a fair field could not be had in either French or English territory, and they applied to Pedro el Ceremonioso of Aragon to provide the lists for them. Pedro acceded to the request and promised to preside, provided there was due cause for a judicial duel and that the arms were agreed upon in advance, and he sent the combatants safe-conducts to come to Aragon. He assigned the city of Valencia as the place of combat, and when there was an endeavor to break off the affair on the ground that it concerned the kings of France and England, he replied that it was now too late and that the battle must take place.[1]

In 1386, the Parlement of Paris was occupied with a subtle discussion as to whether the accused was obliged, in cases where battle was gaged, to give the lie to the appellant, under pain of being considered to confess the crime charged, and it was decided that the lie was not essential.[2] The same year occurred the celebrated duel between the Chevalier de Carrouges and Jacques le Gris, to witness which the king shortened a campaign, and in which the appellant was seconded by Waleran, Count of St. Pol, son-in-law of the Black Prince. Nothing can well be more impressive than the scene so picturesquely described by Froissart. The cruelly wronged Dame de Carrouges, clothed in black, is mounted on a sable scaffold, watching the varying chances of the unequal combat between her husband, weakened by disease, and his vigorous antagonist, with the fearful certainty that, if strength alone prevail, he must die a shameful death and she be consigned to the stake. Hope grows faint and fainter; a grievous wound seems to place Carrouges at the mercy of his adversary,

---

[1] Bofarull y Mascaró, Coleccion de Documentos ineditos, VI. 355–59.

[2] De Laurière, note on Loysel, Instit. Coutum. Lib. VI. Tit. i. Règle 22.

20

until at the last moment, when all appeared lost, she sees the avenger drive his sword through the body of his prostrate enemy, vindicating at once his wife's honor and his own good cause.[1] Froissart, however, was rather an artist than an historian; he would not risk the effect of his picture by too rigid an adherence to facts, and he omits to mention, what is told by the cooler Juvenal des Ursins, that Le Gris was subsequently proved innocent by the death-bed confession of the real offender.[2] To make the tragedy complete, the Anonyme de S. Denis adds that the miserable Dame de Carrouges, overwhelmed with remorse at having unwittingly caused the disgrace and death of an innocent man, ended her days in a convent.[3] So striking a proof of the injustice of the battle ordeal is said by some writers to have caused the abandonment of the practice; but this, as will be seen, is an error, though no further trace of the combat as a judicial procedure is to be found on the registers of the Parlement of Paris.[4]

Still, it was popularly regarded as an unfailing resource. Thus, in 1390, two women were accused at the Châtelet of Paris of sorcery. After repeated torture, a confession implicating both was extracted from one of them, but the other persisted in her denial, and challenged her companion to the duel by way of disproving her evidence. In the record of the proceedings the challenge is duly entered, but no notice whatever seems to have been taken of it by the court, showing that it was no longer a legal mode of trial in such cases.[5]

In 1409, the battle trial was materially limited by an ordonnance of Charles VI. prohibiting its employment except when specially granted by the king or the Parlement;[6] and

---

[1] Froissart, Liv. III. chap. xlix. (Éd. Buchon, 1846).

[2] Hist. de Charles VI. ann. 1386.

[3] Hist. de Charles VI. Liv. VI. chap. ix.

[4] Buchon, notes to Froissart, II. 537.

[5] Registre du Châtelet de Paris, I. 350 (Paris, 1861).

[6] Que jamais nuls ne fussent receus au royaume de France à faire gages de bataille ou faict d'armes, sinon qu'il y eust gage jugé par le roy, ou la cour de parlement.—Juvenal des Ursins, ann. 1409.

though the latter body may never have exercised the privilege thus conferred upon it, the king occasionally did, as we find him during the same year presiding at a judicial duel between Guillaume Bariller, a Breton knight, and John Carrington, an Englishman.[1] The English occupation of France, under Henry V. and the Regent Bedford, revived the practice, and removed for a time the obstacles to its employment. Nicholas Upton, writing in the middle of the fifteenth century, repeatedly alludes to the numerous cases in which he assisted as officer of the Earl of Salisbury, Lieutenant of the King of England ; and in his chapters devoted to defining the different species of duel he betrays a singular confusion between the modern ideas of reparation of honor and the original object of judicial investigation, thus fairly illustrating the transitional character of the period.[2]

It was about this time that Philippe le Bon, Duke of Burgundy, formally abolished the wager of battle, as far as lay in his power, throughout the extensive dominions of which he was sovereign, and in the Coutumier of Burgundy, as revised by him in 1459, there is no trace of it to be found. The code in force in Britanny until 1539 permitted it in cases of contested estates, and of treason, theft, and perjury—the latter, as usual, extending it over a considerable range of civil actions, while the careful particularization of details by the code shows that it was not merely a judicial antiquity.[3] In Normandy, the legal existence of the judicial duel was even more prolonged, for it was not until the revision of the coutumier in 1583, under Henry III., that the privilege of deciding in this way numerous cases, both civil and criminal, was formally abolished.[4] Still, it may be assumed that, practically, the

---

[1] Monstrelet, Liv. I. chap. lv.

[2] Nic. Uptoni de Militari Officio Lib. II. cap. iii. iv. (pp. 72-73).

[3] Très Ancienne Cout. de Bretagne, chap. 99, 129–135 (Bourdot de Richebourg).

[4] Ancienne Cout. de Normandie, chap. 53, 68, 70, 71, 73, etc. (Bourdot de Richebourg).

custom had long been obsolete, though the tardy process of revising the local customs allowed it to remain upon the statute book to so late a date. The fierce mountaineers of remote Béarn clung to it more obstinately, and in the last revision of their code, in 1552, which remained unaltered until 1789, it retains its place as a legitimate means of proof, in default of other testimony, with a heavy penalty on the party who did not appear upon the field at the appointed time.[1]

During this long period, examples are to be found which show that although the combat was falling into disuse, it was still a legal procedure, which in certain cases could be claimed as a right, or which could be decreed and enforced by competent judicial authority. Among the privileges of the town of Valenciennes was one to the effect that any homicide taking refuge there could swear that the act had been committed in self-defence, when he could be appealed only in battle. This gave occasion to a combat in 1455 between a certain Mahuot and Jacotin Plouvier, the former of whom had killed a kinsman of the latter. Neither party desired the battle, but the municipal government insisted upon it, and furnished them with instructors to teach the use of the club and buckler allowed as arms. The Comte de Charolois, Charles le Témé-raire, endeavored to prevent the useless cruelty, but the city held any interference as an infringement of its chartered rights; and, after long negotiations, Philippe le Bon, the suzerain, authorized the combat and was present at it. The combatants, according to custom, had the head shaved and the nails pared on both hands and feet; they were dressed from head to foot in a tight-fitting suit of hardened leather, and each was anointed with grease to prevent his antagonist from clutching him. The combat was long and desperate, but at length the appellant literally tore out the heart of his antagonist.[2] Such

---

[1] Fors et Cost. de Béarn, Rubr. de Batalha (Bourdot de Richebourg, IV. 1093).

[2] Mathieu de Coussy, chap. cxii.—Ol. de la Marche, ch. xxii. Such a case as this justifies the opinion quoted by Olivier de la Marche, "que le

incidents among roturiers, however, were rare. More frequently some fiery gentleman claimed the right of vindicating his quarrel at the risk of his life. Thus, in 1482, shortly after the battle of Nancy had reinstated René, Duke of Lorraine, on the ruins of the second house of Burgundy, two gentlemen of the victor's court, quarrelling over the spoils of the battlefield, demanded the *champ-clos;* it was duly granted, and on the appointed day the appellant was missing, to the great discomfiture and no little loss of his bail.[1] When Charles d'Armagnac, in 1484, complained to the States General of the inhuman destruction of his family, committed by order of Louis XI., the Sieur de Castlenau, whom he accused of having poisoned his mother, the Comtesse d'Armagnac, appeared before the assembly, and, his advocate denying the charge, presented his offer to prove his innocence by single combat.[2] In 1518, Henry II. of Navarre ordered a judicial duel at Pau between two contestants, of whom the appellant made default; the defendant was accordingly pronounced innocent, and was empowered to drag through all cities, villages, and other places through which he might pass, the escutcheon and effigy of his adversary, who was further punished by the prohibition thenceforth to wear arms or knightly bearings.[3] In 1538, Francis I. granted the combat between Jean du Plessis and Gautier de Dinteville, which would appear to have been essentially a judicial proceeding, since the defendant, not appearing at the appointed time, was condemned to death by sentence

gaige de bataille fut trouvé par le diable pour gagner et avoir les âmes de tous les deux, tant du demandeur que du deffendeur" (Traité du Duel Judiciaire, p. 4, communicated to me by George Neilson, Esq.).

[1] D. Calmet, Hist. de Lorraine.

[2] Jehan Masselin, Journal des États de Tours, p. 320.

[3] Archives de Pau, *apud* Mazure et Hatoulet, Fors de Béarn, p. 130. There may have been something exceptional in this case, since the punishment was so much more severe than the legal fine of 16 sous quoted above (Fors de Morlaas, Rubr. IV.).

of the high council, Feb. 20, 1538.[1] The duel thus was evidently still a matter of law, which vindicated its majesty by punishing the unlucky contestant who shrank from the arbitrament of the sword.

Allusion has already been made to the celebrated combat between Chastaigneraye and Jarnac, in 1547, wherein the death of the former, a favorite of Henry II., led the monarch to take a solemn oath never to authorize another judicial duel. Two years later, two young nobles of his court, Jacques de Fontaine, Sieur de Fendilles, and Claude des Guerres, Baron de Vienne-le-Chatel, desired to settle in this manner a disgusting accusation brought against the latter by the former. The king, having debarred himself from granting the appeal, arranged the matter by allowing Robert de la Marck, Marshal of France, and sovereign Prince of Sedan, to permit it in the territory of which he was suzerain. Fendilles was so sure of success that he refused to enter the lists until a gallows was erected and a stake lighted, where his adversary after defeat was to be gibbeted and burned. Their only weapons were broad-swords, and at the first pass Fendilles inflicted on his opponent a fearful gash in the thigh. Des Guerres, seeing that loss of blood would soon reduce him to extremity, closed with his antagonist, and being a skilful wrestler speedily threw him. Reduced to his natural weapons, he could only inflict blows with the fist, which failing strength rendered less and less effective, when a scaffold crowded with ladies and gentlemen gave way, throwing down the spectators in a shrieking mass. Taking advantage of the confusion, the friends of Des Guerres violated the law which imposed absolute silence and neutrality on all, and called to him to blind and suffocate his adversary with sand. Des Guerres promptly took the hint, and Fendilles succumbed to this unknightly weapon. Whether he formally yielded or not was disputed. Des Guerres claimed that he should undergo the punishment of the gallows and

[1] D. Calmet, Hist. de Lorraine.

stake prepared for himself, but de la Marck interfered, and the combatants were both suffered to retire in peace.[1] This is the last recorded instance of the wager of battle in France. The custom appears never to have been formally abolished, and so little did it represent the thoughts and feelings of the age which witnessed the Reformation, that when, in 1566, Charles IX. issued an edict prohibiting duels, no allusion was made to the judicial combat. The encounters which he sought to prevent were solely those which arose from points of honor between gentlemen, and the offended party was ordered not to appeal to the courts, but to lay his case before the Marshals of France, or the governor of his province.[2] The custom had died a natural death. No ordonnance was necessary to abrogate it; and, seemingly, from forgetfulness, the crown and the Parlement appear never to have been divested of the right to adjudge the wager of battle.

In Italy many causes conspired to lead to the abrogation of the judicial duel. On the one hand there were the prescriptions of the popes, and on the other the spirit of scepticism fostered by the example of Frederic II. The influence of the resuscitated Roman law was early felt and its principles were diffused by the illustrious jurists who rendered the Italian schools famous. Burgher life, moreover, was precociously developed in the social and political organization, and as the imperial influence diminished with the fall of the House of Hohenstaufen, the cities assumed self-government and fashioned their local legislation after their own ideals. The judgments of God were not indigenous in Italy; they were not ancestral customs rooted in the prehistoric past, but were

---

[1] Brantôme, Discours sur les Duels. An account of this duel, published at Sedan, in 1620, represents it as resulting even less honorably to Fendilles. He is there asserted to have formally submitted, and to have been contemptuously tossed out of the lists like a sack of corn, Des Guerres marching off triumphantly, escorted with trumpets.

[2] Fontanon, I. 665.

foreign devices introduced by conquerors—first by the Lombards and then by the Othos.   There were thus many reasons why the trial by combat should disappear early from the Italian statute books.   There is no trace of it in the elaborate criminal code of Milan compiled in 1338, nor in that of Piacenza somewhat later; in fact, it was no longer needed, for the inquisitional process was in full operation and in doubtful cases the judge had all the resources of torture at his disposal.[1]

Although by the middle of the fourteenth century it had thus disappeared from the written law, the rulers retained the right to grant it in special cases, and it thus continued in existence as a lawful though extra-legal mode of settling disputed cases.   Where suzerains were so numerous there was thus ample opportunity for belligerent pleaders to gratify their desires.   Even as late as 1507 Giovanni Paolo Baglioni, lord of Spello (a village in the Duchy of Spoleto, near Foligno), granted a licence for a month to Giovanni Batta Gaddi and Raffaello Altoviti to settle their suits by fighting within his domain with three comrades.[2]   Two years after this, Julius II., in issuing a constitution directed against duels of honor, took occasion also to include in his prohibition all such *purgationes vulgares*, even though permitted by the laws; the combatants were ordered, in all the States of the Church, to be arrested and punished for homicide or maiming according to the common law.[3]   In 1519 Leo X. reissued this bull with vastly sharper penalties on all concerned, but in his additions to it he seems merely to have in mind the duel of honor, which was habitually conducted in public, in lists prepared for the purpose, and in presence of the prince or noble who had granted licence for it.[4]   The legal combat may be considered to have virtually disappeared, but the duel of honor which

---

[1] Statuta Criminalia Mediolani e tenebris in lucem edita, Bergomi, 1594. —Statuta et Decreta antiqua Civitatis Placentiæ, Placentiæ, 1560.

[2] Patetta, Le Ordalie, p. 449.

[3] Julii PP. II. Bull. *Regis pacifici* § 2, 1509 (Mag. Bull. Rom. I. 499).

[4] Leon. PP. X. Bull. *Quam Deo*, 23 Julii, 1519 (Ib. p. 596).

succeeded it inherited some of its sanctions, and in the learned treatises on the subject which appeared during the first half of the sixteenth century there are still faint traces to be found of the survival of the idea of the judgment of God.[1]

In Hungary, it was not until 1486 that any attempt was made to restrict the judicial duel. In that year Matthias Corvinus prohibited it in cases where direct testimony was procurable: where such evidence was unattainable, he still permitted it, both in civil and criminal matters.[2] In 1492 Vladislas II. repeated this prohibition, alleging as his reason for the restriction the almost universal employment of champions who sometimes sold out their principals. The terms of the decree show that previously its use was general, though it is declared to be a custom unknown elsewhere.[3]

In Flanders, it is somewhat remarkable that the duel should have lingered until late in the sixteenth century, although, as we have seen above, the commercial spirit of that region had sought its abrogation at a very early period, and had been seconded by the efforts of Philippe le Bon in the fifteenth century. Damhouder, writing about the middle of the sixteenth century, states that it was still legal in matters of public concern, and even his severe training as a civil lawyer cannot prevent his declaring it to be laudable in such affairs.[4] Indeed, when the Council of Trent, in 1563, stigmatized the duel as the work of the devil and prohibited all potentates from granting it under pain of excommunication and forfeiture

[1] Patetta, op. cit. pp. 438–46.

[2] Eph. Gerhardi Tract. Jurid. de Judic Duellico c. ii. § 11.

[3] Quia in duellorum dimicatione plurimæ hinc inde fraudes committi possunt; raro enim illi inter quos illud fit judicium per se decertant, sed pugiles conducunt, qui nonnunquam dono, favore, et promissis corrumpuntur.—L. Uladis. II. c. ix. (Batthyani, I. 531).

[4] Reperio tamen indubie vulgarem purgationem sive duellum in casu sine scrupulo admittendum quum publicæ salutis caussa fiat: et istud est admodum laudabile.—Damhouder. Rer. Crimin. Praxis cap. xlii. No. 12 (Antverp. 1601).

of all feudal possessions,[1] the state Council of Flanders, in their report to the Duchess of Parma on the reception of the Council, took exception to this canon, and decided that the ruler ought not to be deprived of the power of ordering the combat.[2]   In this view, the Council of Namur agreed.[3]

In Germany, in spite of the imperial legislation referred to above (p. 212), feudal influences were too strong to permit an early abrogation of the custom.   Throughout the fifteenth century the wager of battle continued to flourish, and MSS. of the period give full directions as to the details of the various procedures for patricians and plebeians.   The sixteenth century saw its wane, though it kept its place in the statute books, and *Fechtbücher* of 1543 and 1556 describe fully the use of the club and the knife.   Yet when in 1535 Friedrich von Schwartzenberg demanded a judicial duel to settle a suit with Ludwig von Hutten, the latter contemptuously replied that such things might be permitted in the times of Goliath and Dietrich of Bern, but that now they were not in accordance with law, right, or custom, and von Schwartzenberg was obliged to settle the case in more peaceful fashion.   Still, occasional instances of its use are said to have occurred until the close of the century,[4] and as late as 1607, Henry, Duke of Lorraine, procured from the Emperor Rodolph II. the confirmation of a privilege which he claimed as ancestral that all combats occurring between the Rhine. and the Meuse should be fought out in his presence.[5]

In Russia, under the code known as the Ulogenié Zakonof, promulgated in 1498, any culprit, after his accuser's testimony

---

[1] Concil. Trident. Sess. xxv. De Reform. cap. xix.   Detestabilis duellorum usus fabricante diabolo introductus.

[2] Anne is usus relinquendus sit arbitrio principis ?   Videtur quod sic, et respiciendum esse principi quid discernat.—Le Plat, Monument. Concil. Trident. VII. 19.

[3] Le Plat, VII. 75.   [4] Würdinger, Beiträge, pp. 17, 19.

[5] Belitz de Duellis German. p. 15.

was in, could claim the duel; and as both parties went to the field accompanied by all the friends they could muster, the result was not infrequently a bloody skirmish. These abuses were put an end to by the Sudebtnick, issued in 1550, and the duel was regulated after a more decent fashion, but it continued to flourish legally until it was finally abrogated in 1649 by the Czar Alexis Mikhailovich, in the code known as the Sobornoié Ulogenié. The more enlightened branch of the Slavonic race, however, the Poles, abolished it in the fourteenth century; but Macieiowski states that in Servia and Bulgaria the custom has been preserved to the present day.[1]

In other countries, the custom likewise lingered to a comparatively late period. Scotland, indeed, was somewhat more forward than her neighbors; for in the year 1400, her Parliament showed the influence of advancing civilization by limiting the practice in several important particulars, which, if strictly observed, must have rendered it almost obsolete. Four conditions were pronounced essential prerequisites: the accusation must be for a capital crime; the offence must have been committed secretly and by treachery; reasonable cause of suspicion must be shown against the accused, and direct testimony both of witnesses and documents must be wanting.[2]

Still the "perfervidum ingenium Scotorum" clung to the arbitrament of the sword with great tenacity. In 1532 Sir James Douglass accused his son-in-law Robert Charteris of treason, and the charge was settled by a judicial duel in the presence of James V., who put an end to it when Charteris's

---

[1] For these details I am indebted to Du Boys, Droit Criminel des Peuples Modernes, I. 611–17, 650. See also Patetta, Le Ordalie, p. 161. The Sachsenspiegel was extensively in use in Poland, and under it duels continued to be lawful until its abrogation early in the sixteenth century by Alexander I. (Ib. p. 162).

[2] Statut. Roberti III. cap. iii. The genuineness of this statute has been questioned, but it undoubtedly reflects the practice of the period. For the evidence, see Neilson (Trial by Combat, p. 256), who further notes the identity of these provisions with those of Philippe le Bel's ordonnance of 1306.

sword broke.[1] Knox relates that in 1562, when the Earl of
Arran was consulting with him and others respecting a proposed accusation against Bothwell for high treason, arising out
of a plan for seizing Queen Mary which Bothwell had suggested,
the earl remarked, "I know that he will offer the combate unto
me, but that would not be suffered in France, but I will do
that which I have proposed." In 1567, also, when Bothwell
underwent a mock trial for the murder of Darnley, he offered
to justify himself by the duel; and when the Lords of the
Congregation took up arms against him, alleging as a reason
the murder and his presumed designs against the infant James
VI., Queen Mary's proclamation against the rebels recites his
challenge as a full disproval of the charges. When the
armies were drawn up at Carberry Hill, Bothwell again came
forward and renewed his challenge. James Murray, who had
already offered to accept it, took it up at once, but Bothwell
refused to meet him on account of the inequality in their rank.
Murray's brother, William of Tullibardin, then offered himself, and Bothwell again declined, as the Laird of Tullibardin
was not a peer of the realm. Many nobles then eagerly proposed to take his place, and Lord Lindsay especially insisted
on being allowed the privilege of proving the charge on Bothwell's body, but the latter delayed on various pretexts, until
Queen Mary was able to prohibit the combat.[2] The last
judicial duels fought in Scotland were two which occurred as
the sixteenth century was closing. In 1595, under a warrant
from James VI. John Brown met George Hepburn and was
vanquished, though his life was spared at the request of the
judges. In 1597 Adam Bruntfield charged James Carmichael
with causing the death of his brother, and under royal licence
fought and slew him before a crowd of five thousand spectators.
Yet even this was not the end of the legal custom, for in 1603
an accusation of treason against Francis Mowbray was ad-

---

[1] Neilson's Trial by Combat, p. 292.
[2] Knox's Hist. of Reformation in Scotland, pp. 322, 446–7.

judged to be settled by the duel, though the combat was pre-vented by Mowbray meeting his death in an attempt to escape from prison, after which he was duly hanged and quartered.[1]

In England, the resolute conservatism, which resists inno-vation to the last, prolonged the existence of the wager of battle until a period unknown in other enlightened nations. No doubt a reason for this may be found in the rise of the jury trial towards the end of the twelfth century, which, as we have seen above (p. 144), furnished an effective substitute for the combat in doubtful cases. As the jury system developed itself in both civil and criminal matters the sphere of the duel became more limited, in practice if not in theory, and its evils being thus less felt the necessity for its formal abrogation was less pressing.[2] It was thus enabled to hold its place as a recognized form of procedure to a later period than in any other civilized land. Already in the first quarter of the thirteenth century Mr. Maitland tells us that in criminal cases it had become uncommon, but the number of examples of it which he gives shows that this can only be in comparison with its greater frequency in the preceding century and that it was still in common use notwithstanding the tendency of the judges to disallow it.[3] At the close of the fourteenth century, when France was engaged in rendering it rapidly obsolete, Thomas, Duke of Gloucester, dedicated to his nephew Richard II. a treatise detailing elaborately the practice followed in the Marshal's court with respect to judicial duels.[4] Even a century

[1] Neilson's Trial by Combat, pp. 307, 310.

[2] Neilson's Trial by Combat, p. 35. See also a very interesting essay on the origin and growth of the jury by Prof. J. B. Thayer in the Harvard Law Review, Jan.–March, 1892.

[3] Maitland's Select Pleas of the Crown, p. xxiv. Whatever may have been the desire of the royal judges, King John himself was not averse to it, for there is a record of two duels between common malefactors ordered to be fought before the king " quia ea vult videre" (Ib. p. 40).

[4] Spelman (Gloss. s. v. *Campus*) gives a Latin translation of this interest-ing document from a MS. of the period.

Mr. Neilson draws (pp. 167, 168) a distinction, which is evidently correct,

21

later, legislation was obtained to prevent its avoidance in
certain cases. The "Statute of Gloucester" (6 Ed. II. cap.
9), in 1333, had given to the appellant a year and a day in
which to bring his appeal of death—a privilege allowed the
widow or next of kin to put the accused on a second trial
after an acquittal on a public indictment—which, as a private
suit, was usually determined by the combat. In practice, this
privilege was generally rendered unavailing by postponing the
public prosecution until the expiration of the delay, so as to
prevent the appeal. In 1486, however, a law was passed to
diminish the frequency of murder, which required the trial to
be finished before the expiration of the year and day, and
ordered the justices, in case of acquittal, to hold the defendant in prison or on bail until the time had passed, so as to insure to the widow or next of kin the opportunity of prosecuting
the appeal of death.[1] Another evidence of the prevalence of
the custom is to be found in the rule which, in the fifteenth
century, permitted a priest to shrive a man who was about to
wage his battle, without regard to the fact as to whose parish-
ioner he might legally be—

> And of mon that schal go fyghte
> In a bateyl for hys ryghte,
> Hys schryft also thou myghte here,
> Thagh he thy pareschen neuer were.[2]

With the advance of civilization and refinement, the custom
gradually declined, but it was not abolished. The last duel
fought out in England is said to be one in 1492 between Sir
James Parker and Hugh Vaughan, arising from a grant of

between what he calls the chivalric duel, conducted by marshals and con-
stables, and the ordinary combat adjudged by the courts of law. The former
makes it appearance in the latter half of the fourteenth century, when the
common law duel was falling into desuetude. As we have seen above, a
somewhat similar development, though not so formally differentiated, is
traceable in France and Italy.

[1] 3 Henr. VII. cap. 1.

[2] John Myrc's Instructions for Parish Priests, p. 26 (Early English
Text Society, 1868).

armorial bearings to Vaughan; it was fought on horseback with lances, and at the first course Vaughan slew his antagonist.[1] Still the old laws remained unaltered, and an occasional appeal to them, while it offended men's common sense, was insufficient to cause their repeal. In 1571 a case occurred, as Spelman says, "non sine magna jurisconsultorum perturbatione," when, to determine the title to an estate in Kent, Westminster Hall was forced to adjourn to Tothill Fields, and all the preliminary forms of a combat were literally enacted with the most punctilious exactness, though an accommodation between the parties saved the skulls of their champions.[2] In 1583, however, a judicial duel was actually fought in Ireland between two O'Connors on an accusation of treason brought by one against the other, which ended by the appellant cutting off the defendant's head and presenting it on his sword's point to the justices.[3]

A device, peculiar to the English jurisprudence, allowed a man indicted for a capital offence to turn "approver," by confessing the crime and charging or appealing any one he choose as an accomplice, and this appeal was usually settled by the single combat. Indeed, even when a criminal had confessed he was sometimes pardoned on condition of his being victorious in a specified number of duels, and thus compounding for his own life by the service rendered to society in relieving it of so many malefactors, as in a case in 1221 where a confessed thief "became approver to fight five battles."[4]

---

1 Stow's Annals, ann. 1492.

2 Spelman, Gloss. p. 103.—Stow's Annals, ann. 1571.

3 Neilson, Trial by Combat, p. 205.

4 Maitland's Select Pleas of the Crown, I. 92. See Neilson, p. 154, for an account of a savage combat in 1456 with an approver who had already caused the hanging of several innocent men. In this case the judge laid down the law that if the approver was vanquished the defendant must be hanged for homicide. This strange ruling is not in accordance with earlier practice. In 1220 an approver accuses seven persons, but is defeated in the first combat and hanged, whereupon the accused are discharged on bail (Maitland, Select Pleas, I. 123). See two other cases in the same year (Ibid. p. 133).

The custom continued to be a feature of criminal jurisprudence sufficiently important to require legislation as late as the year 1599, when the Act 41 Eliz. chap. 3 was passed to regulate the nice questions which attended appeals of several persons against one, or of one person against several. In the former case, the appellee, if victorious in the first duel, was acquitted; in the latter, the appellor was obliged to fight successively with all the appellees.[1] In civil suits the last case on record, I believe, is that of Claxton v. Lilburn, which shows curiously enough the indisposition to put an end to what was regarded by common consent as a solecism. A valuable estate in Durham, said to be worth more than £200 a year, was the subject in dispute. Claxton had been unsuccessful in a suit for its recovery, and had brought a new action, to which Lilburn responded, Aug. 6th, 1638, by producing in court his champion, George Cheney, in array, armed with a sandbag and battoon, who cast into the court his gauntlet with five small pence in it, and demanded battle. Claxton rejoined by producing a champion similarly armed, and gaged his battle. The court was nonplussed, putting off the proceedings from day to day, and seeking some excuse for refusing the combat. The champions were interrogated, and both admitted that they were hired for money. King Charles demanded the opinion of the Chief Justice and all his barons whether this was sufficient to invalidate the proceedings, but they unanimously replied that after battle was gaged and sureties given, such confession was no bar to its being carried out. The King then ordered his judges if possible to find some just way for its prevention, but they apparently could do nothing save procrastinate the matter for years, for in 1641 Lilburn petitioned the Long Parliament, setting forth that he had repeatedly

---

[1] Hale, Pleas of the Crown, II. chap. xxix. According to Pike (Hist. of Crime in England, I. 286 sq.), the record shows that approvers almost invariably either died in prison or were hanged in consequence of the acquittal of the party whom they accused. It was very rare that a combat ensued.

claimed his right of battle and had produced his champion, but was ever put off by the judges finding some error in the record. Parliament thereupon ordered a bill to be brought in taking away the judicial combat.[1] It was not enacted however, and Sir Matthew Hale, writing towards the close of the century, feels obliged to describe with considerable minuteness the various niceties of the law, though he is able to speak of the combat as "an unusual trial at this day."[2]

In 1774, the subject incidentally attracted attention in a manner not very creditable to the enlightenment of English legislation. When, to punish the rebellious Bostonians for destroying the obnoxious tea, a "Bill for the improved administration of justice in the province of Massachusetts Bay" was passed, it originally contained a clause depriving the New Englanders of the appeal of death, by which, it will be remembered, a man acquitted of a charge of murder could be again prosecuted by the next of kin, and the question could be determined by the wager of battle. The denial of this ancestral right aroused the indignation of the liberal party in the House of Commons, and the point was warmly contested. The learned and eloquent Dunning, afterwards Lord Ashburton, one of the leaders of opposition, defended the ancient custom in the strongest terms. "I rise," said he, "to support that great pillar of the constitution, the appeal for murder; I fear there is a wish to establish a precedent for taking it away in England as well as in the colonies. It is called a remnant of barbarism and gothicism. The whole of our constitution, for aught I know, is gothic. . . . . I wish, sir, that gentlemen would be a little more cautious, and consider that the yoke we are framing for the despised colo-

---

[1] Rushworth's Collections, Vol. I. P. i. pp. 788–90, P. iii. p. 356. The gloves presented by the champions in such trials had a penny in each finger; the principals were directed to take their champions to two several churches and offer the pennies in honor of the five wounds of Christ that God might give the victory to the right (Neilson's Trial by Combat, p. 149).

[2] Hale, loc. cit.

nists may be tied round our own necks!" Even Burke was heard to lift a warning voice against the proposed innovation, and the obnoxious clause had to be struck out before the ministerial majority could pass the bill.[1] Something was said about reforming the law throughout the empire, but it was not done, and the beauty of the "great pillar of the constitution," the appeal of death, was shown when the nineteenth century was disgraced by the resurrection of all the barbaric elements of criminal jurisprudence. In 1818, the case of Ashford *vs.* Thornton created much excitement. Ashford was the brother of a murdered girl, whose death, under circumstances of peculiar atrocity, was charged upon Thornton, with much appearance of probability. Acquitted on a jury trial, Thornton was appealed by Ashford, when he pleaded "Not guilty, and I am ready to defend the same by my body." After elaborate argument, Lord Ellenborough, with the unanimous assent of his brother justices, sustained the appellee's right to this as "the usual and constitutional mode of trial," expounding the law in almost the same terms as those which we read in Bracton and Beaumanoir.[2] The curious crowd was sorely disappointed when the appellant withdrew, and the chief justice was relieved from the necessity of presiding over a gladiatorial exhibition. A similar case occurred almost simultaneously in Ireland, and the next year the Act 59 Geo. III. chap. 46, at length put an end to this remnant of Teutonic barbarism.[3]

America, inheriting the blessings of English law, inherited also its defects. The colonies enjoyed the privilege of the appeal of death, against the abrogation of which, in the province of Massachusetts Bay, Dunning protested so vehemently. At least one instance of its employment is to be found here,

---

[1] Campbell's Lives of the Chancellors of England, VI. 112.

[2] I. Barnewall & Alderson, 457.—In April, 1867, the journals record the death at Birmingham of William Ashford the appellant in this suit. Thornton emigrated to America, and disappeared from sight.

[3] Campbell, Chief Justices, III. 169.

when in 1765, in Maryland, Sarah Soaper appealed a negro slave named Tom for the murder of her husband. The negro, however, was probably not aware of his privilege to demand the wager of battle, so he submitted to be tried by a jury, and was duly condemned and executed.[1] John C. Gray, Jr., Esq., of Boston, to whom I am indebted for calling my attention to this and some other sources of information on the subject, informs me of a tradition that a disputed question of boundary between two townships in New Hampshire was once settled by combat between champions ; but the most conservative State in this respect appears to be South Carolina. An act of that colony, in 1712, enumerating the English laws to be held in force, specifically includes those concerning appeal of death, and Dr. Cooper, in his "Statutes at Large of South Carolina," writing in 1837, seems to think that both the wager of battle and appeal of death were still legally in force there at that time.[2] So Chancellor Kilty, in his Report on English Statutes applicable to Maryland, made in 1811, apparently considers that the appeal of death was still legally existent, but regards it as unimportant in view of the pardoning power and other considerations.[3]

[1] I. Harris and McHenry's Md. Reps. 227.
[2] Cooper's Statutes at Large of S. C. II. 403, 715.
[3] Kilty's Report on English Statutes, Annapolis, 1811, p. 141.

APPENDIX.

THE JUDICIAL DUEL AND COMPURGATION: DOCUMENTS IN TRANSLATION

The following materials were originally translated by Arthur Howland in his pamphlet *Ordeals, Compurgation, Excommunication and Interdict*, University of Pennsylvania Translations and Reprints from the Original Sources of European History, Vol. IV, no. 4 (1897). A wide variety of original materials may be found in Petrus Browe, *De Ordaliis,* Pontificia Universitas Gregorians Textus et Documenta, Series Theologica, nos. 4 and 11 (Rome, 1932, 1933). For further reading, see the Introduction (Part I, no. 7 has been translated by the Editor).

I

COMPURGATION

1. TWO FORMS OF COMPURGATORIAL OATH.

(a) Form. Turon., M.G. LL., Sec. V, p. 154. Latin. 8th century.

[Defendant made oath denying the crime.] Likewise, witnesses of his own order, who were eye-witnesses and cognizant of the facts in the case, swore after him that the aforesaid N.

had given a true and satisfactory oath in what he had sworn regarding the matter.

(b) Thorpe's Ancient Laws of England, I, p. 180. 10th century.

By the Lord, the oath which N. has sworn is clean and without falsehood.

2. COMPURGATION OF QUEEN FREDEGONDA IN 585.

Gregory of Tours, Hist. Franc. Lib., viii, v. 9, M.G. SS. Mer., p. 330.

On the assassination of Chilperic I. king Gontran became guardian of his brother's infant son. Doubts were entertained as to the child's legitimacy, especially as Chilperic was said to have been murdered by a paramour of queen Fredegonda. The latter, however, fully established the paternity of the child by a compurgatorial oath, and thus prevented the kingdom of Neustria from passing into the hands of Gontran.

After this the king [Gontran] went to Paris and openly addressed all the people, saying: "My brother Chilperic on his death is said to have left a son, whose governors begged me at the mother's solicitation to stand sponsor for him at the baptismal font on the day of the festival of our Lord's birth; but they did not appear. Next they asked me to have him baptised at Easter, but the child was not brought then. For the third time they prayed me that he might be presented for the sacred rite on St. John's Day, but the child was still kept back. And so they have compelled me to leave home at this disagreeable season of the year. Therefore I have come, and behold, the boy is concealed, he is not shown me. For these reasons I feel certain that matters are not as they have been represented, but that the child is, as I believe, the son of some one of our nobles. For, if it had been of our race, it would have been brought to me. Know, therefore, that I will not acknowledge it until I receive satisfactory proofs of its paternity." When queen Fredegonda heard this she summoned the chief men of her kingdom, namely, three bishops and three hundred nobles, and with them made oath that Chilperic was the father of the child. By this means suspicion was removed from the king's mind.

3. COMPURGATION OF THE BROTHERS OF ADELHER.

Passio S. Bonifatii, in Jaffé, Bibliotheca Rer. Germ., III, p. 475. Latin. 11th century.

This story illustrates one of the abuses to which the system of compurgation lent itself, and at the same time shows how the clergy attempted to overcome it by emphasizing the danger of immediate punishment to the perjurer.

Some time after this it happened that a certain priest named Adelher was stricken with great weakness. He was indeed deeply devoted to the bishop [Boniface] on account of his noble character, and knowing the latter's secrets he served him truly. And when he perceived the end of life approaching, by the council of the man of God he gave what property he had inherited to St. Martin of Mainz. After this, his sickness increasing, he died. Afterwards his brothers violently seized what he had given to St. Martin in the following places, ... And when they had been summoned and questioned regarding their action, they promised to prove by an oath that the property was rightly theirs; and the bishop promised to be present. On the appointed day they brought together a large number of their relatives. The man of God was likewise there, and when the brothers had fetched their compurgators to the altar he is reported to have said: "If ye will swear, swear alone; I do not desire that ye should cause the damnation of all these." But the brothers took the oath. And immediately the bishop turning to them said: "Have ye sworn?" "We have," they replied. Then to the elder he said: "Thou wilt shortly be killed by a bear;" but to the younger, "Never wilt thou see son or daughter from they seed." Both of the prophecies proved true. And so the church of St. Martin received the heritage given to it.

4. COMPURGATION OF BISHOP NORGAUD OF AUTUN.

Hugh of Flavigny, Chron. Lib. II, M.G. SS., VIII, p. 494.   Latin.

Norgaud, Bishop of Autun, had been accused of simony by his canons, and had attempted to clear himself by the oath-helpers; but the compurgators were deterred by fear of the charge of perjury, and Norgaud was deposed.   He refused to resign his office, and in the following year succeeded in being reinstated by purging himself in the absence of his enemies.   The incident shows another form of abuse of the system.

In the year of our Lord 1101 John, bishop of Frascati, was sent by the pope into England to look after the papal property. . . . .   The cardinals had now returned to Rome openly confirming the sentence of deposition against the invader of the see of Autun and pronouncing it to be canonical by authentic proofs, when the bishop of Lyons began openly and publicly to condemn their action.   As he was setting out on a pilgrimage to Jerusalem in company with the bishop of Chalons-sur-Sâone and the simoniacal bishop of Autun, he was met on the way by the aforesaid bishop of Frascati who, in the absence of accusers and outside the boundaries of his province, received the purgation of him of Autun.   The bishop of Lyons aided and confirmed the oath as follows: "I believe that Norgaud, bishop of Autun, has sworn the truth, so help me God."   The bishop of Chalons-sur-Sâone also assisted and swore the same thing.   I am astonished that the good judgment of so great a man,* renowned everywhere for his inborn goodness and honesty, whose unvarying constancy is venerated by the Gallican church, could be deceived by the man to such an extent that even to the present time he takes his part as a compurgator, cherishes and protects him, and is almost the only one in the world to believe good of him, although an almost universal sentiment condemns such a favorable opinion.

* I. e., the bishop of Lyons.

5. PUNISHMENT FOR PERJURY.

Lex Fris., xiv, 3, M.G. LL., III, p. 668. Latin. About 800.

As the efficiency of the whole system of compurgation depended upon the confidence that could be placed by the court in the word of the oath-helpers, it was necessary to make the penalty for false swearing as severe as possible. The punishment for perjury varied in different codes. That mentioned in the Frisian law is here given.

He who seeks the composition for homicide,* let him swear on the relics of the saints that he will not accuse any one of this except those whom he suspects of the murder; and then let him accuse of homicide one, two, or even three or four or how-ever many there may have been that wounded him who was killed. But, though there were twenty or thirty, yet no more than seven can be accused, and let each one of these who has been accused swear with his twelfth hand,† and after the oath let him show himself innocent by the judgment of God in the ordeal of boiling water. Let the one who swore first go first to the ordeal, and so on in order. He who shall be found guilty by the ordeal, let him pay the composition for homicide, and to the king double his *wer-gild;* let the others who were his oath-helpers pay the fine for perjury as has been previously enacted.‡

* In the case of a man killed in a crowd.
† I. e., with eleven compurgators.
‡ This fine consisted of a single *wer-gild* each. Vid. Tit. X, eadem lege.

6. REFORM OF INNOCENT III.

Corp. Jur. Can., cc. 5 and 13, Extra, V, 34. Latin.

Although by the 13th century compurgation had come to be looked upon with suspicion by royal judges, it yet continued for a long time an ordinary method of trial for the clergy. Innocent III. introduced certain reforms which did away with some of the dangers of perjury, but he thereby weakened the force of the oaths and dealt a mortal blow to the system.

We believe you are not ignorant of how many times the bishop of Trent has been accused of simony. But the accusers though producing a writing were unable to bring forward witnesses according to canonical form to prove that he had given the church of St. Peter to the presbyter P. for four measures of corn. We decree to the common council of our brethren that he ought to purge himself of the aforesaid simony with three of his own order and four abbots and regular priests. Now the manner of purgation shall be as follows: First, the bishop shall swear on God's sacred Gospel that, for giving the church of St. Peter to the presbyter P., he has received no price personally or by the hand of a subordinate, nor to his knowledge has any one accepted anything for him. Then the compurgators shall swear upon God's holy Gospel that they believe he has spoken the truth.

But those who are brought forward to purge another of infamy are held to affirm this alone by their oaths; namely, that they believe that he who is being purged speaks the truth.

7. THE LIFE OF AUSTREGISIL, ARCHBISHOP OF BITONTO, SEVENTH CENTURY.

At that time there was in the king's palace a certain powerful official, savage and proud, named Bethelenus, who had taken for himself certain things belonging to the king. When he was challenged before the king for having done this, he showed the king a false authorization. "Who gave you this authority," asked the king. And Bethelenus said, "Austregisil, your servant." Austregisil, when he was interrogated, denied having done so. Hearing these conflicting accounts, the king in a fury ordered them to go from him to another place so that the judgment of God should show whose account was false. Then the day for the trial came. Austregisil rose up, armed with a shield and spear by his servants, and proceeded to the field where the king was accustomed to witness such ordeals. He went first to the basilica of Saint Marcellus where he was accustomed to pray for grace. He entered the church, prayed, and armed himself with the banner of the cross, which is the weapon of God Confident in the justice of his cause and in the just judgment of God, he went out at last, undaunted and quickly. As he was awaiting the arrival of his adversary, behold! One of the servants of Bethelenus came running up, out of breath and with a grief–stricken expression, announcing to the king that Bethelenus was dead.

II

JUDICIAL DUEL

I. EXAMPLE OF JUDICIAL DUEL IN GERMANY.*

Wiponis Vita Chuonradi Imp., c. 33, ann. 1033. M.G. SS., XI, p. 271.

The emperor having levied a force in Saxony marched upon the Luitzes,† a people who were formerly half Christians but who have wickedly apostatized and are now become thorough pagans. In their district he put an end to an implacable strife in a wonderful manner. Between the Saxons and the pagans at that time fighting and raids were being carried on incessantly, and when the emperor came he began to inquire which side had first broken the peace that had long been observed inviolate between them. The pagans said that the peace had been disturbed first by the Saxons, and they would prove this by the duel if the emperor would so direct. On the other side the Saxons pledged themselves to refute the pagans in like manner by single combat, though as a matter of fact their contention

---

*For a good example of the judicial duel under Otto I. see Widukind, Saxon Chronicle, ann. 938, trans. in Emerton's *Introduction to the Middle Ages*, p. 83.

† A Wendish tribe living on the east side of the river Elbe.

was untrue. The emperor after consulting his princes permitted the matter to be settled between them by a duel, though this was not a very wise act. Two champions, each selected by his own side, immediately engaged. The Christian, trusting in his faith alone, though faith without the works of justice is dead, began the attack fiercely without diligently considering that God, who is the Truth, who maketh His sun to shine upon the evil and the good, and the rain to fall upon the just and the unjust, decides all things by a true judgment. The pagan on the other hand resisted stoutly, having before his eyes only the consciousness of the truth for which he was fighting. Finally the Christian fell wounded by the pagan. Thereupon his party were seized with such elation and presumption that, had the emperor not been present, they would forthwith have rushed upon the Christians; but the emperor constructed the fortress Werben in which he placed a garrison of soldiers to check their incursions and bound the Saxon princes by an oath and by the imperial commands to a unanimous resistance against the pagans. Then he returned to Franconia.‡

‡ For a discussion of this incident see Jahrbücher d. deutschen Geschichte, Konrad II., II, 94 sq.

2. THE JUDICIAL COMBAT IN SPAIN.

Rodericus Toletanus, Lib. VI, c. 26. Bel: Rerum Hispanic. Script., I, p. 241. Latin. 13th century.

The old Gothic or Mozarabic ritual long preserved its place in the churches of Spain, but Gregory VII. on his accession determined to substitute the Roman in place of the old national service in Castile and Leon. The supporters of the papal policy were not at first able to carry their point by means of argument, and resort was had to single combat between champions, one representing the Roman, the other the Gothic ritual.*

But before the recall [of the legate Richard] the clergy and people of all Spain were thrown into confusion by being com-

* See Hefele, Conciliengeschichte, V, pp. 158 and 200.

pelled by the legate and the prince to accept the Gallic ritual. On an appointed day the king, the primate, the legate, the clergy, and a vast multitude of people came together and a long altercation took place, the clergy, soldiery and people firmly resisting a change in the service, the king, under the influence of the queen, supporting the change with threats and menaces. Finally the demands of the soldiers brought matters to such a crisis that it was decided to settle the dispute by a duel. When two soldiers had been selected, one by the king, who contended for the Gallic ritual, the other by the soldiery and people, who were equally zealous for the ritual of Toledo, the king's champion was defeated on the spot to the exultation of the people, because the victor was the champion of the Toledo service. But the king was so far persuaded by queen Constantia that he did not recede from his demands, adjudging the duel to be of no weight. . . . . And when thereupon a great tumult arose among the soldiers and the people, it was finally decided that a copy of the Toledo ritual, and one of the Gallic should be placed in a great fire. When a fast had been imposed upon all by the primate, legate, and clergy, and all had devoutly prayed, the Gallic office was consumed by the fire, while the Gothic leaped up above the flames and was seen by all who stood there praising the Lord to be wholly uninjured and untouched by the fire. But since the king was obstinate and stiff-necked he would not turn aside either through fear of the miracle or through supplication of the people, but, threatening confiscation and death against those who resisted, he ordered the Gallic office to be adopted in all his dominions. Whence arose from the grief and sorrow of all the proverb, *Quo volunt Reges, vadunt Leges.*

3. LAW OF FREDERIC II. ABOLISHING WAGER OF BATTLE IN SICILY.

Const. Sicular., Lib. II, Tit. 33. H.-Bréholles: Op. cit., vol. IV, part I, p. 105. Latin.

We will that the single combat, or duel, as it is commonly called, shall never be adjudged between men subject to our jurisdiction, except in a few specified cases: for it cannot be called so much a real proof as a sort of divination, which is not in accord with nature but is opposed to universal law and inconsistent with just reason. For it is almost if not quite impossible for two champions to come together so equally matched that the one is not wholly superior to the other in strength or does not excel him in some other way by greater vigor and courage or at least in cleverness. But we exclude from the benefit of this humane edict murderers who are charged with having caused the death of others by using poison or some other secret means; and even against these we do not sanction the wager of battle at the beginning of the trial, but command that ordinary proofs be first adduced against them if there be any such at hand, and that only then, as a last resort, when the crime cannot be fully established by other proofs after a thorough investigation by the officials of the court, resort may be had to the judgment of battle to decide the above charges: and we wish all these things to be arranged through the medium of a judge fully cognizant of the proceedings, that he may carefully and diligently investigate the proofs brought out by the inquisition. And if the charges shall not be proved as stated let him grant the accuser permission to offer battle, if nothing was brought out in court prejudicial to the accuser's right. But if the accuser should first offer to prove the crime by witnesses and their testimony should be insufficient, the trial shall not take place by the double method of inquisition and battle, but the defendant, not being convicted of guilt and being presumably innocent, shall be set free; because we wish the same law to be observed among all, both Franks and Lombards, and in all cases. In our new constitution, indeed, wager of battle has been sufficiently recognized in the case of the knights and nobles of our kingdom and of others who are able to offer battle. For we except the crime of treason, respecting which we preserve the judicial duel   Nor is it strange if we subject traitors, secret murderers and poisoners to the duel (though not so much as a method of judgment as to terrify them) ; not because our Serenity deems that just in their case which it has declared unjust in others, but because we desire that such homicides as have not feared to lay secret plots against human life, which God's power alone can call into existence, should be publicly subjected to this terrible method of proof in the sight of all men as a punishment and an example to others. Those also we exclude from the terms of our leniency who do not hesitate to plot against our peace in which the peace of all the rest is involved.